The Indians Were Prosperous

Documents of Salish, Pend d'Oreille, and Kootenai Indian History, 1900-1906

The Indians Were Prosperous

Documents of Salish, Pend d'Oreille, and Kootenai Indian History, 1900-1906

edited by
Robert Bigart
and
Joseph McDonald

published by
Salish Kootenai College Press
Pablo, Montana

distributed by
University of Nebraska Press
Lincoln, Nebraska

Publication of this book was made possible through the generosity of the Oleta "Pete" Smith Endowment Fund of the Montana Community Foundation.

Cover design: Corky Clairmont, artist/graphic designer, Pablo, Montana.
Cover illustration: Joseph Dixon walking over the Flathead Reservation, designed by Robert Bigart using material from *The Anaconda Standard*, September 4, 1904, editorial section, page 1.

Library of Congress Cataloging-in-Publication Data:
Names: Bigart, Robert, editor. | McDonald, Joseph, 1933- editor.
Title: The Indians were prosperous : documents of Salish, Pend d'Oreille, and Kootenai Indian history, 1900-1906 / edited by Robert Bigart and Joseph McDonald.
Description: Pablo, Montana : Salish Kootenai College Press, [2021] | Includes bibliographical references and index.
Identifiers: LCCN 2021007486 | ISBN 9781934594285 (paperback)
Subjects: LCSH: Salish Indians--Montana--History--20th century--Sources. | Kalispel Indians--Montana--History--20th century--Sources. | Kootenai Indians--Montana--History--20th century--Sources. | Indians of North America--Montana--Government relations--1869-1934--Sources. | Flathead Indian Reservation (Mont.)--History--20th century--Sources.
Classification: LCC E99.S2 B543 2021 | DDC 978.6004/979435--dc23
LC record available at https://lccn.loc.gov/2021007486

Published by Salish Kootenai College Press, PO Box 70, Pablo, MT 59855.

Distributed by University of Nebraska Press, 1111 Lincoln Mall, Lincoln, NE 68588-0630, order 1-800-755-1105, www.nebraskapress.unl.edu.

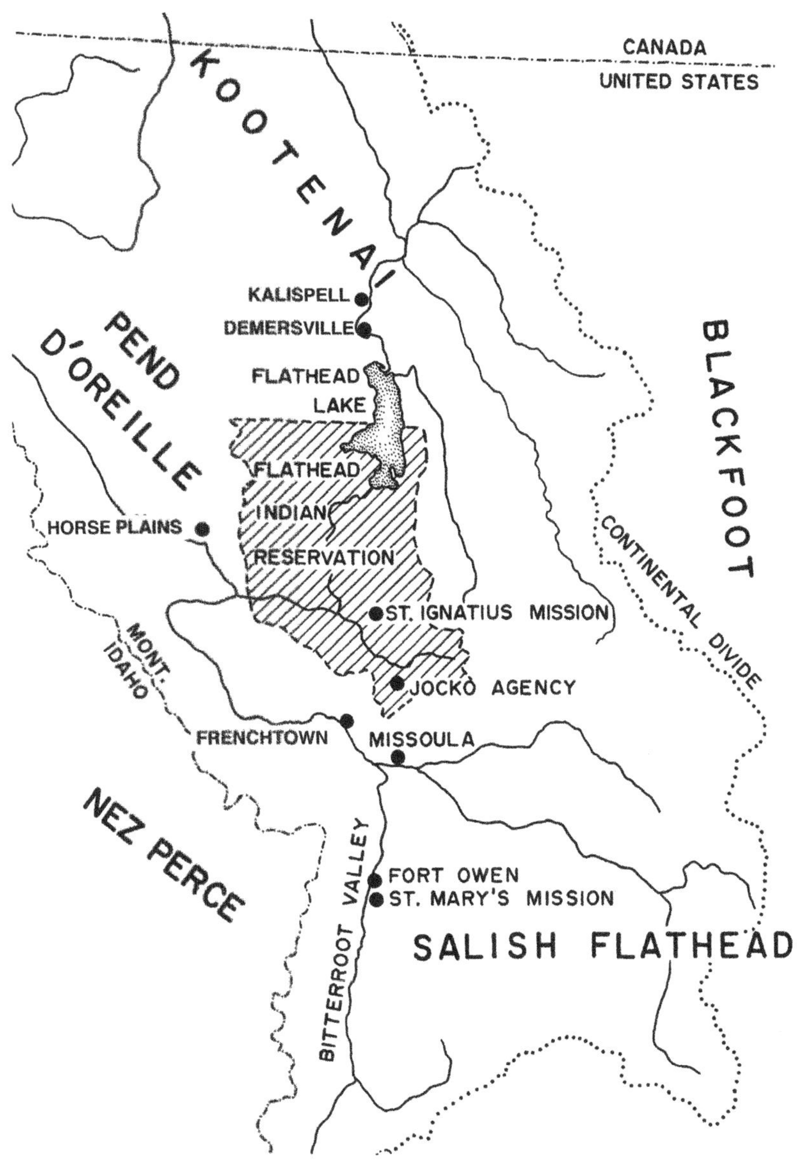

Flathead Indian Reservation
Showing Tribal Territories
and Surrounding Towns

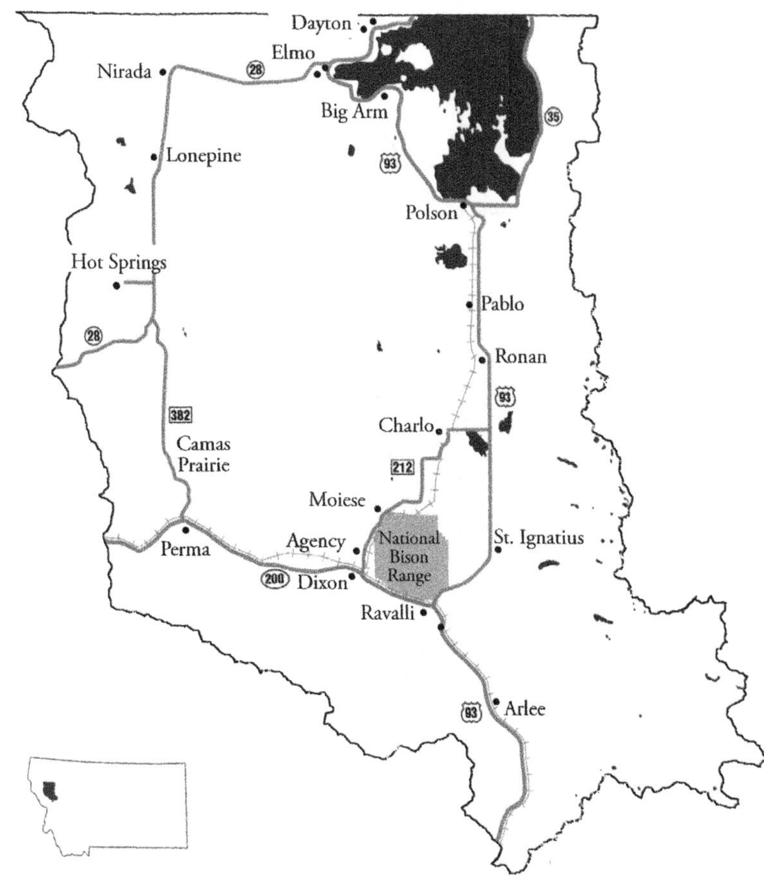

Flathead Indian Reservation, Montana

Map by Wyatt Design, Helena, Montana.

Table of Contents

Detailed Table of Contents

Introduction

By the beginning of the twentieth century the crescendo of economic change on the Flathead Reservation was reaching a climax. Income was not distributed equally on the reservation, but by 1905 the Indians were basically self-supporting and most of the poorer tribal members had enough to get by.

But the surrounding white community cast covetous eyes on tribal assets — especially the land. In 1903, Congressman Joseph Dixon led an assault on the tribes to force the sale of reservation land to white homesteaders at far below its real value. Tribal leaders realized they were being robbed and protested vigorously — but to no avail. With the loss of their assets in land, the tribes' future income declined, leaving them poorer than white rural Montanans. As part of the allotment policy, tribal members wrestled with a formal enrollment to determine who had rights on the reservation. White businessmen also moved to claim possession of the dam site at the foot of Flathead Lake.

While the tribes were fighting against the coerced allotment, they fought the State of Montana over taxes and hunting rights. In the background, alcohol and crime impacted some tribal members. The written documents give only glimpses of everyday life on the reservation, but some of the information is important.

The 1900 to 1906 period saw both the culmination of their efforts to develop a new economy based on livestock and agriculture and the frustration of having their economic progress sabotaged by the theft of tribal assets. The period set the stage for decades of disappointment and success as the tribes fought to influence government policies on the reservation and to control how tribal assets were managed.

Cautions, Biases and Selection Strategies

The documents of Flathead Reservation history in this collection were selected because they offered valuable information about the tribes. However, because they were written records, they also reflect the biases and bigotry of the white men and women who wrote the records. The readers need to look beyond the bigotry to see the specific incidents being described.

The editors have given preference to statements by individual Indians or chiefs or descriptions of specific activities. The documents chosen needed to be readable and make sense on their own. Normally historians often rely on many small, short references in diaries or newspaper articles which do not tell a full story.

The documents have not been edited to remove all bigoted words or references. However, an offensive term describing Indian women has been rendered as "s...."

The editors have tried to use "sic" as infrequently as possible. It is usually only used when we felt the reader might be confused about whether the mistake was in the transcription or in the original manuscript.

The most important sources for tribal history are the oral traditions of the elders. The written sources contribute towards telling history, but they do not give the history. Hopefully, the documents reproduced here will supplement the oral tribal histories currently being collected and written by the Séliš–Ql̓ispé Culture Committee in St. Ignatius and the Kootenai Culture Committee in Elmo, Montana.

The Flathead Reservation Economy, 1900-1906

By 1900 the livestock industry dominated the reservation economy. Sales of both horses and cattle were important, but most of the documents in this collection relate to the cattlemen.

On July 30, 1901, Special Agent Frank Armstrong submitted a report to the Secretary of the Interior describing a trip noting the farms and livestock herds in different parts of the reservation. (Document 14) A year and a half later, Special Indian Agent Charles McNichols listed the major livestock owners on the reservation and the number of acres each had enclosed. (Document 27) The biggest herds and farms belonged to mixed bloods and white men who had married into the tribes.

Newspaper reports in 1900 and 1904 described the sales of horses to off-reservation buyers which freed up more grazing for cattlemen. (Document 1; Document 50) The cattle owners were happy to have more grass but objected strenuously in 1903 to a grazing tax on the larger cattle and horse herds. In the spring of 1903 a delegation of cattlemen led by Duncan McDonald travelled to Washington, D.C., to protest the new tax. The government refused to repeal the tax. (Document 30) On July 2, 1903, Flathead Agent W. H. Smead proposed a per capita payment to tribal members from the proceeds of the grazing tax. (Document 33) In November 1903, Joe Morigeau was removed from the reservation by troops from Fort Missoula. He quickly settled his tax debt and returned home. (Document 37) Cattle owners Arthur Larravie, Angus P.

McDonald, and Maxime "Mike" Matt were ordered off the reservation in 1904 for failing to pay their grazing tax. They promptly paid up to avoid expulsion. (Document 52)

In 1904 the prices for reservation cattle were depressed, (Document 56) but in September 1905 there were large shipments of cattle from the reservation. (Document 81) William Q. Ranft, a Missoula attorney publicizing land sales on the reservation, left a detailed description of reservation cattle roundups in the early twentieth century. (Document 82)

One sideline of the reservation livestock industry was the Pablo-Allard buffalo herd. In 1902, J. B. Monroe visited Pablo's ranch and buffalo and also recorded sales of animals from the herd. (Document 21) During the summer of 1902, Charles Allard, Jr., used the buffalo as a star attraction for a wild west show. The show toured around Montana and the Midwest during the summer of 1902, but went broke that fall in Iowa. (Document 22)

Newspapers reported bountiful crops on the reservation in 1905 — mostly grain. (Document 79) In June 1905, Indian Inspector Arthur Tinker reported on the reservation economy that, "the Indians of this reservation, with but few exceptions, live in good log houses and have fair out buildings. Judging from all visible indications I should say they were prosperous and in good financial condition. Most of them are industrious and for Indians are good farmers." Tinker also said almost every Indian owned stock of some kind. (Document 71)

Battles with Missoula County and the State of Montana

The success of the Flathead Reservation tribes in the early twentieth century attracted predatory interest from Missoula County and Montana State officials. Missoula County made repeated efforts to tax mixed blood tribal members and the state tried to control Indian off-reservation hunting.

The federal government defended tribal members against Missoula County efforts to tax the mixed bloods. Taxes assessed against Alexander Matt, Michel Pablo, and Allen Sloan were struck down by the Missoula courts. (Document 4; Document 65; Document 66) Oliver Gibeau, who had moved onto the reservation in his late teen years, was declared a United States citizen and liable for county taxes. (Document 15)

The tribe also fought against the State of Montana over off-reservation hunting rights. In 1903 the state tried to enforce a new law forbidding Indians from being armed off the reservation. Presumably, if Indian hunting was restricted, there would be more game left for white sports hunters. In September 1903 the Missoula game warden confiscated Alex Bigknife's gun and ammunition while Bigknife was in Missoula buying supplies for his fall hunt. Bigknife was outraged and returned to the reservation. Bigknife and the chiefs promptly hired a Missoula attorney and sued the game warden. The state was able to keep the case tied up in legal technicalities, but they stopped enforcing the law that would have crippled tribal hunting rights. (Document 34)

In autumn 1905 Indian hunting parties traveled through Missoula. (Document 80; Document 84) Most bought Montana state hunting licenses, but a few were arrested for hunting without licenses. (Document 84; Document 85) Indian hunters did benefit from the state bounty for killing bears. (Document 58; Document 62)

Allotment Policy Imposed on Reservation

Flathead Agent W. H. Smead had long supported opening the Flathead Reservation to white homesteaders, but the actual imposition of the policy was the work of freshman Congressman Joseph Dixon in the fall of 1903. The chiefs and other tribal leaders had made clear their opposition to land sales in 1901 when the Crow, Flathead, Etc., Commission tried to buy the northern part of the reserve. (Document 11)

But, despite the clear opposition of tribal leaders, in December 1903, Dixon submitted a bill to allot the reservation and open the unallotted lands to white homesteaders. Apparently the first version of the bill provided for tribal member consent before the reservation was opened. (Document 39) Dixon wrote to five prominent mixed blood tribal members on December 19, 1903, asking for their suggestions for the bill. Dixon made it a point to mention the recent Lonewolf decision of the U.S. Supreme Court declared that Congress could alter Indian treaties without the consent of the tribes. Only one mixed blood, Joseph Allard, approved of the allotment. Duncan McDonald replied that he was "dissatisfied and disgusted and would have to take my medicine." Michel Pablo wrote that he was too busy caring for his cattle to make any comments. Allen Sloan and Angus P. McDonald apparently did not reply to Dixon's letter. (Document 40) Dixon did have the active support of the white Missoula business community. (Document 39)

Dixon used the Lonewolf Supreme Court decision and an obscure provision in the 1855 Hellgate Treaty to justify passing the allotment bill without asking for tribal consent. Article six of the treaty allowed the President to survey the reservation land into individual lots and sell the "surplus" land to white settlers. However, the transcript of the 1855 treaty negotiations does not show that this provision was explained to the chiefs. The bill was signed into law by President Theodore Roosevelt in April 1904. The Flathead allotment law provided for the sale of the "surplus" lands to white homesteaders under terms of the federal laws to convey public lands to white settlers for less than the real value of the land. Consequently, white homesteaders got the land for far less than the full value and the Indians were robbed. (Document 49)

Charlo and the other chiefs protested vigorously against the opening of the reservation. (Document 63) Despite tribal objections, the government moved quickly to survey the reservation land. (Document 67) In June 1905, Magpie was arrested for interfering with the survey, but Magpie apparently apologized and was released. (Document 72)

By 1906, William Q. Ranft, a Missoula attorney who had worked on the tribal enrollment, had formed the Flathead Reservation Information Agency. The agency gathered information on the lands open for homesteading and made the information available to prospective white settlers. (Document 91)

Formal Tribal Enrollment Lays Groundwork for Allotment

One prerequisite for allotment was establishing a formal roll of all the Indians who were recognized as tribal members. The first roll, compiled by Special Indian Agent Charles McNichols, was rejected by the Indian Office and in 1905 Special Indian Agent Thomas Downs completed a second roll which was accepted. (Document 26; Document 28; Document 70)

Two problem areas for the roll were the Camas Prairie Kalispel and the enrollment claims of a number of mixed blood families. The Camas Prairie Kalispels refused to deal with the agency or government agents, because they felt the government had lied to them in the past. The final roll included these Indians' names based on information gathered indirectly. Some of the chiefs objected to enrolling mixed blood families who had small amounts of Indian blood from the confederated tribes. Most of the families who were questioned submitted evidence and were added to the roll. Some families hired white attorneys, especially William Ranft, to prepare their enrollment cases. One record was found of Ranft soliciting legal business relating to enrollment in a Missoula saloon. (Document 47)

The enrollment of Flathead Indian reservation residents from other tribes was determined by formal councils of the chiefs to consider adoptions. The proceedings of two of these councils are included in this collection. (Document 55; Document 60)

Another spin off from the Flathead allotment bill was the disposition of the Flathead Lake dam site. If the dam site was part of the public domain after the reservation was opened, any white man could claim the site as private property. Almost as soon as the allotment bill was signed, white businessmen started making claims for the site. Fortunately, however, the federal government reserved the site for the tribes — or for the irrigation project. (Document 59; Document 68; Document 95)

Crime on the Reservation

Since major crimes on the reservation were tried in federal courts, news of reservation crimes was a staple of newspaper coverage. There is no way to tell how biased the white courts were, but most of the crimes were Indian on Indian and relied on Indian testimony. A number of the murder charges were dismissed on the basis of self-defense. (Document 17; Document 42; Document 53) Many charges related to bringing whiskey on the reservation. (Document 44; Document 57) In one case in December 1903 a white man was convicted of stealing an Indian's horse. (Document 38) An Indian was drunk in Missoula in November 1902 and attacked a Missoula residence. (Document 25) In August 1906 Peter Matt was arrested for shooting a white boy in the ankle while trying to force the boy to dance for spectators. (Document 77) On October 27, 1903, an article in a Kalispell newspaper described the use of whipping as a punishment on the reservation. (Document 36)

One of the most famous crimes on the reservation was the autumn 1902 robbery of a prominent Indian cattleman named rich Michel who was robbed of an estimated $18,000 to $22,000 in cash. (Document 24) In June 1903 an Indian was arrested for the crime. (Document 32) The robbery was even reported in the *New York Times*.

A poignant case was the 1906 theft of one of Kootenai Chief Koostatah's work horses by an Indian named Gingras. Gingras took the horse to Kalispell and sold it to a white man. The white man refused to surrender the horse to Koostatah without a formal court order. This left Koostatah without a full team of horses to do his spring plowing, and Koostatah did not have the money to purchase a replacement. (Document 92)

Glimpses of Everyday Life on the Reservation

The written sources have only limited information about everyday life on the reservation between 1900 and 1906. The oral histories being compiled by the Séliš–Ql̓ispé and Kootenai Culture Committees will provide much more information about the normal activities of tribal members and attitudes of the Indian people about the dramatic changes impacting the tribes in the beginning of the twentieth century. The written documents do give us some glimpses into the lives of tribal members on the reservation.

A detailed newspaper article gave a description of the ceremony and pomp surrounding the arrival of Montana Bishop John Brondel for the 1902 St. Ignatius Day celebration. (Document 23) Another article described the 1905 school closing ceremonies for the St. Ignatius Mission schools. (Document 74) Church festivals and holidays were important community events attended by most tribal members.

The 1905 Fourth of July celebration at Arlee received extensive coverage in the newspapers. One report told of a Kootenai Indian named Darsoe who died of cramps after strenuous dancing. (Document 75)

A newspaper article and a report by Special Agent Frank C. Armstrong outlined the basic details of tribal and government efforts to fight the 1901 smallpox epidemic on the reservation. Unfortunately, some lives were lost to the disease. (Document 13)

Missoula newspapers related how tribal members spent their money from the sale of their Bitterroot allotments. Some spent the money on farm machinery while others purchased alcohol. (Document 29; Document 64) In 1905, Indians visited Missoula to dig bitterroot in the Missoula Valley. (Document 69) Later that year, tribal members gathered in Missoula to attend a circus that was visiting the city. (Document 78)

In 1901, Father Augustine Dimier left several detailed descriptions — from his point of view — of his pastoral visits to the Kootenai village on Flathead Lake. (Document 10) In 1904 and 1905, William and Henry Matt and a Kootenai, who took the professional name of Two Feathers, wrestled professionally in Missoula and other Pacific Northwest cities. Many tribal members traveled to Missoula to attend the matches and bet on the outcomes. (Document 61)

Some other aspects of reservation life in the early twentieth century were described in the written documents. In 1956 Blind Mose related his memories of the cycle of fishing and hunting with his family in his childhood years. (Document 7) In a local history of the Libby, Montana, area, Mrs. Jacob Boothman gave a meal to an Indian visitor who later dropped off a string of trout for Boothman in return. (Document 8) Joe Barnaby was killed in a railroad accident in August 1900. He had operated a store at the agency before his death. (Document 5) In May 1901, Chief Charlo took his first ride in an automobile in Missoula. (Document 12) A newspaper reporter described a visit with Duncan McDonald at Ravalli while waiting for the train. McDonald regaled the visitors with traditional Indian stories. (Document 18) In July 1904, the newspaper reported that a full-blood Indian from the reservation purchased a piano. He wanted the piano for his daughter who had learned to play piano at the Carlisle Indian School. Unfortunately, the reporter did not give the Indian's name. (Document 54)

Conclusion

The full history of the Salish, Pend d'Oreille, and Kootenai Indians at the start of the twentieth century will be found in the oral histories being compiled now by the tribal culture committees on the reservation. The written historical documents tell only part of the story. However, the documents do tell a tale of crisis as Congressman Joseph Dixon and neighboring white businessmen moved to force the tribes to sell their land to white voters for less than its true value. By 1905, the tribes had made remarkable progress in developing a new economy based on livestock and farming. In 1905, the tribes were basically self-supporting, but with the forced loss of their assets — the land — their future income declined and the tribal community became poor. Tribal leaders recognized that they were being wrongly treated, but could not stop the opening of the reservation. Despite disappointments, the tribes never stopped complaining about harmful government policies and fought to have their voices and interests heard.

Chapter 1

Documents of Salish, Pend d'Oreille, and Kootenai History Between 1900-1902

Document 1

Indians Sell Cayuses to Make Room for Cattle February 27, 1900

Source: "They Spoil the Range," *The Anaconda Standard*, February 27, 1900, page 16, col. 2.

Editors' note: Agent W. H. Smead worked hard to develop a market for the small cayuses that dominated the livestock herds on the reservation range. The reservation cattlemen supported Smead in order to make more grass available for cattle herds.

They Spoil the Range
The Cayuse Problem Is a Serious One.
A Menace to Cattle
Their Number Is Steadily Increasing and There Is No Sale for Them.
Five Hundred Fed to Fatten Hogs.

Missoula, Feb. 25. — What to do with the cayuses has been a problem that has vexed the range people of this end of the state for several years. This has been especially true of the ranges west of Missoula, where the influence of the Indian reservation is felt. There are tens of thousands of these little horses on the reserve and the region that borders upon it. They spoil the range for valuable stock, but there seems to be no good way of getting rid of them and they have multiplied till they are a menace to the cattle herds. There has been no sale for them, and the number has been steadily increasing for four or five years, till now the ranges are covered with them. There has been talk of offering a bounty for their hides, as for other animal pests, but this has not found general favor, and it has never been more than a suggestion. Still, there has not till recently been any practical suggestion made for the reduction of the size of these cayuse herds and for their disposal in a way that would not meet with the opposition of their owners, who are not disposed to give away these horses, though they are not worth what they are assessed for.

Within the past six months C. C. Willis of Plains has found a use for the cayuse that promises to dispose of some of them, and he has succeeded in getting away with nearly 500 of them. He buys them from the Indians and feeds them to the hogs. In this way he has disposed, as stated, of about 500, and the results have been satisfactory. The hogs thus fed make good pork that is readily marketable, and Mr. Willis sells the hides at a profit. When asked the other day about this branch of his business Mr. Willis said to a Standard man:

"I first began to talk to the Indians about this matter some eight months ago. At first they would not listen to the proposition. They had not yet got out of the idea that the cayuses were worth as much as they used to be and they wanted old-time prices for them. When they came to think it over, however, they changed their minds, and after a couple of months, they began to bring in the animals. Since then I have had no trouble in getting all I want of them. The first lot that came in was driven down to my corral, and when I counted them I found there were 65 of the little fellows. I made a dicker with the Indians for them and at once began to feed them to the hogs. I thought that the 65 would last all winter, but I soon found that this was not so. I had to get more, and up to date I have bought and used in this way nearly 500.

The average cost of the cayuses has been $1.75 a head. The hides bring about $2 a piece, so that the cost of the meat is practically nothing. At first I was opposed to feeding the hogs on this meat, but I found that they like it and that it makes good pork. The hogs like the feed and do well on it. We kill the cayuses in the hog pasture and skin them there. When the hogs are ready for market I feed them on grain for a couple of weeks so that they will be solid and not shrink in shipment. I have found, too, that this improves the quality of the pork. I have just shipped a carload of hogs thus handled to the Seattle market and this netted me $947. I will ship another soon.

"This plan is all right for the winter, but this summer I will have to move the pasture to my hill ranch, so as to get them away from the houses. I expect to build a cooking house up there with a bag vat, so that the horse meat can be cooked before it is fed. In this way we will be able to use up with the meat all the culled vegetables that are too small for market, potatoes, turnips, beets and so forth. This will make better pork and will dispose of a lot of waste stuff from the ranch.

"Alex Dow of Arlee has been following the same plan and has found it successful. I talked with him not long ago about it, and his opinion was that the cooked meat is better than the uncooked. Not long ago there was a large shipment of cayuses fed at Plains, en route from the coast to the South, where they were to be sent to Cuba. These were not as good as the range cayuse of this part of the country, and I had a talk with the shipper as to supplying him from local ranges. I found that we could furnish him with much better horses at a less price than he had paid in Oregon for the lot that he was then shipping. Last week I had a letter from him, and I expect that we will make up a trainload for him from the ranges around here. This will get rid of a lot of the cayuses and save the ranges for the cattle. I have also had some correspondence with the horse meat canners of Oregon and think that we will be able to do business with them before the end of the season. But the most profitable way of disposing of the cayuse seems to me to be the plan that I have adopted. It consumes a lot of them and the business is profitable. The pork is good and we have had no trouble in getting a good price for our hogs that have been fattened in this way. I think that will solve the question of how to get rid of the cayuse. It is an important one, as the rapid increase of these animals threatens to make the ranges worthless for cattle unless it is checked at once."

Document 2

Charles Allard, Sr., Estate Divided

May 14, 1900

Source: "Order of Distribution," *The Anaconda Standard*, May 14, 1900, page 12, col. 2.

Editors' note: Allard, Sr., left a large estate to be divided among his heirs after his death in 1896. The estate was probated in a Montana state court.

Order of Distribution
Made by Judge Woody in the Allard Estate.
Accounts Are Approved
Twenty Thousand in Cash and an Undivided Half-Interest in the Buffalo Herd — An Appraiser Appointed.

Missoula, May 12. — Judge Woody has made the following order in the estate of Charles Allard, in accord with the will filed for probate at the time of his death:

Louise Allard Stinger and Michael Pablo, executrix and executor, respectively, of the said Charles Allard, deceased, having heretofore filed their petition for partial distribution, and the heirs of the said Charles Allard, the persons entitled to share in the distribution of this estate, having entered their appearances and consented thereto; and it appearing to the satisfaction of the court and from the petitions and account heretofore filed and approved that there is at this time in the hands of the personal representatives of said decedent and which should be distributed the sum of $20,000 in cash and an undivided one-half interest in a herd of buffalo estimated to be 250 head; and,

It further appearing to the satisfaction of the court that under and by virtue of the will of said decedent heretofore admitted to probate in this court that said funds and property should be distributed as follows, to-wit:

To Joseph Allard, son of the decedent, one-fourth of said sum and an undivided one-fourth of the undivided one-half of the said herd of buffalo, or in other words, an undivided one-eighth interest in the whole of said herd of buffalo.

To Charles Allard, son of the decedent, one-fourth of said sum and an undivided one-fourth of said undivided one-half interest in said herd of buffalo, or an undivided one-eighth interest in the whole of said herd of buffalo.

To Louise Allard, now Stinger, lately widow of the said decedent, one-sixth of said sum and an undivided one-sixth of the undivided one-half of said herd of buffalo, or an undivided one-twelfth interest of the whole of said herd of buffalo.

To Eva May Allard, daughter of said decedent, one-sixth of said sum and an undivided one-sixth of said undivided one-half interest in said herd of buffalo, or an undivided one-twelfth interest in the whole of said herd of buffalo.

To Louise Anna Allard, daughter of the said decedent, one sixth of said sum and an undivided one-sixth of said undivided one-half interest in said buffalo, or one-twelfth interest in the whole of said herd of buffalo.

And the court is sufficiently advised in the premises, it is hereby ordered that the prayer of said petition be granted; that said money and property be distributed among the heirs of the said Charles Allard, deceased, as hereinafter provided, which is in accordance with provisions of the will of said decedent.

It is further ordered, adjudged and decreed that there be a partial distribution of said estate and that the executrix and executor hereinbefore named are ordered, directed and required to pay to Joseph Allard the sum of $5,000, to Charles Allard the sum of $5,000, to Louise Allard Stinger the sum of $3,333, to John M. Keith, guardian of Louise Anna Allard, for the said Louise Anna Allard, the sum of $3,333.

It is further ordered, adjudged and decreed that there be and hereby is set apart and distributed to Joseph Allard an undivided one-eighth interest in that certain herd of buffalo on the Flathead reservation known as the Pablo-Allard herd of buffalo, and to Charles Allard an undivided one-eighth interest in that certain herd of buffalo on the Flathead reservation known as the Pablo-Allard herd of buffalo; and,

To Louise Allard Stinger an undivided one-twelfth interest in that certain herd of buffalo on the Flathead reservation known as the Pablo-Allard herd of buffalo; and,

To John M. Keith, guardian of Eva May Allard, for said Eva May Allard, an undivided one-twelfth interest in that certain herd of buffalo on the Flathead reservation known as the Pablo-Allard herd of buffalo; and,

It is further ordered, adjudged and decreed that John L. Sloane be appointed an appraiser of this court to ascertain and determine the amount of inheritance taxes due from said estate and to report the same in writing to this court; and when said report has been approved by this court said amount to be paid by the above petitioners to the treasurer of Missoula county and his receipt taken therefor; and,

Said executrix and executor will file in this court receipts and vouchers for the payments made hereunder.

Document 3

Flathead Reservation Cattle and Horse Herds

June 29, 1900

Source: "A Trip to Selish," *The Kalispell Bee*, June 29, 1900, page 1, col. 5.

Editors' note: This writer commented on the large herds of cattle and horses on the reservation in 1900. He also described some of the sales of Indian owned horses to off-reservation buyers.

A Trip to Selish
Down Flathead River and Over the Lake to Polson.
A Delightful Trip.
The Flathead Indian Reservation a Splendid Tract of Land, Wonderfully Productive.

At this season the traveler will find a most delightful and picturesque trip in taking the lake and river voyage from Kalispell to Selish. The distance is about one hundred miles and is made in one day from Kalispell. The steamer Klondyke leaves Demersville, three miles from Kalispell, three times each week at six o'clock in the morning and winds down the Flathead river at a speed which is entirely satisfactory, giving enough time to admire both banks of this beautiful stream. About nine o'clock you pass the bar of the Flathead lake and are then on the bosom of what is the largest body of water in the Rocky mountain region and is a sight which one will never tire of praising. The landing place is Polson, at the foot of the lake and about thirty-eight miles from Selish. Polson is not much of a town, consisting only of a few houses and a general store, in which is the hotel and postoffice. This store does a good business with the Indians.

The trip from Polson by stage to Selish is through the finest range country in Montana, or the entire west for that matter. Thousands of cattle belonging to the Indians graze on the luxuriant grasses and at this season they are rolling fat. The "big prairie," as it is called, is a stretch fifteen miles of as fine land as any state can boast. It is watered plentifully by hundreds of small lakes and where it is cultivated at all it shows wonderful productive qualities. Almost the entire reservation of nearly three million acres is used only for range purposes. It belongs to the Flathead Indians, of course. There are 1800 full bloods and about 400 half breeds at present on the reservation and it is likely to be many years before this rich land will be opened for settlement. A great number of these Indians are stocking up with the very finest cattle, while others cling to the horses. The latter they sell in large bands for as low as $2 a head. G. C. Jamison, representing Thewett Bros. of St. Paul, made a shipment to his firm yesterday from Selish. The train was made up of about 25 cars, which will average 30 head to each car, not counting the colts, which are usually thrown in by the Indians to make good measure. This firm has shipped over 100 cars of horses the past four months from Selish, all of them being purchased from the Indians. On the road to St. Paul they are unloaded at Billings and Mandan and fed, watered and classified. These cayuses will be sold as western range horses at a big sale in St. Paul on July 5. The farmers within 200 and 300 miles of St. Paul will attend this sale, as over 20,000 head of all sorts of horses will be sold. The Montana horses are represented as being unbroken. The farmers of Minnesota will doubtless find this statement a fact.

Selish is reached at about six o'clock in the evening. The stage usually connects with the Northern Pacific train for the west, due at that time, and the east-bound train leaves at 7:30 the next morning. It is about the quickest way to make the journey to Butte and the east unless you are hampered with baggage.

Document 4

Alexander Matt Not Subject to County Taxes

July 2, 1900

Source: "United States v. Higgins, County Treasurer. (Circuit Court, D. Montana. July 2, 1900.) No. 576," *The Federal Reporter*, vol. 103 (Sept.-Oct. 1900), pages 348-352.

Editors' note: This decision forced the Missoula County to stop attempting to tax many of the mixed blood tribal members who lived on the reservation. The decision also includes a short biographical sketch of Alexander Matt.

United States v. Higgins, County Treasurer.
(Circuit Court, D. Montana. July 2, 1900.)
No. 576.

Taxation — Liability of Half-Breeds to State Laws.

> One born of a white father and an Indian mother, and who is a recognized member of the tribe of Indians to which his mother belongs, is an Indian, and not subject to taxation under the laws of the state in which he resides.

W. B. Rodgers, U.S. Dist. Atty.

Marshall, Stiff & Denny, for defendant.

Knowles, District Judge. This is a suit brought by the United States against George Higgins, the treasurer and tax collection of Missoula county, to enjoin him from collecting a tax from one Alexander Matt. It appears from the evidence in the case: That said Matt is the owner of a number of horses and cattle ranging upon the Flathead Indian reservation, sometimes called "Jocko Indian Reservation," in the state of Montana. That in the year 1897 one W. R. Hamilton, the then assessor of Missoula county, listed said property as that of the said Matt for taxation, and that the amount of the taxes assessed upon the same for state and county purposes was the sum of $10.50. The said assessment was duly returned upon the proper assessment roll for said year to the then tax collector of Missoula county. The said Matt refused to pay this tax, and after the same became delinquent said George Higgins, as treasurer and tax collector of said county, seized two head of cattle, the property of said Matt, and advertised the same for sale at public auction, with a view to securing money sufficient to pay said tax, penalty, and the cost of collection thereof. The government brought this suit for the purpose of enjoining this sale, alleging that said Matt is an Indian and its ward. No contention has been made that the United States cannot maintain this suit, if such is the fact. The defendant contends that said Matt should be classed as a white man, and not an Indian, and that, as that part of the Flathead reservation where Matt resides lies within the exterior boundaries of Missoula county, he should list his property and be taxed in that county. The question here presented is, should Alexander Matt be classed as an Indian or a white man? If an Indian, he is not subject to taxation in said county.

From the evidence it appears: That the father of Matt is a Canadian Frenchman. That his mother was a Piegan Indian, and that Alexander Matt was born somewhere in the northeastern part of what is now known as "Montana" in the year 1853, at which time it was all known and classed as Indian country. His father moved to Colville, then in the territory of Washington, and seems to have lived there several years, and then returned to Montana some time in 1864, and lived in various places within the limits of what is now the state of Montana, coming to Stevensville, in the county of Missoula, in 1866 or 1867. At that time the Flathead Indians were the principal inhabitants of the Bitter Root valley. Shortly after the arrival of the father and mother of Matt in the Bitter Root valley, his mother was adopted into the Flathead tribe. She made application to be so admitted or adopted to Victor, the head chief thereof, who called a council of the leading men of his tribe; and by them, and with the consent of the chiefs of the tribe, it was declared that she was a member thereof. From that time on she and her children were recognized as members of the Flathead tribe. The father of Matt was a blacksmith, and generally followed that trade, and instructed his son therein. Subsequently the whole family moved to the Flathead Indian reservation, sometimes called "Jocko Indian Reservation," and said Matt has lived there since that time, — some 26 years. By article 2 of the treaty between the United States and the Flathead, Kootenai, and Upper Pend D'Oreille Indians, concluded July 16, 1855 (12 Stat. 976), it was provided that other friendly tribes and bands of Indians in the territory of Washington might be consolidated under the common designation of the Flathead nation, with Victor as head chief, upon the said Flathead Indian Reservation. The evidence shows that the said Matt had and has been recognized as a member of the Flathead tribe of Indians ever since his residence therein. It is claimed that notwithstanding these facts, the father of Matt being a white man, Matt would follow the condition of his father, and must be treated as a white man. It is undoubtedly true that a white man, although adopted into an Indian tribe, and treated by them in all respects as and like an Indian, cannot escape his responsibilities as a white man, and must be subject to the laws and taxing power of a government of white men, embracing the section of the country where he lives. But is it true that under our laws a child will always be classed as of the same color and race as his or her father? It is well known and settled that, if a mother is a slave, her children follow her condition. A government under which persons of the half-blood may reside can determine the status of such half-bloods, — as to whether they shall be classed as white people or as Indians. In the case of U.S. v. Holliday, 3 Wall. 419, 18 L. Ed. 182, the court held that in the treatment of the Indians it is the rule of this court to follow the action of the executive and other political departments of the government. In the Case of The Kansas Indians, 5 Wall. 756, 18 L. Ed. 673, the court said:

> "But the acts of the political department of the government settles beyond controversy that the Shawnees are as yet a distinct people, with a perfect tribal organization. As long as the United States recognize their national character, they are under the protection of treaties and the laws of congress, and their property is withdrawn from the operation of state laws."

In the case of U.S. v. Boyd (C. C.) 68 Fed. 580, it was said:

> "In determining the attitude of the government towards the Indians, — all Indians, — the courts follow the action of the executive and other political departments of the government, whose more especial duty it is to determine such affairs."

In determining as to what class half-breeds belong, we may refer, then, to the treatment and recognition the executive and political departments of the government have accorded them. On August 4, 1824, the government made a treaty with the Sac and Fox Indians (7 Stat. 229), in which it is provided that certain land therein described should be set apart as a reservation for the use of the half-breeds of the Sac and Fax confederated Indian tribes. It will be observed that these half-breeds were described as belonging to said tribes. On June 30, 1834 (4 Stat. 740), these half-breeds were given permission to sell these lands. These Indians were again described as half-breeds belonging to those tribes. On April 27, 1816 (6 Stat. 171), an act of congress was passed for the relief of Samuel Manac, and he is described therein as "a friendly Creek Indian of the half blood." On March 3, 1837 (Id. 692), congress passed an act for the relief of James Brown and John Brown, half breeds of the Cherokee nation of Indians. On September 29, 1817 (7 Stat. 163), the United States made a treaty with the Wyandot and other Indian tribes, and therein provision was made for the children of one William McCollock, and these children are described as quarter-blood Wyandot Indians. At the same time, and in the same treaty, provision was made for the children of one Isaac Williams, who is described as a half-blood Wyandot Indian. At the same time, and in the same treaty, provision was made for one Anthony Shane, who is described as a half-blood Ottawa Indian. On October 6, 1818 (Id. 191), in a treaty with the Miami Indians, there was a reservation of lands made in favor of Ann Turner, Rebecca Hackley, William Wayne Wells, Mary Wells, and Jane Turner Wells; each of them being described as a half-blooded Miami Indian. On November 15, 1824 (Id. 233), in a treaty with the Quapaw Indians, a reservation of land is made in favor of one Saracen, who is described as a half-breed Quapaw Indian. On June 2, 1825 (Id. 240), the United States made a treaty with the Osage Indians, and therein is made a provision for half-breeds. The language and scope of the treaty show that these half-breeds were persons of that tribe. On June 3, 1825 (Id. 245), in a treaty with the Kansas Indians, a reservation of land is made for a large number of persons, named and described as half-breeds of the Kansas nation. On August 5, 1826 (Id. 291), in a treaty with the Chippewas a reservation of land is made for the benefit of a large number of persons named therein, described as half-breeds and Chippewas by descent. On October 16, 1826 (Id. 298, 299), in a treaty with the Pottawatomie Indians, a reservation of land is made for certain persons therein, described as half-breeds and Indians by descent. On October 23, 1826 (Id. 302), in a treaty with the Miami Indians a reservation of land is made for certain persons therein, described as the children of a half-blood Miami Indian woman. Similar descriptions of half-breeds as being Indians of the tribe with whom they lived will be found in the following Indian treaties: August 1, 1829 (7 Stat. 324), treaty with Winnebago Indians; July 15, 1830 (7 Stat. 330), treaty with Sioux Indians; August 30, 1831 (7 Stat. 362), treaty with Ottawa Indians; September 15, 1832 (7 Stat. 372), treaty with Winnebago Indians; September 21, 1832 (7 Stat. 374), treaty with Sac and Fox Indians; October 27, 1832 (7 Stat. 400), treaty with Pottawatomie Indians; March 28, 1836 (7 Stat. 493), treaty with Ottawa, etc., Indians; July 29, 1837 (7 Stat. 537), treaty with Chippewa Indians; September 29, 1837 (7 Stat. 539), treaty with Sioux Indians; November 1, 1837 (7 Stat. 545), treaty with Winnebago Indians; October 4, 1842 (7 Stat. 592), treaty with Chippewa Indians; October 18, 1848 (9 Stat. 952), treaty with Menominee Indians; March 16, 1854 (10 Stat. 1045), treaty with Omaha Indians; February 22, 1855 (10 Stat. 1169), treaty with Chippewa Indians; February 27, 1855 (10 Stat. 1174), treaty with Winnebago Indians; September 29, 1865 (14 Stat. 689), treaty with Osage Indians; October 14, 1865 (14 Stat. 705), treaty with Cheyenne Indians; March 21, 1866 (14 Stat. 756), treaty with Seminole Indians. On September 24, 1857 (11 Stat. 731), in a treaty with the Pawnee Indians it is provided that the half-bloods of that tribe who remain with them shall have equal rights with the other members thereof; that those who do not reside with the tribe shall be entitled to script in lieu of lands. On March 12, 1858 (12 Stat. 999), in a treaty with the Ponca Indians it is provided that the half-breeds of that tribe residing with them shall have the same rights and privileges as the other members thereof, and that those residing among the whites in civilization shall be entitled to land script in lieu of lands.

In an act of congress approved June 5, 1872 (17 Stat. 226), the following provision is made in regard to the Flathead Indians:

> "It shall be the duty of the president as soon as practicable, to remove the Flathead Indians (whether of full or mixed blood) and all other Indians connected with said tribe and recognized as members thereof, from the Bitter Root valley in the territory of Montana to the general reservation, commonly known as the Jocko reservation, which by a treaty was set apart and reserved for the use and occupation of said confederated tribes."

Alexander Matt
Source: Virginia Matt Brazill, Arlee, Montana

The Jocko reservation, here referred to, is the Flathead reservation named in the treaty with these Indians on the 16th day of July 1855, above referred to. At the time this statute was passed the mother of Matt, according to the evidence, had been adopted into the Flathead tribe. Matt was undoubtedly a half-breed connected with that tribe, and was recognized as a member thereof. This statute recognized mixed bloods of the Flathead tribe as Indians. They are to be removed from the Bitter Root valley, which at that time was being settled by whites. They were distinguished from the whites, as not being entitled to reside there. Considering the history of the Indian tribes throughout the United States, I am satisfied it will be found that the half-bloods of all tribes were the children of what was recognized as Indian marriages between white men and Indian women. But few instances can be found in which white women intermarried with Indian men. Considering, then, the treaties and statutes above referred to, I think it evident that the executive and political departments of the government have recognized persons having at least one-half Indian blood in their veins, whose fathers were white men, which half-bloods lived and resided with the tribes to which their mothers belonged, as Indians. Considering the treaties and statutes in regard to half-breeds, I may say that they never have been treated as white people entitled to the rights of American citizenship. Special provision has been made for them, — special reservations of land, special appropriations of money. No such provision has been made for any other class. It is well known to those who have lived upon the frontier in America that, as a rule, half-breeds or mixed-blood Indians have resided with the tribes to which their mothers belonged; that they have, as a rule, never found a welcome home with their white relatives, but with their Indian kindred. It is but just, then, that they should be classed as Indians, and have all the rights of the Indian. In 7 Op. Attys. Gen. 746, it is said, "Half-breed Indians are to be treated as Indians, in all respects, so long as they retain their tribal relations."

Entertaining these views, I hold that Alexander Matt should be treated as an Indian, and as such he is not subject to taxation under the laws of the state of Montana. The prayer of the bill will be granted. Let the injunction heretofore issued be made perpetual.

Document 5

Joe Barnaby Killed in Railroad Accident

August 22, 1900

Source: "Joe Barnaby Killed," *The Anaconda Standard*, August 22, 1900, page 12, col. 2.

Editors' note: In 1883 the tribal members had been promised free rides on the railroad running through the reservation, but this promise was soon forgotten. Tribal members who tried to get the free rides they were entitled to were often harassed or forced to take unauthorized rides with tragic consequences. Note that Barnaby operated a small store at the agency before his death.

Joe Barnaby Killed
His Mangled Remains Found Near Arlee.
Dragged by the Train
It Is Supposed That He Was Stealing a Ride When the Accident Occurred.
He Was a Halfbreed With a Record.

Missoula, Aug. 21. — The mangled remains of Joe Barnaby were found this morning by a railway bridge gang at the first crossing of the Jocko, about a mile below Arlee. The body had evidently been dragged some distance by the train. There were traces of its course the entire length of the railway bridge and the bruised and mangled mass of flesh and bones was found in a heap at the west end of the bridge.

The coroner was notified at once and Deputy Corner Marsh went out to the scene of the accident this forenoon. The evidence of the cause of the death was so apparent that it was not considered necessary to hold an inquest and the remains were buried at the agency cemetery on the reservation.

Barnaby was a well know half-breed, having lived with the Indians on the Bitter Root reservation before their removal to the valley of the Jocko on the Flathead reservation. He was thrifty and had accumulated considerably money at different times. His inordinate thirst, however, generally caused him to lose all he had saved in his weeks of soberness. About a year ago he received a considerable sum of money from the distribution of funds due the Bitter Root

Indians, his share being $500. He came to Missoula and bought wine and a new hat and then proceeded to blow in the rest in the most approved style. He went to the places where they charge double price for wine, and he was a king for a night. He bought wine for the ladies and was a popular idol. When he came to himself in the morning all that he had to show for his $500 was a wine headache and the new hat that he had bought. He did not howl, however. He simply said that the hat was all he wanted anyway, and it wasn't everybody that could spend $500 in a night for wine. He went back to the reservation and the experience was a closed incident.

Since then he has not been in Missoula much till yesterday. He spent the day here and the last that any one remembers having seen of him was on West Front street here about 10 o'clock last night. At that time he was very drunk. How he met his death nobody seems to be able to explain, unless he went out to Arlee on the front end of a baggage car on the north coast limited last night. That train does not stop at Arlee and it may be he tried to get off the train as it passed the station and was killed and his lifeless body dragged along the track till it was reduced to pulp.

Louis Pablo was the last man who saw him in town. He was then, as stated, on Front street much the worse for booze. Mr. Pablo went to Evaro, the station this side of Arlee, on the limited last night. He says that he did not see anything of Barnaby, but that he might have been upon the front end and escaped his notice. He thinks that he saw him when the train reached Evaro, but is not sure. The only conclusion that can be reached is that he was riding the blind baggage and either fell from the train or tried to get off as it passed Arlee and was caught under the wheels. In the pockets of his clothes were found the broken fragments of three bottles — two quarts and a pint — that had evidently contained whiskey. Recently Barnaby had been running a small store near the agency.

Document 6

Charlo and Kakashe Complain About Agent Smead August 25, 1900

Source: "Letter and Statements of Flathead Chiefs Sharlo & Ki-ki-is-see," enclosure number 1 in Cyrus Beede to Secretary of the Interior, August 25, 1900, U.S. Department of the Interior, "Reports of Inspection of the Field Jurisdictions of the Office of Indian Affairs, 1875-1900," National Archive Microfilm Publication M1070, reel 11, Flathead, 6597/1900.

Editors' note: These statements include Chief Charlo's and Baptiste Ka-ka-shee's complaints about their treatment by Agent W. H. Smead and Flathead Agency policies in 1900.

Statement of Sharlo, Chief of Flathead Indians

I spoke to agent Smead about cattle and horses of white men on the reservation and told him it was his duty to keep them off. He replied "Sharlo, You have no brains. You are opposed to me. He said I was just like a horse." I said "if I am a horse you ought to take care of me and when you call me a horse I think you are not a fit man to be the Agent." Another time I told him where some white men had driven cattle on the reservation and suggested that the Agent have them removed — the Agent said "Wait a little while." This was over a year ago but the agent did nothing to remove these cattle. The half breeds and the Agent stand in together.

Last year Agent Smead and Alex Dow the trader rounded up all the horses and cut the Stallions; when they found horses without brands on they appropriated them. The chiefs tried to stop this rascality but we were powerless. Smead said he had authority from Washington to round up the horses & take those which were not branded. Many of these unbranded horses belonged to old people & children living on this reservation, who had not been able to round up & brand their horses. Eighteen of our head men tried to stop this round up of Smead & Dow but we couldn't stop it. They brought these horses to Alex Dow's field, about 200 & Alex Dow Killed them & fed them to his hogs. Agent Smead said he would take the money Dow gave for these horses & divide it up among poor Indians, but none of the poor Indians ever got any of it.

Sharlo, his x mark

Witnesses to mark, Oscar Anderson, L Geis

I hereby certify that I acted as interpreter for Sharlo & that the preceding statement was written at his dictation & that he fully understands the contents thereof.

Paul Shawaway
Interpreter.

* * * * * * * * *

Judge Baptiste Kakashe, Pend d'Oreille
Source: Photograph Archives, Montana Historical Society, Helena, Montana, detail from photo 954-528

Statement of Ki-Ki-is-see Chief of Flathead Indians

Last spring I came to this agency & saw a band of cattle in a field near there about 100 — They told me they belonged to Agent Smead. Their brand was H. I told the agent there was a thief stealing horses near the foot of the lake. Smead asked me if I knew the man. I said yes, his name is Owl, which is all the same as thief. I said two men can prove he is a thief. Agent Carter had driven him out once, but he came back again. Smead said he would see about it but the man is there yet. I told him about last May.

Agent Carter used to do something but Smead does not help the Indians at all. I could give much more information if there was time to look around & get names.

Ki-Ki-is-see, his x mark

Witnesses to mark, Oscar Anderson, L Geis

I certify that I acted as interpreter for Ki-Ki-is-see and fully explained to him the contents of the above statement & that I wrote it at his dictation.

Paul Sha wa way
Interpreter.

Document 7

Blind Mose Remembered His Childhood Travels

1900, ca.

Source: Blind Moses, "Reminiscences of Blind Moses, Confederated Salish and Kootenai Tribes of the Flathead Reservation, Montana," South Dakota Oral History Center, Department of Native Studies, University of South Dakota, Vermillion, S.D., AIRP 563.

Editors' note: In this November 7, 1956, interview with Robert C. Carriker and Father Thomas Connolly, S.J., Mose talked about his memories of the cycle of fishing and hunting during his childhood years. The interview took place on the Flathead Reservation and was translated by Celina Goolsby, Spokane, Wash.

Years ago when I was a very small child my uncles, my aunts, my grandparents, they were people [unintelligible] my Uncle John Big Smoke, [unintelligible] who was the son of [unintelligible] is old Joe Andrew and all their wives [unintelligible] we would get on the canoes, three or four of them, make out of bark, not wood. Then we would make our annual trip down the river we would go, all the way down to the lake, to the larger lake that is off of the river, Ponderray River. They would go, we would go to pick, we would go to store up on fish, [unintelligible] which is white fish. That's where they would dig holes, yeah dig holes and braid their traps. They would braid their traps and in these traps they would dig holes and the fish would go in and they would catch them in these large cones. They would stay there for several days and then they would leave to the other end of the lake. And they would hunt for deer, elk, bear, they would trap beaver, they would leave from Cusick early in the spring and they would stay at the Ponderray Lake for two or three months, they be there all summer long. From there they would come back and they would come back to a place called Swayee and, which was a little island and this island they would pack their canoes and all of their provisions and walk over the island and then from the other side they would then again set their canoes with all the provisions and start in again. There was in those days there was no white people, none whatsoever all the way from here clear down to the Ponderray Lake. In my childhood I remember seeing only four people who were white. And then when they arrived here, back here is Kalispel, they would stay here about two months and then in the fall when the first snow came, everybody from this valley would leave, to go hunting for the deer; that's when me and my uncles and my grandfather and all my other relatives we would cross the mountains at [unintelligible]. They would, we would go on horseback, they would pack all of the horses, tying everything onto the horse. After they had everything tied onto the horse they would put me on top of the horse, tied on and that was the way I travelled. I don't know what lake this is? Oh I do . . . And there we would camp at the lake and there again we hunted and fished and got ready for the coming winter. There was a certain way that we prepared the salmon after, or the fish after we caught them. We put them on sticks and stand them in the water, I imagine the water was pretty cold so they kept everything real . . . I went down and I was watching my father as he was doing this with the fish and as I was watching him here came a large fish and I jumped in after it. I didn't really jump in, as I reached out to get it, I fell in the river or fell in the lake and drifted down. The wind was blowing and drifted me down but I caught the salmon and my father pulled me out. . . Everything was prepared there, everything was butchered out, dried on racks, the deer, the elk, the fish, the beaver. We would pack up our horses and come back and by the time we came back to [unintelligible] there would be a lot of snow if we came back by the mountains, the snow would be clear up to the tops of the horses' legs as they came over the mountains. Indians, the people walked on ahead of the horses to make trails for the horses because it was hard for the horses to plow through the snow. They wore snow shoes as they made trails for these horses. There would be three men at the head who made the trail. And I remember that I was always tied onto the horse and being led by my father. As we made our way over the pass and came down where there was less snow, we would camp there. We would camp at least two days and from there try to wind our way home. That is what I remember of the camping trips and those who were from Flathead, my uncles would go back. . . . My uncles and my grandparents went back to [unintelligible]. They went clear as far as where there today is a dam. They passed, yeah, over where this dam is, they passed this one island. They had to go by boat because on both sides of this river there is nothing but rock cliffs. There they came down, they didn't go far, they didn't go far and one of the canoes broke, they hit the rock on the island very hard because the river was running very swiftly. Their canoes tipped and on the, tipped over and they hit the side of the island with their birch canoes. They'd landed on the rock, everything was broken and they tried to get on their feet. The father got on his feet and pulled the other one up to the island . . . Everything was gone all of the provisions that they had worked so hard for was all gone, all of their food, everything was gone. Their food, their furs, everything was gone into the river, their birch canoe was in slivers. They sat on the island for two days, the father told his son, we can sit here forever and we are gong [gone], we'll perish. When I jump into the river, you will follow me. And that's a good word [unintelligible], whatever may happen to us. He watched his father as he jumped into the river, his father was just about across the river and he knew that his father would make it so he jumped in too. They landed someplace called [unintelligible], I don't know, and they started back. They came back through very brushy places where there were no trails. They were, they took at least two days and those that were remaining at home, they said that they would be back in three days. The wife of [unintelligible] said that, they said that they would return in three days, it is now five days and they aren't back. So Big Smoke and his son John started down the river to try to find them. I don't know what the name of the little town was but this is where Big Smoke and his son John went, that was where they saw, they met the two men. They were in a very sad state of affairs, they were hungry, their moccasins were wore out and their feet were blistered. This is what I know of the early days of my childhood.

Blind Mose
Source: Séliš–Ql̓ispé Culture Committee, St. Ignatius, Montana

Document 8

Feeding an Indian Visitor in Libby Area

1900, ca.

Source: Mrs. Jacoba Boothman, "An Indian Visitor," Libby Pioneer Society and Libby Woman's Club, *Nuggets to Timber: Pioneer Days at Libby, Montana* (Libby, Mont.: Libby Litho and The Western News, 1970), pages not numbered.

Editors' note: A white woman settler in the Libby area described her encounter with an Indian visitor. She shared food and fish hooks with the man and he later repaid her with a string of fresh fish.

An Indian Visitor

One day I was washing the dishes, the kitchen was suddenly darkened and I looked up to see an Indian peering in at me through the window, completely shutting off the light as he put his arms up over his head, the better to see what was inside. He frightened me for a moment, his appearance was so sudden. But apparently satisfied with what he had seen he disappeared as suddenly as he had come. A moment later he was on the porch. I could hear the soft pad, pad of his moccasined feet coming toward the door, and then the rattling on the knob told me that he intended to come in. What should I do? Lock the door? Why, people in this mountain country never lock their doors! At least, not unless they are going to be away for several months, and then of course they put a padlock on. Why how would your tired neighbor, on his way home from town, or from a hunt get in to get a "snack" if you happened to have gone to town for the day, if the door was locked? No, they never lock their doors out here, so there was no lock and key and I couldn't have locked the door if I had wanted to.

This wasn't the day of tomahawk and war paint anyway, so if I was afraid, I wasn't going to let him know it if I could help it.

"Hello, John," I said as he entered the cabin. "What you want?"

"Me want eat," he said pointing to the table where the bread and butter and a few remnants from dinner still remained.

"All right," said I, "You sit down there and I'll get you something to eat." And I prepared to fry some meat and warm over some potatoes.

"Coffee,["] he said as he pointed to the coffee pot on a shelf behind the stove.

"Oh, you want coffee, too, do you John. All right." And I took down the coffee pot and put it on the stove with fresh coffee and hot water from the teakettle. I wished the red giant would sit down, but he didn't, he kept watching me as I prepared his meal. He was a big fellow, at least six feet tall. As he watched me, he walked around the room, looking at everything and touching every thing, then putting them back. Finally he came to my husband's tobacco on the mantle shelf. "Me smoke," he said, and I gave him some in a little sack, fearing that if I didn't he might be tempted to take it all; but he didn't seem to want to take anything that wasn't given to him.

When the meal was ready I told him to "sit up." He ate like a half-starved man, he seemed to try to eat every bit of it but he couldn't. So, producing a little sack from somewhere, he put the rest of the bread and meat in and stowed it away out of sight. Then taking up the knife he had been eating with, he felt of its edge and shaking his head stepped up to the mantle shelf again, picked up a whet stone and begun to sharpen its edge, feeling of it from time to time. Finally with a grunt of satisfaction, he put the whet stone down. Then picking up the fork, he put them both in a little sack with bread and meat! "Here," said I. "That's not yours."

"Sure, you give me," said he.

"Oh, but I only gave you those to eat with."

"Sure," said the Indian and he put them into his pocket.

"You got fish hook?" he asked next, looking along the shelf. shelf. [sic]

"All right," I said, "I'll get some fish hooks." And I opened a little box in the corner. He held out both hands for the whole box. But I selected several hooks and some line and gave them to him. Then he looked around again.

"Where your man?" he asked.

"Oh," said I. "He's over there in the timber, be home soon."

"Huh, your papoose?" he asked, looking at Sonny asleep in the crib.

"Yes," I said laughing, "My papoose."

Then apparently satisfied, he opened the door and went out as quietly as he had come in.

In the evening he appeared again just as suddenly and unexpectedly as before, and this t[i]me he had a nice string of trout, and laying them on a bench in the yard said, "For you," and went on his way toward town.

Mrs. Jacoba Boothman

Document 9

Bitterroot Trip Brought Memories to Tribal Elder 1900, ca.

Source: Don Matt, "A Visit Back to Chief Charlo's Days," *Char-Koosta* (Dixon, Mont.), vol. 6, no. 10 (September 15, 1976), page 4.

Editors' note: Louise Vanderberg's 1976 trip to the Bitterroot Valley brought back memories of years of hunting and traveling through the valley.

A Visit Back to Chief Charlo's Days
by Don Matt

The only three surviving members of Chief Martin Charlo's band recently returned to visit the area along the Continental Divide where one of their members was buried while the band was on a hunting party about 1900.

Pete Pierre, Mary Ann Coombs, and Louise Vanderburg recently went into the area along the west fork of the Bitterroot and placed a stone which the Tribal Council had donated on the grave of Plaussee, or Francis Adams, who died at the approximate age of 80.

Modern transportation got some of the group up there and back in a day, but Mary Ann Coombs wasn't sure if she liked that or not. "You're shrinking our land," she told Councilman Louis Adams. It used to take four days for Martin Charlo's band to make the trip. Louise Vanderburg said there were only three of the band left and told a few of her memories and things she had heard.

She said Chief Martin Charlo was the last of the regular Chiefs. It was said he always allowed Plaussee (Francis Adams) to go along on these trips even though he had trouble with his feet and could not walk. Louis Adams (not the present councilman) and Louis Coombs used to help carry Plaussee and lift him on and off his horse. The band used to hunt on the other side of the divide in an area called "Deep Creek." Blacktail deer were abundant there. When Plaussee died they brought him up over the divide to bury him closer by the old campground there. At the same location, Louise's aunt, Martine Swasa also buried infant twins and returned to the gravesite in the spring to bring them back here.

On the trip Louise also saw a large butte where they used to hunt bighorn sheep. She claims there was a different kind of plant there similar to bitterroot, but with bigger roots, more flowers, and a stronger taste. Fool's hens were plentiful in the area too. She remembers fishing and catching big fish using meat for bait. She says they caught trout, whitefish, and suckers. She comments that whitefish are rarely seen now. The suckers were caught for the meat on the head. One time her brother Jerome saw a big fish and tried to catch him with meat but it wouldn't bite. They finally caught it with snowberries. Roasting white pine cones in the fire for their seeds is another memory that came back to her. Sometimes, however, food was not always plentiful on the trips. She remembers one trip where young Paul Charlo got so hungry that he roasted grasshoppers.

Louise, who is now 78, says the band went on the trips from her earliest memories until about the time she was 10. These trips in the fall lasted up to a month. Because she was small, her mother tied her into the saddle with shawls. When she was about six, the saddle slipped. She remembers hanging upside down under the horse screaming and crying. On this trip she saw a rock that sometimes provided entertainment for the band as they passed. Bets were placed on who could lift it and a contest followed. There is a legend connected with this, and another one with the sleepy child area she saw on the trip. Since tales are not told until after snow falls, she can't tell the stories. Snake might get her.

The trip included Mr. & Mrs. Pete Pierre, Mary Ann Coombs, Pascal Charlo, Louise [Louis] Adams, and his daughters, Maxine and Arlene. The group went in by a four wheel drive vehicle and some by horseback.

Document 10

Jesuit Priest Visits Flathead Lake Kootenai Indians March – April 1901

Source: Robert Bigart and Clarence Woodcock, eds., "St. Ignatius Mission, Montana: Reports from Two Jesuit Missionaries, 1885 & 1900-1901: (Part II)," *Arizona and the West*, vol. 23, no. 3 (Autumn 1981), pages 271-278.

Editors' note: In these letters Father Augustine Dimier described his 1901 trips to minister to the Flathead Lake Kootenai Indians. The letters were originally published in Italian in a private Jesuit publication, *Lettere Edificante* (Turin, Italy), (1901), pages 79-86. Translation by Eliodoro Rodoni and Beatrice Steinmann, who in 1981 were faculty members at Western Montana College, Dillon. Footnotes in the 1981 edition have been omitted here.

St. Ignatius Mission (Montana)
March, 1901

Reverend Father Provincial.
Dear Father,

I send you this short report of our Mission here in St. Ignatius as you wished.

On the fourth of March I went to visit a Kootenai Indian band. The band consists of 150 Indians and is located 51 miles from the Mission. I arrived at Flathead Lake at around eight in the evening and spent the night at the house of a Canadian merchant [Henry Therriault]. A terrible snow storm started up during the night and lasted the entire next day.

In the morning I said the Mass in the house of my host and then got ready to continue my journey. I had to cross the [Lower Flathead] river that comes from the lake so I got on a boat with my horse and coach. The boatman [probably Baptiste Ignace] said to me: "It will be impossible to cross the river today, because the wind is so strong that we would not be able to disembark. We will see how it is tomorrow morning." So I had to wait the whole day, which was a Saturday. Rather than disturbing my host again by asking him to take care of me and my horse, I went somewhere else, about 4 miles away, and spent the night. In this Mission, a Father who travels is always well received wherever he goes. The people treat him courteously and even take care of his horse. Such hospitality is never paid for with money, but on the other hand, we never get anything from them — not even a cent — for baptisms, matrimonies, funerals, and for giving assistance to the dying sometimes 60 miles away from the Mission. I said the Holy Mass on the next day, a Sunday, and about 10 people were present, two of whom received the Holy Sacraments. Immediately afterwards I went back to the river and crossed it in the boat.

I arrived at the Kootenai camp at about 5 in the evening. They live communally in conical shaped tents. Only a few of them live in log cabins. I stopped at the first teepee I came to and heard a voice saying: *kin nka nkne mali* [Hail Mary, Full of Grace], etc., and other voices which responded: *Sancta Maria, Mater Dei* [Holy Mary, Mother of God], etc., in the Kootenai language. They were saying the Hail Mary and other prayers. I was curious to see what was going on, so I entered. I saw the body of a man wrapped in blankets with a small wooden cross over it. There were 12 people in the teepee who were praying and who were, in turn, succeeded by another 12 who came to pray and sing for the deceased until late at night. That Indian died the night before; the bad weather prevented me from getting there while he was still alive so that I could give him the last Sacraments. I remained awhile there in the teepee and then I went to the Church.

In the meantime the news had got around that the Black Robe had arrived. All of the Indians, coming out of the teepees and huts, gathered around me to shake my hand even though they had never seen me before. I did not know one word of their language. Fortunately though, some of the educated children could speak English and served me as interpreters.

After these initial greetings, I directed my horse toward the Church, located about 200 meters from the camp. The Church is made of wood and has two small rooms behind the altar for the missionary. However, I found that all of the windows were broken. Who did this" I do not think the Indian kids were responsible for such a thing; I believe that the whites did it since the Church is situated right on the borderline of the reservation. Because of all the broken windows I could not spend the night there, so I went back to the camp and took shelter in a teepee. On the next day I said the Mass, not in the Church, which was open to all winds, but in the largest cabin in the village, where more than 200 people were crammed together.

After the Mass I celebrated the funeral rites for the deceased Indian whose body had been taken to the same large cabin. I then said a few words about death, by means of an interpreter who repeated everything I said in English in Kootenai. For the remainder of the day I made a list of questions in Kootenai so I could hear their confessions; hearing their confessions was a long job, I read the questions in Kootenai and the penitent answered with a *yes* or a *no*.

On the following morning there were 150 who received Communion during the Mass. I taught for awhile with an interpreter, gave 50 others Communion, preached, baptized a few babies, and brought the Holy Sacrament to the sick. An old Indian lady led me to a corner where, quite mysteriously, she opened a small sack made of cloth and took from it a number of pages from a newspaper which were sewen together in the shape of a book. Between one page and another there were sacred images and sculptures. I had met this woman six years ago in the Blackfeet tribe where she had married a heathen. She had three sons and sent them to our school. Within the span of just a few years her husband and two of her sons died. Her husband, though, was baptized while on his death bed. After all of these misfortunes she returned to her tribe, where I ran into her. Opening the pages of the paper, the good lady said to me in a low voice: "You see, Black Robe, this sacred image belonged to Joseph, and this one to Philip, and this crucifix belonged to my husband. The Black Robes gave them to my sons and to my husband. They are precious remembrances for me. I am now burdened with afflictions and cannot find comfort on earth." Thus she went on telling me her troubles. Others came up to me to ask for a rosary or a medal, etc.

Kootenai Chief Isaac Big Knife
Source: Kootenai Culture Committee, Elmo, Montana

At about 5 in the evening when I was about to leave, the Kootenai chief [Isaac Big Knife] came to me with his police, who were 9 in all, so that I could give them a special blessing. I did as he wished. These policemen are chosen by the chief to maintain order in the village. After having shook nearly everyone's hand, I finally left and promised to return sometime in the month of May.

The Kootenai speak a language which is totally different from the Flathead language. Of the three Fathers that are here in this Mission, not one of us understands it. There are only about 150 of them here. Their tribe is located in the Canadian territory and is under the care of the Oblate Fathers who know the language. These Kootenai were either rejected from their tribe or they went on their own for some unknown reason many years ago. They came to this Flathead Reservation but do not mix with anyone. They are all alone in a corner of the reservation where they lead a rather miserable life. They are very poor and hardly have enough to live on. Their land could be very good, but they are lazy and do not cultivate the land. Besides this, the government does not help them, it does not furnish them with the necessary implements to work the land. Therefore, they live on fishing and hunting or on selling horses. Quite often they starve.

However, they still have a lot of faith; every evening they gather together in a hut where they recite prayers together and sing songs. They also have much respect and veneration for the Black Robes. They listen willingly to the advice we give them and seem to understand our words. They are so far away from the Mission that they cannot come to hear the Holy Mass. The weather permitting, they make it to Church for Christmas and Easter. The entire village comes to the Mission then, and they put up their teepees and stay for a couple of days. It is therefore necessary for the missionary to go to visit them two or three times a year. Sometimes they call for one of us to assist a dying person. It takes at least two days to go and come back. . . .

* * * * * * * * *

St. Ignatius Mission
April, 1901

Reverend Father Provincial.
Dear Father,

In this letter I will give you some news about our dear Indians of the St. Ignatius Mission. We are presently suffering from a smallpox epidemic, five have already died of it and many others have come down with the sickness. The danger of the infection spreading is quite great so the government has sent a few huge tents which have been put up in a location separated from the tribe. Everyone who has smallpox is taken there. The necessary help and medicine is not lacking; there are assisting nurses and visits by the doctor. No one is allowed to enter except the Priest. These Indians do not know how to take care of themselves when they are sick and are not always willing to take the medicine that the doctor prescribes. They prefer their own medicines made from various herbs; sometimes they use the medicine prepared by their own *Indian doctor.*

Last month, March, I went to the Kootenai tribe where a diphtheria epidemic was raging. Their medicine man had prepared a medicine which, according to some Indian woman, was very good. This medicine let off a very pleasant smell which was taken by breathing it in through the mouth. This whole procedure only temporarily revived the sick person. The medicine was a resin that they had extracted from trees. This medicine was used with much confidence, yet five died. In the meantime the American doctor also gave some medicine to his patients who also died. The second time the doctor came the Kootenai said to him: "We do not need you, everyone who took you medicine died." This is how these Indians reason; however, they will always have confidence in their medicine man even though his patients die as well. It often happens that these medicine men mix superstitions with medicines and we still have not been able to rid our Christians of these beliefs.

Many times I have gone to bring the last Sacraments to our smallpox patients and have not contracted the sickness, thank God. I take various precautions when I have to enter these tents. I cover myself entirely, except my head, with a waxed canvas; sometimes I even use camphor. They do not take the dead to the Mission's cemetery, instead they bury them right where they die for fear of spreading the smallpox germs. The Indians, though, do not take any precautions, they touch the sick person with their hands and they gather around as if there were no danger.

These Indians pray a lot for those who die, they do not forget this sacred duty. A few days ago an American told me that a dead man had been found in the train and that no one knew whether he was Catholic or Protestant. There was one of our Indians among those who were burying him, and when the others were about to put him into the hole without ceremony as one would do with a dead dog, the Indian said: "Wait a minute, I want to pray for his soul." "He is not Catholic," said the others, even though they knew nothing about it. But the Indian replied: "One minute, one minute, if he is Catholic, my prayer will do him some good; if he is not Catholic, it will not hurt him." So, they let him pray for the dead man. This Christian act made a good impression on everyone who assisted in this moving incident.

The chief of the Kootenai, the old Ignatius [Eneas Big Knife], died last year; he was certainly a good Christian soul. He was baptized by the first missionaries that came to the Rocky Mountains and he always remained a very good Christian. Having been confined to his bed during the last years of his life, he could not exercise his authority as chief. Because of this many abuses had been introduced among the Kootenai, one of which was gambling. They let themselves become blinded by passion, and they gambled away the little bit of money they had. When they lose all their money they use their gun with which to gamble, then the bed cover, and even their horses, etc.

Now, one of the sons [Isaac Big Knife] of the old Ignatius has been elected as his successor. The first thing he did as chief was to restore the use of the whip, which had been put aside during his father's last years. According to the custom of the tribe, whoever commits a bad crime or a public offense is called to come before the chief and his policemen and is whipped a number of times proportionate to the seriousness of the crime. A violator is never whipped on his bare skin, thus he has the right to wear thick clothing, if he has any. I was told that once someone wore two pair of pants in order to protect his skin since the person who does the whipping does it without mercy. The new chief, then, restored this former method of punishment, and this did a lot of good to many of the wrongdoers.

Last year in August, I went to their camp. I arrived at the end of the day and came upon a large number of people, about 20 men and women, earnestly gambling. They did not see me arrive and they did not expect me, but the first one to notice me immediately shouted from a distance to the gamblers warning them to stop. I spurred my horse and surprised them as they were still concentrating on their game. I gave them a quiet reprehension. The following morning after Mass, which had been assisted by everyone, I was preparing to return to the Mission. It was a Saturday. One of the policemen came and asked me to stay until the next day, but I refused saying that they did not deserve it, and so I left. When I returned in January I praised the new chief for his vigor; he had restored the use of the whip and had abolished every game of the kind.

Even though these Kootenai only get 5 or 6 visits a year by the missionary, they still faithfully recite their prayers morning and night, and each time I go to see them they confess themselves and receive Communion. For the confessions I have a list of questions that I ask them, but with these questions alone it is hardly possible for me to maintain the integrity of the confession. Yet, without this list I would have to absolve them without any confession whatsoever. I understand the language of the Flatheads, but these Kootenai have a totally different language. When I preach to them I speak in English while one of the students of the Mission school repeats what I say in Kootenai.

Last March I went to visit them again, but since they had moved their camp to the bank of Flathead Lake, I had to say the Mass there. Since there was no church I said the Mass in a tent which remained open during the Sacrifice so that everyone could see the altar. The people stayed outside, they sat down or else knelt on the bare ground even though it was still quite cold. No one budged. After the Mass I preached for at least 25 minutes, and no one left until I finished, no one except the *Indian doctor* [Bull Robe]. When I began talking against the superstitious practices behind the Indian medicines, the medicine man rose to his feet and left immediately. No one else followed him though, and I could go on with my sermon without bother. In fact, no one was offended besides the one who got up and walked away.

Here at the St. Ignatius Mission we have two schools for the girls, one which is under the care of the Ursuline Sisters, and the other by the Sisters of Providence, each school has about 50 pupils. Our school for the boys also has about 50 pupils. At the present, the Government no longer helps us maintain these schools, so the American Bishops have asked the Catholic population of the United States to help the Missions and the Indian schools. However, the donations collected in Church do not amount to much when they have to be divided among all of the Missions. Perhaps a few rich and charitable people will help us. Whatever the case may be, for the finances of these schools we now depend entirely on Divine Providence. Even the agent [W. H. Smead], or should I say the chief of the entire reservation, is trying to do harm to our school. He established one of these so-called state schools which can hold about 30 pupils, boys and girls. The Indians do not want to send their children to that school so the agent had to send his policemen to private homes in order to come up with these 30 children. When many of the parents heard about this they lost no time and sent their children to our school before the policemen arrived. The agent, against his will, actually does us some good. In general, the Indians do not send their children to school. They do not understand the importance of education. Because of this, many of our students are mixed-bloods. All of them speak English, have had some instruction, and can better understand the advantages of education.

We are expecting many scholastics from Spokane to come here towards the end of next June to spend a two-week vacation. Among them will be philosophers, theologians, and teachers. They have a number of large tents that they can set up in some nice mountain area. Having at their disposal a few horses, they will be able to run around the country and get back into shape and be able to go back to their jobs fresh. . . .

Document 11

Reservation Chiefs Reject Sale of Northern Part of Reservation April 18, 1901

Source: James H. McNeely, et. al., to Commissioner of Indian Affairs, April 18, 1901, letter received 22,670/1901, land division, RG 75, National Archives, Washington, D.C.

Editors' note: Fortunately, this letter included the transcripts of the January and April 1901 meetings between the Crow, Flathead, Etc. Commission and the Flathead Reservation chiefs. The chiefs made plain their unwillingness to sell the northern part of the reservation. The chiefs pointed out that the government had not kept the promises it had made in earlier agreements and also realized that selling land was not in the best interests of the tribes.

Hon. W. A. Jones,
Commissioner of Indian Affairs,
Washington, D.C.
Sir: —

We have the honor to report that this Commission held a general council with Indians of this Reservation at St. Ignatius Mission on the 3d instant. This council was called at the request of a number of Indians who were not satisfied with the result of the general council held in January last at the same place, and who were not represented at that time. Two or three days prior to the date first named (April 3d) requests were made of us for a further postponement of two months, with the statement that Chief Charlos had forbidden these Indians to act, or even talk to the Commissioners about an agreement, stating that he and others intended to go to Washington before any agreement was made. These requests we did not see our way clear to grant, and hence informed the Indians that the council would be held according to public notice.

The different bands were fairly well represented at the council, but it was plain from the start that the same opposition (Chief Charlos and the cattlemen) had complete control of the influential Indians. We have good reason to believe that quite a sum of money was used in defeating our propositions, one Indian having gone so far as to tell an employe at the Agency that he was approached with such an offer and asked to work against the Commission.

The portion of the Reservation selected by the Commission as the most advantageous for the Indians to dispose of was a strip off of the north end containing some 450,000 acres. With the exception of the Kootenais, who do little or no farming, that portion is very little used by any number of the other Indians. It is nearly all taken up by white men married to Indians, and a few half-blood cattle-men, most of whose rights on the reservation we believe are questioned. The tribes as a whole receive no benefit from the use of all this land, and we are informed that Charlos and his band, who are our chief opposition, have not been on the land referred to for twenty years. A number of these cattle-men sell live stock every year to the amount of many thousands of dollars.

For these reasons your Commission deemed it for the best interest of the Indians as a whole to dispose of this land, and we still hold the same opinion, although we consider it unwise to try and negotiate with them further at the present time and under the present circumstances, as they have rejected all our propositions. We are still fully satisfied that a large majority of them realize the conditions and are in favor of selling, but are held back by the leaders whom they have been so long accustomed to obey.

Under the circumstances we would ask that the work here be discontinued for the time being, and would respectfully make the following recommendations for the general good of these people, believing, too, that they would have a tendency if adopted to break up the opposition to an agreement, which we are satisfied would improve the condition of these Indians materially.

Recommendations.

1st. — That this Reservation be surveyed and allotments in severalty be made to all entitled to them, at once.

2d. — That the rights of white men and half-breeds who are now using the northern part of this reservation be determined, and that if possible the tribe in general be remunerated by the parties so using the land held in common by the Indians.

We would further state that the Agent [W. H. Smead] is in full accord with the above recommendations.

We would respectfully ask for further instructions.

With this report we transmit copies of proceedings of the two councils held at St. Ignatius in January last and on the 3rd of this month respectfully.

James H. McNeely, Commissioner and Chairman.
Charles G. Hoyt, Commissioner.
B. J. McIntire, Commissioner.

Flathead Agency,
Jocko P. O., Montana,
April 18, 1901.

* * * * * * * * *

Enclosure number 2:

The Council with Flatheads, and other tribes of the reservation, assembled at A. L. Demers' store, St. Ignatius, on Thursday, January 3d. 1901. Commissioners Hoyt, McIntire and McNeely, and Agent Smead were present representing the Government. The Kalispells and Kootenais were not represented.

Agent Smead introduced the Commissioners and stated object of the Council.

The Indians selected Joseph McDonald as interpreter, and Michel Revais, the official interpreter, acted for the Commission.

Commissioner Hoyt, addressing the Indians, said he was glad to see so many present. Since last council two of the Commissioners and the Agent have been to Washington and learned the wishes of the Great Father. We asked to be sent back here for the Indians' benefit. They can make a better deal with the Commissioners than to go to Washington. We heard last night that some one had reported that allotments could not be made unless a majority of the Indians consent. This is a mistake, as the Great Father has a right to do as he pleases for the benefit of the Indians. He has a right to make them allotments at any time. The time will come when he will take these matters into his own hands and do what he thinks best for them without a council.

At the last council we offered a certain price for a part of the reservation, and have heard since that the Indians didn't think the price was high enough. We have now prepared an agreement by which, if the Indians will accept, they will get all the land will bring. The Indians can sell the land themselves. Say we figure on the northern part of the reservation — everything north of the line between Missoula and Flathead counties — a line just North of the Sub-agency at Ronan. Fewer full-blood Indians live there than any place else on the reservation. Say we arrange to sell in this way, a commission of three Indians will be appointed, with their Agent a member. Then, if any persons want to buy a farm they can come to this Indian commission and say, we want to buy this land, on which no Indians are settled. No home will be taken from an Indian without he consents and is paid for improvements. This Indian commission will then put a price on the land for so much money. Then if the buyer will pay the price the money will be sent to Washington, and when enough is paid in there, $^1/_2$ of which will amount to ten dollars for each Indian here, old and young, this will be paid to them. After ten years the Government will buy the remainder of the land, at an appraised price to be settled by the Secretary of the Interior. Half of the money received is to be paid to the Indians in cash as fast as it amounts to ten dollars each, and the balance is to be expended for the benefit of the Indians, under direction of the Secretary of the Interior. If people who want the land will not pay the price fixed in cash the land will not be sold, and nobody can buy more than enough for a home, not for speculation, and must live on it, except timber and grazing land.

The Flatheads are sensible people. Many of them are educated. We have presented this matter on business principles. If I want to buy a horse from Michel I have to pay his price. In this way the Indians will get all they think their land is worth. This agreement continues ten years and then any unsold land will be bought by the Government at a fair price.

The rights of any Indians like the Kalispells who haven't been sure of their rights will be established. Indians and half-breeds living on the reservation, whom the Indians wish to live here, will be granted full rights. The agreement provides for paying the Flatheads $6000.00. for letting the Kalispells of Camas Prairie remain on the Reservation.

Duncan McDonald asked: "Who are meant by Flatheads?"

Hoyt's reply: All others except Kalispells — Chief Michel's band. The $6000, to be paid to the other Indians for allowing the Kalispells to remain with full rights on the reservation, is to be expended in buying stallions for improving the breed of horses. Also $10,000.00. is to be paid to the Kalispells for expenses in removing to this reservation. Also $5,000.00. to pay the Kootenais for removing onto the unsold part of the reservation if they wish to leave their present homes.

Also allowing Charlos' band $1200. for certain things that he says were promised him for removing from Bitter Root Valley to this Reservation, this money to be expended for cattle for Charlos' band.

Charlos — "If these things had been paid for I would have had a larger band.

Hoyt — We will provide so he will be satisfied. The agreement also provides that no Indians will be required to move from their homes unless they wish; none will be forced to move, and if they do the Government will pay for their improvements what they are worth. Mr. Hoyt repeated the provisions of the proposed agreement and stated that the Commission of Indians would be paid $25. a month each for their services.

This is a business proposition which the Indians ought to think over. It is intended for their best interests.

Mr. Hoyt then introduced Commissioner McIntire, who said he was pleased to meet with the great chiefs and part of their people. He appreciated the discomforts of coming long distances in such cold and snowy weather to attend this council. Their homes are in the same country as his and he trusted that they would be friends. He wished to see the Indians of this reservation prosper to the greatest extent. It is necessary that they shall have money. The northern portion of the reservation is very thinly settled by Indians. For this reason the Great Father has selected it to be sold. There is a great amount of land there for each Indians — more so than in the Southern part. Most of the land in the Northern part is not occupied or used by Indians. The Great Father wishes to sell part and give money to the Indians. They have no annuities or other sources of income. He wishes to provide for Indians, food, clothes, houses, cattle, etc. When the treaty is made they will not only have all the land they need, but money besides. They will fix prices on their land. The Great Father thinks they have a right to set prices on land as they have on a horse. We think that this is the last offer to be made to the Indians. That this is the last Commission that will be sent to them. *[Handwritten insert in original document: "?? This plan was emphatically condemned in I.O."]* Indians' rights will be protected. They can select homes where they please. If they remove their improvements will be paid for. Land in Northern part of the reservation brings them in little or nothing. If land is sold they will not only have money but the value of their other property will be increased. On the Yakima reservation Indians are prosperous, since lands were allotted, by leasing or working themselves. The Great Father wishes the Indians to fix values of land without white influence. We shall now be glad to hear from Chiefs and head men and report what they say to the Great Father.

Chief Charlos — You all know that I won't sell a foot of land. Washington is not far from here and when we want to sell we can go there. Washington is our father, and why does he want to take our land from us ("by force," according to Duncan McDonald's interpretation?) I know by the papers who has a right to represent Washington, and demand that they be shown. (The agreement was here shown) I want to see credentials with big seal on.

Duncan McDonald explained by stating how one Corey, who represented himself as a special agent, several years ago swindled people on this reservation, which made Charlos suspicious.

Charlos — I have been told when any commissioners come here to require him to show his credentials.

The commissioners all said they possessed credentials but didnt have them here.

Commissioner McIntire said that Agent Smead knew the commissioners, and that they were authorized to treat with these Indians. He asked whether Charlos would take the Agent's word.

Charlos said he would not. *["!!" handwritten in original.]*

McIntire — If Charlos refuses to negotiate without seeing the seal, the Commission will report the refusal to the Great Father. We will produce it as soon as we can get the commissions.

Charlos — The boundary lines have been surveyed three times, and the reservation has been set aside for the Indians forever.

Agent Smead assured Charlos that the commissioners were all authorized to treat with these Indians. He said he wouldn't allow anybody on the reservation under any circumstances unless duly authorized. He had seen the papers of all three commissioners. He had known Commissioner McIntire ten years. He had been to Washington and talked about these commissioners. They are from the Great Father, and sent here to treat with the Indians. He said that the commission would be glad to listen to all chiefs and head men.

Duncan McDonald — Charlos forbids them to speak.

Commissioner McIntire — Ask them whether they wish to talk of the matter amongst themselves tonight.

Commissioner McNeely — This is entirely agreeable to the commissioners.

Agent Smead — I think it wise for Indians to hold a council tonight amongst themselves, and consider the commissioners' proposition very carefully. Don't arrive at a wrong conclusion. The commissioners are servants of the Great Father in Washington. He sends them to you. Treat them with respect. They want to do what is best for the Indians. The Great Father is the Indians' friend. He may not send another commission to treat with you. Don't make the Great Father angry with you. If you don't understand the agreement ask the Agent or Commissioners. Send for the agent if he can help you or explain anything.

The Council then adjourned to re-assemble tomorrow, (Friday) at ten o'clock forenoon.

* * * * * * * * *

Friday, January 4, 1901, 11 a.m.

Agent Smead called the Council to order. He asked the chiefs for the conclusion of their council last night.

Charlos — When we were in Judge Joseph's house we studied and talked about the matter and looked all about the reservation. We have been mistreated and so concluded not to sell any part of the reservation. Other Indians besides himself have got the worst of it in dealing with the Government. We have not got pay for our lands in Bitter Root Valley. We have talked with this Commission and do not wish to do them any wrong. The Flatheads have always been a peaceful tribe. There is no white men's blood on their hands. We saw the first white man in my grandfather's time and have always treated them right.

Commissioner McIntire — Is there anything wrong about the Commission's proposition?

Charlos — Our tribes and other tribes have been deceived by the Government, and for this reason we have no confidence that we will be treated right, judging by the past.

McIntire — Do you still dispute the authority of this commission?

Charlos — I do still doubt it.

McIntire — If the Great Father does just as he proposes will you be satisfied then?

Charlos — If I could go to Washington myself I would talk the matter over with the head men there.

McIntire — Don't you know that the agreement if made goes to the Great Father before it becomes final, the same as all treaties?

Alexander Matt made an explanation to Charlos of the commissioners' meaning, and still Charlo repeated that he did not wish to sell the land.

McIntire — Does he refuse to sell under any circumstances?

Charlos — Yes.

McIntire — Do any other Indians wish to talk now?

Judge Lewissohn — Three commissions have been here. I have been all over the reservation and talked with the Flatheads, Kalispells and Kootenais. They have never got what they were promised and we are all afraid to make a treaty.

McIntire — Do you understand the proposed treaty, and do you think it a fair proposition?

Lewissohn — I don't think you went at it in the right way. If you want to buy land why don't you come with money?

McIntire — Do you want to sell under any circumstances?

Lewissohn — No.

McIntire — Do you take us for boys who don't know what to do or how to do it?

Lewissohn — No.

McIntire — Do you mean to say that you won't sell even for money?

Lewissohn — It depends on the chiefs, and what they decide to do the tribes will follow.

McIntire — Have the chiefs instructed you what to say?

Lewissohn — No; I form my own opinions. Many others of these people hold back.

McIntire — Hasn't the Great Father made a fair proposition if carried out?

Lewissohn — If we could see the Great Father and he would tell us what to do we would study the matter over seriously. A few days ago the Agent went to Washington and I would have liked to go with him but he didn't ask me. In making our old treaties we knew this time would come and we would be asked to sell our land. When the Stevens and Garfield treaties were made we thought the reservation was ours forever. Then other tribes were brought in here to live on our reservation.

McIntire — Does anybody else wish to talk, mixed bloods included? Any person has a right to talk here. The reservation is going to be thrown open; it is only a question of time, *["!!" inserted in original]* and educated Indians, who have considerable at stake, ought to express themselves.

Duncan McDonald — I wish to talk to the Indians in their own language and will not refer to the Commission but the Government. They think the Government is a big wolf, from their point of view. When they made a treaty with Governor Stevens he had a sweet mouth. He made a line around the reservation but it has since been made smaller; a slice of land down by Paradise was cut off. Stevens promised things that the Indians have never received. Afterward Garfield held a council with these Indians with the same result. He was plausible like this commission. Charlos' land in Bitter Root Valley is still unsold. Washington has lots of money while these Indians are living from hand to mouth as best they can. Indians are starving while waiting for money promised to them. The Flatheads have always been friendly to whites and have clean hands while the Government has been kicking them around. Other tribes that have fought the Government have been treated much better than the Flatheads. The Indians feel this way and are afraid to sign an agreement, for fear they will be treated as heretofore. In a few years the Government will want to make another treaty and buy more land.

McIntire — Will you please express you own opinion of the fairness of the proposed treaty?

Duncan McDonald — Poor Michel and Charlos have been treated cruelly. Promises made to them were similar to yours. When half-breeds wish to talk, full-blood Indians say they must not.

Joseph McDonald — Indians don't understand the $10. proposition.

McIntire explained it to the interpreter (Jo McDonald) who in turn explained to the Indians.

Alex Matt (educated half-breed): The Indian chiefs wish to seld [send] a delegation to Washington and prove for themselves whether the Government wishes to make a treaty. That is the reason why they don't want to make a treaty now. They also wish to collect their back pay, and to tell the authorities themselves what was promised to the Indians. He also expressed himself in favorable terms toward this Commission and its proposed agreement.

McIntire — We have listened to the Indians' proposition to go to Washington. The Great Father has sent us here to treat with you, but you have refused to recognize us. It would do no good to go to Washington. The law provides for you to treat with this Commission and with nobody else. We will say to the Great Father that you have not treated us with proper courtesy and respect. You have denied our authority and papers, and said you do not believe the Agent's word. *["!" inserted in original.]* We do not come here to beg you but to state facts for your own good.

We will also report to the Great Father that a large portion of your land is being occupied and used by cattle-men who are not Indians and have no rights on the reservation. Their right, if they have any, will be settled. We believe that it is largely through the influence of these stock=men that no treaty has been made. You can't accuse us of not being plain in our talk. We will try to make good our words in this and other matters.

The full-bloods and half-bloods are poor, yet they are satisfied to go to the stock=men and get a few cattle on shares and be their slaves, instead of owning their own land and receiving pay for its products. The northern part of the reservation is occupied mostly by cattlemen who are getting rich at the expense of the Indians.

Agent Smead then spoke — I have been your agent three years, and when I see the poor way in which the Indians live I feel sympathy for them. I wrote to Washington about affairs on the reservation and called attention to the conditions. A few things were sent here but not enough to take care of the poor and sick. I asked for good stallions to improve the breed of horses, and for cattle that the Indians could sell. The answer was that the Indians had no money like other tribes who had sold land that they didn't need. Last month I went to Washington, after talking to Charlos and other chiefs. I saw the authorities at Washington and pleaded for the Indians. The answer was that the Flatheads had been neglected but the fault was with the Great Council which didn't appropriate enough money. Our hearts are with the Indians. I told the authorities at Washington that the Indians didn't want to sell the reservation or any part of it. They replied that if there is a small part of the reservation that the Indians can spare they might sell to this Commission. Also that the Indians said they had not been offered enough for land. The Great Father wants to pay all that it is worth and the Indians ought to be paid the full value. If Indians will sell land they will have money, cattle, stallions and other things that they need. This is the reason why the Commission is here today.

I am sorry to see them sell any part of the reservation. It is like a man selling part of his farm. — he dislikes to do so, where he has lived all his life, but if he is in need of necessary articles and has no other way to get them, he had better sell and buy what he needs. The question is, hadn't you Indians better sell part of the reservation and buy what you need? I have figured that the land that the Government wants to buy ought to bring a million dollars, or nearly $700.00. for every man, woman and child on the reservation. One-half would be paid in money, the other half to be spent by the Secretary of Interior for blooded horses, cattle, houses, etc.

Under this agreement you would sell this land yourselves, through three of your number and your Agent. The money would be divided twice a year so long as there is land to sell. Unsold land would belong to you. At the end of ten years the Government would buy the unsold land in the ceded strip and pay you its full value. This money would amount to a great deal. A man, his wife and two children would receive about $2800.00.; with four children $4200.00., half cash, the other half to be spent to buy articles that you need. In addition, your remaining lands would be surveyed and allotted. Any old person could rent his or her share and receive cash. Allotments could be made on the ceded strip or on the unsold portion of the reservation.

Other Indians who have sold their lands — the Crows, Nez-Perces, Blackfeet, Bannocks, Shoshones, Umatillas, etc., have money and think it was a good thing to sell. You have the opportunity to do this today, and don't you think that you had better do it? I, as your Agent, have explained the agreement honestly. Think it all over, and if you don't sell I will not be angry with you. If Charlos and his poor people had money I wouldn't advise you to sell. It is now for you to decide for yourselves.

McIntire — Does any other Indian wish to talk? There was no response.

Agent Smead read an extract from the Stevens treaty of 1855. He also referred to the General Allotment act. Both of these empower the Great Father to allot lands and sell surplus lands without the consent of Indians. *["?" inserted in original.]*

Lewissohn — I am sorry that we can't go to Washington. Indians go there to see about big things. We are afraid of each other. *["Distrust" inserted in original.]* You don't want me to go to Washington.

The Council then adjourned without date.

* * * * * * * * *

Enclosure number 1:

Proceedings
Of a General Council Held with Indians of the Flathead Reservation at Saint Ignatius, Montana, April 3, 1901, (Wednesday).
at Predieux & Demers' Store.

The Council assembled at 3 o'clock p.m. Present, Commissioners McNeely (chairman), Hoyt and McIntire; also Agent W. H. Smead.

Interpreters, Michel Revais (official for the Reservation), Gustave (Statah) for the Kootenais, Louis Camille, Ed Dishon and Maud S.

Commissioner Hoyt — This Council has been called for the Indians' benefit. We had a council last January, but the Kootenais and Kalispels were not here. The Commissioners thought they would go away and not return, as no agreement was made, but some Indians came to the Commissioners and asked them to have another council, and we wrote to Washington and asked if we should come and have this council. Washington told us to come back again. This council is for the Indians and not for the Commissioners. We come at the time the Indians asked us to come — the week before Easter Sunday. We are here for the good of the Indians, and want to talk over the same matters as last time.

Some Indians on the upper part of the Reservation have their money from their Bitter Root lands. Chief Charlos has his money. We heard that Charlos wanted this council put off, and that he said he was going to Washington. Charlos can't go there without a permit. If he goes without, the President will not see him. We don't think the President will issue him a permit. Some time ago the Commission asked the President to let some of these Indians go to Washington, but he said No. He said if they went to Washington they would have to come back and made a deal with the Commissioners. We can't put off a council because Charlos or any other Indian wants us to do so. Our orders are to deal with all the Indians and not with one. Washington don't believe that Charlos or any one else has a right to stop these Indians from making a deal. If the Kootenais want to sell part of their land, the Indians at Charlos' end of the Reservation have no right to say they sha'n't. Charlos has received his money and he has no right to stop the Kootenais and other Indians from getting money for their land. Charlos doesn't seem to take an interest in his Indians as I don't see him here to-day.

It won't be a great while until the Government will allot these lands. *["?" inserted in original.]* Washington has a right to allot lands at any time it thinks best for the Indians. It would be better for the Indians to sell part of their land before the Government allots. They can make a better deal now and get more for it than to have the Government sell it for them. This is the reason we have come back. It is better for the Indians.

We have the same plan as when we were here last time. I want to make it as plain to you as I can. The land we have in mind is the northern portion of the Reservation, north of the Sub-Agency. We want to allow the Indians to sell that land at a price they make themselves. The Indians now have three Judges. We want to appoint three Indians more to put prices on those lands, these Indians to be paid for their time the same as the judges are paid for their time. These three Indians are to go over the land and put prices on the different parts of it. Then, if some one wishes to buy a quarter=section he goes to this Indian Commission and asks the price of it. These three Indians then find out which piece of land the man wishes to buy, and they and their Agent put a price on the land and tell the white man the price. If he won't pay this price he can't buy it. Some pieces of land will be worth more than other pieces. If the white man pays the price asked, the money will be sent to Washington. As soon as there is enough there, the Secretary or President will send it out and have it divided amongst the Indians. Half will be paid to the Indians in cash and the other half will be spent by the President for things that the Indians need. The money should be distributed at least twice a year. The Indians will get the benefit of all money paid in. Nobody else will receive any of this money except these Indians. I want to have this plain, as we were misunderstood the last time. Some Indians thought they would receive only one payment. The Indians will receive payment after payment as long as money is received.

Commissioner Hoyt repeated what Agent Smead said in his talk at the last council:

"I have figured that the land ought to bring a million dollars, or nearly $700 for every man, woman and child on the reservation. Half would be paid in money, the other half in blooded horses, cattle and other articles that the Indians would need. Under this arrangement you would sell land through three Indians and the Agent. The money would be distributed twice a year as long as there is land to sell. This money would amount to a great deal. A man, his wife and two children should receive about $2800. Half would be in cash and half in articles that you need. After ten years, if there was land left, the Government would buy it and the pay the Indians for it."

Com'r Hoyt then said: We have other provisions in the Agreement, and called for questions.

A Pend d'Oreille Indian replied that he thought everybody understood. (The foregoing was interpreted into Kootenai and the other dialects.)

Commissioner Hoyt: I now want to talk about the Camas Prairie (Lower Kalispel) Indians. They made a deal some years ago at Sand Point, Idaho. The great Council in Washington never said Yes to that agreement. No agreement is good until the great Council says yes to it. Washington has always been very sorry that the big Council didn't say yes to that agreement, and we were instructed to put a provision for the Camas Prairie Indians in the new agreement. We have put in, that Washington is to send Michel's band $10,000. This money is to be used to buy cattle and other things that Michel's Band needs. It is in this paper, and anyone who can read can see it. It doesn't come out of land sales, but is to be sent from Washington. It is to make right the old agreement.

In addition, Washington is to spend $6000 for all three of the tribes in what they may need.

In addition, Washington is to spend $1200 for Charlos' Band for things he claims were heretofore promised but not paid.

If this deal is made, the Kootenais may have to leave where they are and come to this part of the Reservation. They don't have to move unless they want to, but will probably want to do so. If they do move to another part of the Reservation south of the line of division, it will be a hardship and expense to them. So we have put in the agreement that if the Kootenais move they are to have $5000, either to be paid in cash or things they need, as the President chooses. This is outside (to Kootenais) of proceeds of sales of lands. They will get their full share of what is paid for land and this in addition. Mr. Hoyt asked —

Question: Do you understand?

Answer by several, "Yes."

Com'r Hoyt: All these Indians are poor and need money and things that money will buy. The Kootenais, Kalispels and nearly all the Indians need money. If they do, why not exchange land that they don't need for money that they do need?

We have offered a fair proposition. We think it the best ever offered any Indians. I have been dealing four years with Indians, and it is the best proposition that I have ever seen. *["!" inserted in original.]* It leaves the sale of land entirely to yourselves. You and the Agent put a price on land, and if a man doesn't want to pay the price he can't have it. If he does pay the price, the Indians get the benefit of every cent he pays. Nobody can take any advantage of you under this agreement.

Chief Isaac (of the Kootenais): Do you intend to make good arrangements with us?

Com'r Hoyt: The best we can.

Chief Isaac: Are you chief?

Com'r Hoyt: We represent the Chief at Washington.

Chief Isaac: I am chief of the Kootenais, and anything I tell my Indians to do they all do. You're off (wrong). When they treated for this reservation, the treaty wasn't this way. Three men were the head men, and when they granted this reservation they didn't grant it to sell. When these three men gave us this reservation it was a big country. When they made lines, white man's place was outside of the reservation. When treaties were made with other Indians they were to get money in their hands, but they never got it. Where is it? All I got was hearsay. I never got money in my hands or saw it with my eyes.

Before we make a new treaty we want to know the boundary lines of this reservation. That is the next thing we ought to work on. Making bargains for the reservation is out of our line. We want to quit making bargains until we find our lines. To-day and afterwards I don't want to hear any more stories, but want the truth. My body is full of your people's lies.

You told me I was poor and needed money, but I am not poor. What is valuable to a person is land, the earth, water, trees, &c., and all these belong to us. Don't think I am poor. Why do you tell me I am poor? Does stock, land, timber, etc., make me poor? I don't consider myself poor, because I don't need anything. Therefore, don't think I am poor and you won't make any bargain with me. We haven't any more land than we need, so you had better buy from somebody else. Maybe some poor people are willing to sell land. Forty-six years ago we made a deal with people who talked the same language that you do.

That is all I have to say, and you had better hunt some people who want money more than we do.

(There were expressions of approval from Indians.)

Com'r Hoyt: The first thing in the agreement is a provision to have the land surveyed. Does anybody else want to talk?

Judge Kackashee: I heard Isaac talk, and I believe none of the Indians want to sell land.

Chief Michel (of Lower Kalispels): Of course the words of the Washington Chief are good and we can't break them. He sympathized with us poor Indians and told us to take good care of our land and not squander it, and said, if you do, you will be poor. We know these were his words. You say he said the words you told us, and we can't answer them.

Com'r Hoyt: Anybody has a right to talk.

An Indian: Children don't want to talk after the head-men have talked.

Com'r Hoyt: We are glad to have heard this talk. Have taken it all down and will send it to Washington. We have offered you a fair agreement as Washington told us to do, and we don't know what Washington will do now. We have offered you a fair agreement and told the truth. We have the best of feeling toward the Indians here, and have carried out all our instructions from

Washington. We shall be glad to furnish more provisions to you this evening and to-morrow.

Judge Lewissohn: Everybody understands well, and the three Indians who spoke told the truth, and all other Indians agree with them. It takes too long to receive our money. We intend to go to Washington, as we now have plenty of money to go with.

At 6 o'clock p.m. the Council adjourned sine die.

Document 12

Chief Charlo Rides an Automobile in Missoula

May 19, 1901

Source: "Old Charlot Rides in an Automobile," *The Anaconda Standard*, May 19, 1901, page 30, col. 4-7.

Editors' note: One of the first automobiles in Missoula caused quite a stir when Chief Charlo took a ride in it.

Old Charlot Rides in an Automobile
Grim Old Flathead Chieftain Whirls Through Missoula's Streets in Style.
He Was a Sight to Behold

When Thomas Jefferson made the Louisiana purchase there were many of his associates and contemporaries who questioned the wisdom of the deal which the great democrat made with Napoleon. Since that time there have arisen at intervals numerous other doubters, who have for some reason or other, expressed a conviction that Jefferson made a mistake. In recent decades the list of these pessimists has, of course, dwindled until it is only among the aboriginal owners of the great empire of the West that any of them are found.

Foremost among the red men who have held to the opinion that Jefferson erred is Charlot, the hereditary chief of the Flatheads. Although the ancestral home of Charlot in the Bitter Root valley was not included in the land that Jefferson bought from Napoleon, the purchase brought United States territory into such shape that the domain of Charlot's people was no longer separated from the eastern territory of the United States by any foreign possessions and the Americans could crowd in and push out the red men. This is just what happened to the Bitter Root Indians and it so came about that Charlot was of the generation that was pushed. That he was deceived and treacherously dealt with by the government there is no doubt and that his proud old heart is full of venom toward the race that defrauded him and his people is no wonder. If he has ever thought about the Louisiana purchase, it is safe to say that he has decided that it was not wise.

If Charlot ever felt in any degree reconciled to the invasion of the home of his people by the whites, it was last Wednesday afternoon when he was whirled through Missoula's streets in the front seat of the very latest sort of automobile. Those who have known the old chief for many years say that they have never seen him before manifest as much enjoyment as he did during his automobile experience. For the first time he seemed to feel that there might be some compensation, after all, in the occupation of the Bitter Root by the white men.

Charlot had been in Missoula all day and, in the afternoon, chanced to see the new automobile in its trip through the streets. Loquacity is not a characteristic of Charlot, but if it were he would have probably voiced some sentiment similar to that famous expression of the Chinaman when he saw a San Francisco cable car for the first time. As it was, he hunted up his old friend, Senator Worden, and inquired of him what sort of creature was the new machine.

Senator Worden explained to the old chief something of the nature of the machine and then induced him to take a ride in it. The old fellow hesitated somewhat but finally yielded and a party was made up for a spin around town. In the party were Chief Charlot and Little Wolf, one of his sub-chiefs, Senator Worden and Mineral Land Commissioner Garrett.

The stern old chief sat up as straight as a New York tiger on the high seat of my lady's cab. He tried to look unconcerned, but the experience was so novel that he could not conceal his interest in the new fangled vehicle. When he thought that nobody saw him, he allowed his features to relax and his face lost its habitual frown. His seat companion was Senator Worden and he really smiled at him once or twice. There is no doubt that the automobile accomplished what nothing else had ever done and Charlot believed that, after all, there might be something about the white man's life that was not entirely objectionable.

The chief's automobile party rolled around through Missoula's thoroughfares, attracting attention everywhere. Missoula had seen Indians riding bicycles, but this was a sight worth watching, for Chief Charlot's only tolerance in civilization's innovations has heretofore been a plug hat. To see him adopt the automobile was something noteworthy.

Senator Worden brought his guests around to the Standard office and there the camera caught them. So benign had Charlot become under the influence of the automobile that he did not object to the camera. He had never before posed willingly for a picture.

It seems possible that the automobile may turn out to be the great civilizing agent for which search has been made all these years. It may be that missionaries equipped with automobiles will find willing converts where now they run up against hungry cannibals and that our conquering hosts in the Orient if mounted on these machines will encounter only Filipino hosts holding up their right hands to take the oath of allegiance instead of an ambushed army pointing Mausers at them. That is the way it is working on Charlot.

Charlot has had some experience in dealing with the federal government. For many years he resisted all attempts made to have him relinquish his loved home in the Bitter Root and when his signature to a treaty of transfer was secured it was only by gross misrepresentations that it was obtained. But few of the government's pledges contained in that treaty have ever been carried out.

The story of the negotiations between the commission sent West by Garfield's administration and Charlot's people is familiar enough to the older residents of Western Montana. Promises without end were made to the resolute chief, but he was suspicious of their sincerity and, even when part of his tribe consented to the removal to the Jacko [sic] valley on the Flathead reservation, he refused to leave the valley that had for many generations been the home of his forefathers.

It required more than one commission to bring to a successful end the negotiations with Charlot. Even the last commissioners, it is alleged, would have failed in their purpose had they not resorted to forgery. Be that as it may, there was trickery galore in the treatment which Charlot's people received from the government at that time and subsequently. He has resented it and has always manifested his distrust of the whites. He is unwilling to entrust the care of his children to the agency schools, and when he is remonstrated with he grimly points to the brown slope where are located the houses of himself and his people and compares it with grassy meadows of the Bitter Root that he and his people left.

The old chief is among those who would have much enjoyed meeting the president had the tour of the Northwest not been abandoned. It would have been a kindly Providence had a meeting been possible, for it would have afforded the broken-hearted old warrior an opportunity of telling the chief executive something of the wrongs that he has endured at the hands of this great government. But this was not to be and Providence has given the sturdy old chief the compensating experience of a ride in an automobile.

Document 13

1901 Smallpox Epidemic on Reservation

June – July 1901

Source: "Victims of Smallpox," *The Anaconda Standard*, June 10, 1901, page 10, col. 2; Frank C. Armstrong, Special Agent, to Secretary of the Interior, July 30, 1901, enclosure in letter received 42,671/1901, finance division, RG 75, National Archives, Washington, D.C.

Editors' note: The 1901 smallpox epidemic on the reservation was a serious event. Tribal members who were infected or suspect were housed in a quarantine hospital camp. As of September 18, 1901, there had been 240 cases and thirty deaths from smallpox on the reservation. Surrounding counties declared the reservation quarantined for the duration and even posted guards along the roads from the reservation to the surrounding white communities.

Victims of Smallpox
How the Disease Spreads Among the Indians.
Grizzly Bear's Medicine
Consulted a Skunk, but Died Just the Same —
Ignorance and Superstition Are Harmful Factors in the Epidemic.

Missoula, June 9. — One of the victims of the smallpox on the reservation this month is old Grizzly Bear, one of the best known of the old medicine men in the reservation country. When the smallpox epidemic broke out this old fellow retired to the mountains and "made medicine." He was an uncle of Duncan McDonald, and the latter says that when Grizzly Bear came back from the mountains he visited his friends and told them that the skunk, which was his oracle, or his "medicine," as he expressed it, had told him how to cure the smallpox.

When his acquaintances spoke plainly to him and told him that the surest way to cure the disease was to shake off the superstition and ignorance of the Indians and pay some attention to the rules of health, the old man was chagrined. He was further offended when he was refused admittance to the house of his nephew, Mr. McDonald, as he had been exposed to smallpox. He withdrew in anger and said that he would cure the people and show that the "medicine" that the skunk had given him was the right stuff. In two weeks he was dead, a victim to his own superstition.

Mr. McDonald tells another story that shows how very difficult it is to take care of the disease among the Indians. A woman up near the lake lost her husband through smallpox. She sent a messenger to Angus McDonald to get a steer, as she wanted to have a funeral feast, according to the custom of her people. Angus sent back word that she must not hold any feast until the danger of infection was past, and urged her to burn all of the contents of her cabin that had been exposed to infection. He explained the necessity for this, and was so successful that he convinced the woman. She postponed the feast and burned her cabin herself. She then went down near the mission to stay with some friends. Soon after smallpox appeared in this family. Investigation revealed the fact that when the woman had burned her cabin she had saved a few trinkets that her husband had had. Some of them had been upon his person when he was sick. These had carried the infection. She had burned the cabin, but had saved just what she should have destroyed. It is this ignorance and superstition that make the reservation situation so serious.

* * * * * * * * *

Department of the Interior,
United States Indian Service,
Jocko Flathead Agency Mont. July 30, 1901

Hon. Secretary of the Interior,
Sir: —

I find that the Agent, Physician, and employees, have used every exertion and care possible, under the adverse conditions, and think they deserve credit for doing all in their power possible.

No reliance whatever can be placed in the police. They will not hunt up or bring in the cases to the quarantine camp, and the Indians will not report such cases, consequently the Doctor and a nurse have to do this work, driving all over the country, and bring the suspects or cases in when found.

There are now in the smallpox camp about 50 cases. Since Feby. about 15 have died, five of them in the hospital camp. Since Feby. and up to date over 80 have been cured and turned out of camp.

Of course some of the cases were light, and now some of the cases in hospital camp are detained, being suspects.

No one is permitted to leave the reservation without a permit, and every efforet [sic] and precaution is being exercised to prevent the disease spreading.

There is a first class white nurse, an immune, in charge of the camp. A man of experience in nursing smallpox for years in Missoula and elsewhere.

The smallpox has been scattered more or less in the towns of this state for over two years, and it was brought to this reservation from the outside. Vaccination has been going on here for two years and I do not think more precaution could have been taken anywhere. The cases have not generally been severe, with a few exceptions. If it continues until winter, I fear it will become worse.

In think that there should be here, until the disease is stamped out an assistant physician, and at least two more white nurses. Only two of the police can be relied on and they are used for interpreters &c. The Agency physician is either at the camp or on the road hunting up cases where ever he hears of one. He and the men he has now cannot stand this work and do it justice. Sometimes they have to drive 50 or 60 miles to get a case. It will be cheaper and far better to give more men and an assistant and scour the entire reservation for cases and suspects, at once, than to have it drag . . . .

Very respectfully,
Frank C. Armstrong
Special and Disbursing Agent
Interior Department

Document 14

Indian Inspector Described Farms and Livestock on the Reservation July 30, 1901

Source: Excerpt from Frank C. Armstrong to Secretary of the Interior, July 30, 1901, letter received 42,669/1901, land division, RG 75, National Archives, Washington, D.C.

Editors' note: This 1901 inspection report took the form of a travelogue around the reservation describing the location of Indian farms and livestock herds on the open range. Among other things note what Armstrong said about the gardens and hay harvested by the Flathead Lake Kootenai and the independence of the Kalispel colony at Camas Prairie. This inspection was made before the expansion of irrigation later in the decade.

Department of the Interior,
United States Indian Service,
Jocko Flathead Agency Mont. July 30th. 1901.

Hon. Secretary of the Interior,
Sir: —

In accordance with your instructions I have investigated the conditions of the Indians of this reservation, the resources of the reservation, classification of the lands with reference to irrigation and allotment, and the portions best suited for farming and grazing, and that portion at which some future date might be purchased as surplus or leased for grazing purposes.

In order to do this I have traveled by team over the reservation the report of which trip I have the honor to submit as follows, —

This reservation contains 1,433,600 acres and is located in Missoula and Flathead counties Montana, has a population of 1734 people, over half of whom are mixed bloods of all grades. There are 442 children of school age. On the 1st. of July of this year there were 160 in the Catholic Mission schools and 40 in the Agency school.

Conditions and Civilization.

The majority of these people are self supporting. I include the mixed bloods who are generally well fixed and have good farms and herds of cattle. Many of this class sell hundreds of beef cattle every year. About one half of the entire population are French mixed bloods. About one fourth of the full bloods are farming and have some cattle. Some of their lands are irrigated in the most primitive manner and not with any regular system. This can be improved and regulated by supervisor of irrigation and regular ditches made. Another fourth of the full bloods have small gardens, large herds of cayuse ponies, some of which they occasionally sell, and make a scant support by cutting hay, gambling, and living on the more prosperous ones.

The remaining half of the full blood element which includes the Kootenai band located in the northern part near Dayton creek and majority of the Bitter Root band under old Chief Charlos located near the Agency are the most nonprogressive and backward Indians on the reservation. Much of this is due to Charlo's bad influence, who is a most nonprogressive Indian, opposed to everything which tends to civilization or advancement among the Indians.

He is bitterly opposed to schools and work, and exerts all his influence against both.

Irrigation, surveys and allotments can in a great measure weaken his influence by drawing off his following and getting the young and better element of his gang on irrigated lands where they can make a sure crop and earn a support. This work should be commenced as soon as possible. The best land being already occupied by the more progressive, it is necessary to provide homes and locations for those who have none and it can only be done by irrigation.

There is an abundance of good land for farming purposes, and water if utilized under a regular system.

There are on this reservation owned by mixed bloods, and s.... men, principally, and a few full bloods, about 25,000 head of cattle.

The full bloods generally own large numbers of ponies which if gotten rid of could be replaced with cattle. This the Agent is making every effort to accomplish and has succeeded getting many ponies sold off the reservation.

I have examined carefully the country suitable for farming marked on the map in red. By examining the map in connection with my trip over the reservation it will give a better idea of the conditions here. After examining the land and settlements around the Agency I drove along the Jocko to Ravalli station to within seven miles of Jocko station. Leaving Jocko river at Ravalli I crossed the divide to the waters of Mission creek examining its branches and head waters to St. Ignatius Mission, the location of the Catholic schools under the Sisters and Jesuits where they have a large establishment, fine farms and gardens, all kept in good condition. They have 160 pupils and could provide for 350 readily.

After a careful examination of the vacant land, water facilities &c north and west of the Mission, I found at least 10000 acres of land could be watered by ditches from Post and Mission creeks, and an excellent location for allotments as this plateau is unoccupied. Passing on northward and crossing Crow creek to the Sub-Agency at Ronan 16 miles from the Mission I found along the foot hills of the Mission range, fine farms and ranches as well as immediately on the creeks above mentioned. These farms under the foot hills have generally enough moisture from springs and seepage and do not require irrigation. These streams come from the Mission range of mountains, have an abundant flow of water all the year, ample to irrigate the lands on the plateau between the streams. Around the Sub-Agency at Ronan are some fine farms well cultivated, partially irrigated but generally not needing it. From the Sub-Agency to the southeast end of Flathead lake in the valley under the Mission mountains is generally well settled and cultivated and with good houses &c. This year these farmers have good crops of wheat, oats, hay, and potatoes and all have cattle, some have large herds which generally run on the range. Passing through these settlements there is as much evidence of civilization, cultivation, and prosperity as will be found in farming sections generally in Montana.

I examined the country &c around Baptice which is the steam boat landing from Kalispell across the lake. Around the south and southeastern part of the lake are fine farms and pastures and no irrigation required. All this country mentioned as being well cultivated &c is occupied by French mixed bloods, nearly white, and s.... men with mixed blood wives. From the Mission to the foot of the lake there are about 40 full blood Indians who are doing fairly well, have farms and cattle. The land marked in red, — a good portion of which is unoccupied and if irrigated the full bloods would be glad to take as it would give homes to every Indian needing them. The land on the east side of the Flathead river is where the majority of the people of this reservation reside.

Crossing the Flathead river at Baptice I found an excellent water fall and power which extends from one to two miles which can be utilized for milling or any other purpose. The country west of the river is better suited for grazing than farming. On Dayton creek on the north end of the reservation, are located the band of Kootenai Indians numbering about 100 who eke out an existance in some way. They have small gardens, sell some hay, and have some ponies but are neither progressive or civilized. They are so far away that unless an additional farmer can be located there among them, it is impossible to do anything with them. There should be a good farmer located there who could give special attention to these Indians, to the lake settlements, and the whiskey traffic, which is carried on extensively in this section of the reservation. Law officers, state and federal, give little heed to it. The country west of the lake and river is high rolling and generally grazing land. There are good streams affording enough water for irrigating small farms and stock ranches. These locations are generally occupied by mixed bloods and s.... men. Some have very excellent stock ranches and large herds of cattle. These people sell large numbers of beef cattle every year and are generally prosperous.

Passing on to Little Bitter Root Creek which rises in the north west portion of the reserve and runs into the Flathead, I crossed to the Hot Springs. Near the head springs of several streams running from the mountain range on the west, I found a number of good small farms and cattle ranches all held by french mixed bloods, a few s.... men and their wives. Some whose rights to be on the reservation are very doubtful. The country outside of the red plats is excellent for grazing, high and rolling, fine range in winter or summer, with ample water for stock at all seasons.

Passing south from Hot Springs I crossed a high range, fine grazing country with good spring lakes on the summit, furnishing plenty of water for any number of cattle. Following along down the creek I came into the Camas Prairie, a basin valley surrounded by mountains. In this valley are located the Lower Kalispell band of over one hundred full bloods under the old Chief Michael. These people have very good houses located around the valley generally where small spring branches run from the mountains, have some very good fields, raise gardens, have some cattle, have large hay fields fenced and are very good workers. They have a colony to themselves, and do not allow the mixed bloods to settle among them. They are about sixty miles from the agency. The station Horse Plains, on the Northern Pacific Railway, is about ten miles from this valley and is a great detriment to these people. It is here where the whiskey traffic is carried on extensively. It is so far from the agency that it is impossible for the agent to prevent it. These Indians are industrious, and if the whiskey traffic could be cut off, in a few years they would be selfsupporting and prosperous.

A good farmer should be located among these people. He should be an active energetic, fearless man, who would look after things generally. A single man who could be in the saddle and if necessary run down a whiskey peddler is the kind of man wanted here.

Passing through this Camas Prairie country over a divide and down a small stream I reached the Flathead river at Perma station on the Northern Pacific Railroad where I crossed at an Indian ferry and traveled along the south side of the river and railroad over hills and broken country suitable only for grazing to Duncan Station. The country from Perma to Duncan is well timbered along the south line of the reservation. From Duncan to Jocko station I found some very good country but the best of the valley is covered by the railroad right of way. At Jocko the Jocko creek flows into the Flathead River. About Jocko Station the valley widens and there are some very good ranches along the south side to Ravalli as well as good grazing lands. From Ravalli I traveled up the Jocko to the Agency.

In no part of the State is there a better country for farming and stock raising then on this reservation and it is only a question of management and labor and the expenditure of some money for irrigating purposes to bring these Indians to comfortable selfsupporting. It is far better to take hold of this matter now than to allow it to drift along, becoming more complicated and difficult to handle. Over half of this population are selfsupporting, the remainder should be compelled to become so.

Lands

The lands marked in red are generally good farming lands, much of it needs no irrigation but in order to give these locations to full bloods without homes there must be some irrigation provided by the government. All these farming lands, whether occupied or not, should be surveyed and no time lost to get at it. The surveys can go on during the winter in these valleys. The irrigation should be commenced on the lands north of the Mission first and also the surveys, as there is a large tract there where Indians who have no places would be glad to locate.

There is much mountain and fine timber land on the west side of the reservation and there will be a very large surplus after the Indians are located. The Indians and settlements will nearly all be on the east side of the Flathead River.

Whether there are any minerals in the mountains can only be determined after they are thrown out and prospected, I have heard of none however.

Ditches &etc.

There should be a regular system of irrigation commenced here, and to do this an irrigating engineer, either Inspector Graves or some of his assistants should be sent here to look it over and make an estimate. Twelve or fifteen thousand dollars might be allowed out of the general irrigation fund to commence this. The Indians can and will do all of the work and thereby get the proceeds of their labor to live on. This would give an opportunity to furnish regular work to the idle full bloods and be a great help in breaking up Charlos influence. Indians will generally work where cash is immediately in sight. The ditch near the agency can be opened out, some new lateral made in the most systematic manner which would give a large increase of acreage under the irrigation.

Surveys and Allotments.

The surveys should commence here at once. It is very evident that many of the mixed bloods and s.... men hold much more land than they are entitled to. Nothing of course in the way of allotments can be done until after the surveys has commenced. It is my opinion that these people will be anxious for allotments when the ditches and surveys are put into operation. Every day that this work is delayed makes more complication and more difficult to settle.

A Complete Roll.

There should be a complete and perfect roll made of these people. Delay brings new difficulty in getting one. A special agent should be put at this work who is familiar with rolls, as it will be several months of hard work to get a correct one. At the Mission Church at St. Ignatius a good record is kept of births, marriages and deaths and valuable information can be obtained there for making a roll. The status of many of these people is similar to that of many of the Civilized Tribes in the Indian Territory and much more difficult to reach as there are no records to follow. This is very important as nothing can be done in the way of allotments until after this roll is completed. The agent here cannot do this work with the force at this command and it requires a Special agent who can give his entire time and attention to business.

Appropriations for Agency.

The appropriations are sixteen thousand dollars per year. After paying employes there remains $10,120.00; out of this all the supplies &c are purchased. The number of Indians rationed here regularly is ninety, old and decrepit. They receive the following rations:

Flour	20 lbs every two weeks
coffee	2 lbs every two weeks
Sugar	3 lbs every two weeks
Beans	4 lbs every two weeks
Bacon	4 lbs every two weeks
Soap	1 lb Issued when called for
Matches	1 box Issued when called for
Candles	Issued when called for
Kerosene	I gal. Issued when called for

The salary of the agency employes amount to $5880.00. The salary of the Sawyer & Miller is $1,000.00 and is paid from Misc'l receipts. The supplies sent to this agency consisting of wagons, plows, harrows, harness, rakes, hoes &c. are issued to Indians who pay for them by labor repairing roads, bridges, delivering logs, hauling freight, cutting wood for agency purposes, and no money is paid out for irregular labor. Also some of these articles are issued to Indians who have commenced to farm and who show industry and thrift.

[The rest of Armstrong's report discusses administrative matters at the agency and recommendations for immediate survey and allotment of the reservation.]

Very respectfully,
Frank C. Armstrong.
Special and Disbursing Agent
Interior Department.

Document 15

Oliver Gibeau Subject to Missoula County Taxes

August 30, 1901

Source: "United States v. Higgins, County Treasurer. (Circuit Court, D. Montana. August 30, 1901.) No. 575," *The Federal Reporter*, vol. 110 (Oct.-Nov. 1901), pages 609-611.

Editors' note: In this decision Judge Knowles decided that Oliver Gibeau was subject to Missoula County taxes because he was largely grown before he moved to the Flathead Reservation as a young man.

United States v. Higgins, County Treasurer.
(Circuit Court, D. Montana. August 30, 1901.)
No. 575.

Indians — Taxation.

One whose father is a white person, and a naturalized citizen, is not an Indian for purpose of taxation, though his mother is a half-breed Indian, and when he is 17 years old goes with her children to an Indian reservation, and has granted her application to be admitted as a member of the tribe, and thereafter lives on the reservation.

Wm. B. Rodgers, U.S. Atty.

Marshall, Stiff & Ranft and Denny & Nolan, for defendant.

Knowles, District Judge. This is a suit brought by the United States against George Higgins, the treasurer and tax collector of Missoula county, Mont., to enjoin him from collecting a tax from one Oliver Gibeau. It appears from the evidence in this case that said Gibeau is the owner of a number of horses and cattle ranging upon the Flathead Indian reservation, sometimes called the Jocko Indian reservation, in the state of Montana; that in the year 1897 one W. R. Hamilton, the then assessor of said Missoula county, listed the said property as that of said Gibeau for taxation, and that state and county taxes were assessed upon the same. Said assessment was duly returned upon the proper assessment roll of said county for said year to the then tax collector of said county. Said Gibeau refused to pay said taxes, and after the same became delinquent said George Higgins, as the then treasurer and tax collector of said county, seized certain live stock, the property of said Gibeau, and advertised the same for sale at public auction, with a view to realizing sufficient money to pay said taxes, penalty, and the costs of collection. The government brought this suit for the purpose of enjoining this sale, alleging that said Gibeau is an Indian, and its ward. No contention has been made that the United States cannot maintain this suit if such is the fact. The defendant contends that said Gibeau should be classed as a white man, and not as an Indian, and, as that part of the Flathead Indian reservation where said Gibeau resides lies within the exterior boundaries of Missoula county, he should list his property and be taxed in and by that county. It appears from the evidence in this case that Oliver Gibeau was born in Missoula county, Mont., in the year 1866; that his father was a white man, and a native of Canada, who in 1877, became a citizen of the United States by naturalization. It also appears from the evidence that Oliver Gibeau's mother was a half-breed Indian woman; her father being a white man, and her mother a Spokane Indian. The father of Gibeau settled upon public land of the United States near Frenchtown, in said Missoula county, and afterwards entered the same in the proper land office of the United States. The mother resided with the father upon this land until 1883, when, with her children, she went to the Flathead Indian reservation, and made application to be admitted as a member of the Flathead Indian Nation. This application was granted. Gibeau was about 17 years of age at the time of going upon the reservation with his mother, and has grown up to manhood there, and has become the chief of the Indian police on that reservation. The father went to live upon the reservation a year after his wife had removed there. The question is presented as to whether or not Oliver Gibeau should be classed as an Indian or a white man. Had he lived in the county of Missoula up to this time, I think he would certainly have been classed as a white man. He would have been entitled to the status of his father. He could have inherited, acquired, and held property. He could have located mining claims. Did the fact of his going upon the reservation with his mother, and adopting the habits of the Indians, change his status? I think not. While there are cases in which quarter-breed Indians have been recognized as Indians by the laws of congress and by the action of the executive department of the government, I cannot refer to any case where a person possessing but one-fourth Indian blood, and who was born among the white people, and lived among them until almost a man grown, has been classed as an Indian. If he had acquired real property, it would have been assessed for taxation and taxed. The fourteenth amendment to the constitution of the United States provides: "All persons born or naturalized in the United States, and subject to the jurisdiction thereof, are citizens of the United States and of the state wherein they reside." Section 1992 of the Revised Statutes also provides: "All persons born in the

United States and not subject to any foreign power, excluding Indians not taxed, are declared to be citizens of the United States." It is stated by Mr. Justice Story, in his work on the Constitution, in regard to Indians:

> "When, however, the tribal relations are dissolved, when the headship of the chief or the authority of the tribe is no longer recognized, and the individual Indian, turning his back upon his former mode of life, makes himself a member of the civilized community, the case is wholly altered. He then no longer acknowledges a divided allegiance. He joins himself to the body politic. He gives evidence of his purpose to adopt the habits and customs of civilized life. And, as his case is then within the terms of this amendment, it would seem that his right to protection in person, property, and privilege must be as complete as the allegiance to the government to which he must then be held; as complete, in short, as that of any other native-born inhabitant."

In the case of U.S. v. Hadley (C. C.) 99 Fed. 437, it is held that a half-breed Indian, raised among the white people as a white man, could not be classified as an Indian, although he had gone upon an Indian reservation to live, and had received an allotment of land in severalty. It has been held that a white man adopted into an Indian tribe by the rules and regulations thereof did not lose his status as a white man, or acquire that of an Indian. The mother of Oliver Gibeau could not, by taking him with her to an Indian tribe, and securing his adoption into the same, deprive her son of the rights of a white man and of a citizen. By Indian polity he might, by them, be classed as an Indian, but not by the constitution and laws of the United States. In the case of U.S. v. Higgins (heretofore decided) 103 Fed. 348, in which it was sought to enjoin said Higgins from collecting taxes from one Alexander Matt, the facts presented were essentially different. Matt was born in the "Indian country." His people never assumed the habits of civilization. It was not shown that his father ever was or became a citizen of the United States. He was one of the class recognized and treated as an Indian in the orders of the executive department of the government to the Flathead Indians to remove from the Bitter Root Valley to the present Flathead or Jocko Indian reservation. For these reasons the injunction heretofore issued should be dissolved, and the complainant's bill dismissed, and it is so ordered.

Document 16

Caroline Grenier Relates Life in Early-day Polson September 1901 plus

Source: Ida S. Patterson, "Polson's No. 1 Woman Recalls Early Days," *The Daily Missoulian,* October 30, 1949, Society Section, page 6, col. 1-5. Reprinted with permission of the *Missoulian*.

Editors' note: Mrs. Caroline Tomfohr Grenier was a white woman who moved to Polson at the start of the twentieth century. Here memories describe early-day Polson, the buffalo roundup, and life and business in the area.

Polson's No. 1 Woman Recalls Early Days

by Ida S. Patterson

Polson, Oct. 29. — This Lake county seat community accords Mrs. Charles Grenier the distinction of being its No. 1 woman on the basis of continuous residence.

Forty-eight years ago last month the then 23-year-old Caroline Tomfohr, tall, blue eyed and blonde, walked from the gangplank of the steamer Klondike onto the Polson dock.

In that September of 1901, Polson consisted of Henry Terriault's trading post and barn, Isaac Cormier's blacksmith shop, Baptiste Eanea's cabin and a few Indian tepees.

The previous year Miss Tomfohr had left her native town of Lake City, Minn., and gone to Kalispell, where she found employment as a housekeeper. In those days there was much discussion at Kalispell about the probable opening to settlement of the Flathead Indian reservation in the lower Flathead valley. The reservation was then regarded as primitive territory, upon which a white person was not allowed to remain without a permit from the Indian agent.

Frequent news of happenings on the reserve interested and intrigued Miss Tomphor [sic] and she resolved to grasp the first opportunity to see this beautiful, wild land of which she had heard so much.

She had joined a Kalispell labor union and at one of its meetings she met a sister of Andrew Stinger. Mr. Stinger, she learned, was a prosperous rancher on the Flathead reservation. His wife was the widow of C. A. Allard, who had been part owner of the famous Pablo-Allard buffalo herd. The Stingers lived on the old Allard ranch on Mud creek about three miles west of Ronan.

Learning from the sister that the Stingers needed a cook, Miss Tomfohr applied for the job and in due time was accepted. Her courage might have failed her but for the fact that a tutor for the Stinger children, Bertha Loder, had preceded her. Caroline was unacquainted with Miss Loder, but with the hope that the young teacher would prove a congenial companion she prepared for the trip by boat to the lower Flathead.

Sails from Demersville

Early on a sunny September morning Miss Tomfohr took the six-horse stage for Demersville, head of navigation on the Flathead river and about three and a half miles east of Kalispell. At 7 a.m. the Klondike, captained by Gene Hodge, Sr., pulled away from the landing. Aboard were 25 passengers, both Indians and whites, booked for the reservation.

As the boat plied the 28 miles of river passage and steamed out on the blue expanse of Flathead lake, Miss Tomfohr stood on the open deck and gazed on the panorama of miles of sparkling water bordered by a forested shoreline of flaming autumn glory and paralleled to the east by the purple shadowed, snow-topped battlement of the majestic Mission range. Caroline felt that adventure was before her.

At noon the boat docked at Polson, where she was met by Mr. Stinger. After lunch at the Terriault trading post they drove over the Polson hill southward to the ranch on Mud creek.

The Stinger home, a large two-story residence, was comfortable and Caroline was kindly welcomed. The household consisted of Mr. and Mrs. Stinger, four children, Miss Loder the teacher, and five or six hired men.

Caroline's job as a cook lasted but a short time. A dressmaker was needed and as she could qualify a man cook was hired and Caroline became the family seamstress. The sewing room was upstairs. The schoolroom, too, was on the second floor. Miss Loder and Miss Tomfohr became fast friends and spent many of their leisure hours riding horseback over the rolling, unfenced grassland of the Mission valley.

At the expiration of Miss Loder's second term she returned to Kalispell, but Caroline stayed with the Stinger family for two years.

Helps in Buffalo Roundup

During the fall of her second year on the ranch some of the Pablo-Allard buffaloes were rounded up and shipped to zoos and parks in various parts of the country. The rounding up, crating and hauling to Ravalli of the great wild creatures was a far more difficult task than was at first anticipated.

Ranging over the rough terrain of the Round Butte and Pend d'Oreille river country, these last monarchs of the plains presented a formidable challenge to horses and hard riding cowboys. At times 45 or 50 men would gather and start about a 100 head to the Stinger ranch. By changing horses and riding hard they sometimes managed to corral 15 or 20 buffaloes.

As all available horses and riders were needed in the roundup, the services of Caroline and Mrs. Stinger were enlisted. Howard Eaton, the man negotiating for the animals, was crippled and as he was unable to ride he volunteered to help cook for the outfit.

Mrs. Grenier recalls that immediately after lunch she and Mrs. Stinger would mount their horses and start out to meet the incoming herd. They would make a wide swing so as to join the semicircle of horsemen to the rear of the buffaloes. Keeping the zigzagging creatures together and headed toward the home corals required all the tactics known to horse and rider.

Mrs. Grenier counts as one of the highlights of her experience those days of helping corral some of this largest and last wild herd of American bison. About 200 were sent to zoos and parks within the United States. Thirty-six comprised most of the nucleus of the Flathead bison reserve. Most of the animals, however, were sold to the Canadian government and formed the original stock of the Athabaska reserve in the dominion.

Goes to Trading Post

Soon after the buffalo roundup in that fall of 1903, Miss Tomfohr left the Stingers and went to work for the trading post at Polson. The business, formerly operated by Henry Terriault, was now owned by Charles Allard, Jr., and Oscar Sedman. Caroline's chief jobs were waitress and maid. However, she sometimes clerked in the store, distributed mail and acted as hostess.

The Klondike came in three times a week. It arrived at noon and travelers would dine at the post before leaving on it for the upper Flathead or going by stage to Ravalli. Usually there were about 25 diners, but Mrs. Grenier recalls that at times she served as many as 85 persons.

Life in Polson was rather quiet in those days, says Mrs. Grenier. Ice on the lake often stopped winter boat traffic for a number of weeks. In such times, nomadic Indians were about the only customers at the trading post. Often for long periods Caroline was the sole woman at the foot of Flathead lake.

Mrs. Grenier recalls one exciting incident of that era. Late on a quiet autumn afternoon a sheriff from Oregon and a deputy from Thompson Falls rode up to the post, tied their horses and strode into the store. They said they were on the trail of two horse thief suspects which the sheriff had pursued from Oregon. They rented a room and prepared to stay for the night.

Dinner was served and a fire was built in the stove in the store, where Mr. Sedman, the officers and five or six other men were conversing.

Shot Shatters Lamp

Caroline finished her work and went into the store. After talking with the men a few minutes she returned to the dining room — which was cut off from the store only by a thin partition — and started reading by the light of a kerosene lamp which was suspended from the center of the ceiling. Instantly the lamp shattered and bits of broken glass and kerosene sprayed the floor. The startled Caroline jumped up and examined the broken lamp. Unable to determine the cause of the crash, she hurried toward the store. Just as she reached the door, it was flung open by a stranger. His left arm was limp and bleeding. His right hand grasped a smoking gun. He pushed her aside, and ran on through the room and out the back way.

Caroline went into the store, but there wasn't a man in sight. She walked on through the room to the front entrance and from Sedman's office on her left a man cried, "Stay out of the fire."

Wonderingly she asked, "What fire?"

Mr. Sedman emerged from his office. From behind boxes, barrels and the counter other heads appeared. Pretty soon all were in the center of the room, all excitedly talking at once.

Caroline was informed that as soon as she quit the group, the two outlaws came into the store. Fleeing to Canada, they had ridden over the Hot Springs trail to the west side of the Flathead river. At a near-by Indian camp they were told about a trading post at the foot of the lake. An Indian boy was hired to take them across the river in his rowboat. Cautioning him to wait at the shore while they bought supplies, they went to the store. On entering, they immediately recognized the officers. Guns flashed, men ducked out of sight and the smell of powder filled the room.

The older desperado's bullet pierced the sole of a boot of the sheriff. The officer retaliated the fire, wounding him in the arm as he ran for the dining room door. The other suspect, a boy of about 16, aimed at the deputy and the shot passed through the officer's hat and the wall beyond, and crashed the dining room lamp.

Escape in Rowboat

The boy escaped through the front door. In hot pursuit, the officers ran to the river — only to see the Indian swiftly rowing the two men to the opposite side of the river where they quickly mounted their horses and fled north.

A few months later, because of an infected arm, the older man entered a Leftbridge hospital, where he died. The boy was arrested, tried and acquitted.

The shooting affray was a topic of conversation for many months at the post, Mrs. Grenier recalls.

In 1905 the trading post was sold to F. L. Gray & Co. An addition was built and the expanded business became the Grandview hotel. Caroline continued with the new management and that year Charles Grenier, a young man from Frenchtown, started clerking at the trading post.

Married in Butte in 1906

On February 14, 1906, Caroline Tomfohr and Charles Grenier were married in Butte. They continued working for Gray & Co. until July when they moved to their farm on the west slope of the Polson hill. There they reared seven children. It is still the family home.

From this vantage point Mrs. Grenier has a clear view of the Mission range of mountains, of Flathead lake and the Lake county seat at its foot. She has watched Polson grow from a trading post to a city of 3,500 residents. For many years she saw the Klondike come through the narrows, cross Polson bay and glide into the city docks. To the south she saw, in days of yore, the six-horse stage from Ravalli jog and bump over the Polson hill.

Then one day the Klondike made its final run; the stage, too, topped the hill for the last time. Auto stages buzzed over improved roads until a branch line of the Northern Pacific pushed its way north from Dixon. After a few years passenger service was discontinued and only freight cars now round the hill. On a new highway below the railroad travelers now come to town in big busses and privately-owned autos. And across the river a city airport gives promise of future airway service.

As Mrs. Grenier looks out upon the much changed scene, she recalls often the days when she was the only woman in Polson.

Document 17

Indian Woman Kills Sac Arlee in Self-defense

September 5, 1901

Source: "Confesses the Killing," *The Anaconda Standard*, September 5, 1901, page 12, col. 5.

Editors' note: The white Montana court system decided that this Indian woman killed Sac Arlee in self-defense and released her.

Confesses the Killing
S.... Admits That She Slew Sac Arlee.
Did It in Self-Defense
Woman Claims That She Did Not Intend to Inflict a Mortal Wound, but That She Struck the Blow to Protect Herself.

Missoula, Sept. 4. — The little courtroom of United States Commissioner Wallace P. Smith was crowded to-day with Indians and spectators who took some part in the preliminary hearing of the Indians accused of murdering Sac Arlee, a Flathead Indian, on the reservation about a month ago. As was stated in to-day's Standard, Agnes, the s.... in the case, acknowledged the murder of the Indian and was held to the federal court. The other Indians have been discharged and will return to the reservation at once.

The story as told by the witnesses is about as follows: On the night of the murder Sac Arlee, Agnes and other Indians had been drinking. It was late that night when it was reported that whiskey had been brought to a tent and was being sold, and that also a game of cards was going to open up. There were several Indians around the place, which is known on the reservation as the Kootenai camp, and a bonfire had been started. Sac Arlee was under the influence of liquor, when he started in pursuit of Agnes, whom he saw pass the place where the gambling was to have been carried on. He caught up with her and insulted her, wanting to go to her tent with her, which insult Agnes resented. The s.... continued to keep away from Sac Arlee and in trying to get away from him was at one time knocked down by him. She then went into a tent of one of the Kootenais and Sac Arlee followed her. As they entered the tent Sac Arlee again knocked Agnes down, and in falling she fell on to the cooking utensils and her hand found a knife. She got up and in defending herself against the assaults of Sac Arlee struck him with the knife. Two blows were struck, one cutting a deep gash on the back of the head and the second cutting his throat. Sac Arlee started to go out of the tent and commenced to sway as he became weak from the wounds. Oyouse Finley, a half-breed, who was in the tent and heard the noise, got up as Sac Arlee came from behind a curtain, where the cutting took place, and caught the Indian as he was falling. He carried him outside of the tent and laid him on the ground. Two other Indians, defendants in the case, were at hand and, picking Sac Arlee up from the ground, laid him up alongside the tent, where he gave a few gasps and died. Sac Arlee being a relation of Mrs. Oyouse Finley, the latter's husband had the remains carried to his home, where they were placed in a coffin and the day following the murder were buried.

The prosecution was conducted by United States Assistant Prosecuting Attorney Carl Rasch of Helena, who for the first time in his life conducted a case of this kind. The gentleman did exceedingly well in examining all of the witnesses and questioned them very closely.

Agent Smead testified to being notified of the murder, of sending the reservation police to arrest those connected with the affair and to what he heard about the manner in which the deed was committed.

J. M. Dixon appeared for Finley and introduced evidence to show that his client was not guilty of the crime and that he bears a good reputation on the reservation, and that he conducts a large farm, employing a number of Indian hands.

D. Dowd, the cattle man, was a witness, but could throw very little light on the murder. He stated that he had heard of the murder and went up to the camp, and found Sac Arlee in the coffin. He was accompanied by some young ladies, and as is the custom with the Indians on occasions like that one, he stepped up to the dead Indian and shook his hand good-bye.

Albert Vincent acted as interpreter, and did well. He understands both languages, and answered the questions fluently. He had some trouble with Agnes, owing to her being a Kootenai.

One of the important witnesses in the case was Michel, who saw almost the whole affair. He stated that the deed was committed after midnight and shortly before daylight. He did not, however, see Agnes hit Sac Arlee with the knife.

Joseph, another Indian, when testifying, produced a picture drawn by himself on a common piece of wrapping paper, of the direction of the tents in which the murder took place, from the house owned by Oyouse Finley, and the direction the fleeing Agnes took when Sac Arlee started after her. One peculiar feature about the picture, and a characteristic of the Indians, is that all their drawings of human beings place then with their heads down. The picture was produced in evidence and was looked at with much merriment by the witnesses.

Agnes told that she did not mean to kill Sac Arlee, but struck him in self-defense, hoping to stop him from assaulting her. When she did strike him she got out of the tent without any one knowing it, and had she not told of her own accord that she did the killing it would have been impossible to secure direct evidence against her. It is understood that Agnes will not be given a chance to secure bail for her appearance in the federal court. The matter was investigated this evening to see if she could get bail if Judge Smith would fix it, but it was found that she could not get it. The case will be tried next month in the United States court at Butte.

Document 18

Visiting with Duncan McDonald at Ravalli Railroad Station October 20, 1901

Source: [no title], *The Anaconda Standard,* October 20, 1901, page 18, col. 1-7.

Editors' note: Travelers stuck at Selish or Ravalli railroad station on the reservation were entertained by Indian tales and personal stories related by Duncan McDonald. McDonald was not convinced that civilization was better than traditional Indian life.

Did you ever have to wait half a day for a train at Selish? May be you don't even know where Selish is. If you don't you certainly have never had to wait there for a train, for if you had you would have Selish so indelibly stamped upon your memory that you would certainly remember where it is. Not that the wait is so disagreeable or unpleasant — on the contrary it is rather interesting. Selish will never be able to contest the reputation of Garrison as a waiting place. Garrison has won a mark in this line that no town will be able to surpass in this generation. Garrison is supreme and will, by force of circumstances, remain so for many years.

Selish, as a waiting place for trains, possesses many points of interest and, always provided that the wait is not too long, the experience of waiting there for a train is an interesting one. Selish is the principal station on the Northern Pacific in the Flathead Indian reservation. From Selish the stage road across the Mission valley take its start, and it is a point of considerable commercial importance. There are always passengers there bound for the Flathead country and it is seldom that there is not a party of Indians present, who are going or coming or else have just come down to the railway as a matter of diversion.

Duncan McDonald's Home.

Selish, too, is the home of Duncan McDonald, well known throughout the Northwest by reason of his great familiarity with the customs and habits of the Indians, their legends and their history. If the wait at Selish were productive of nothing more than a visit with Duncan McDonald one would be fully repaid, for a chat with him is always full of interest. His store of Indian tales and his recollections of early experiences before the railway had penetrated the reservation are so interesting that one forgets that there is a late train and, when the wait is ended, he is almost sorry that it couldn't have been longer.

On Wednesday afternoon of last week there was a larger party of waiters at Selish station than usual and the wait was more than ordinarily long. There had been a collision or something in Idaho and the eastbound overland was about 10 hours late. In the party of waiters was a group of Indians who were on their way to Butte to appear as witnesses in the federal court, where there were two Indian cases, one a murder in which an Indian woman was the accused, and the other a case of cattle stealing.

The prospective witnesses appeared to be more deeply interested in the outcome of the cattle case than in the one in which a woman's life was at stake. The woman had killed a man in defense of her honor — had stabbed only when he had laid violent hands upon her — but there was not the interest manifested in that case that was apparent in connection with the cattle thieves' trial.

Beside the Camp Fire.

Across the right of way from the station there was burning a camp fire against a dry log. The fire was a small one, but it wasn't smoky and it gave out grateful warmth that was attractive. Two Standard men were cordially invited by Mr. McDonald to join the group that sat or lay about the fire and the invitation was accepted.

Duncan sat upon a log near the fire, and in various positions around lay half a dozen Indians who, like the Standard men, were waiting for the train. They were philosophical about the wait, however, and their only anxiety was lest they should be late in getting to court and thus render themselves liable to punishment. In their own language they discussed all sorts of things. That is, it appeared as if they did, but their words were not intelligible to their visitors.

"How are you?" was the cordial greeting of Duncan McDonald as he rose to shake hands with the new arrivals. "It was too close up there in the station, so we came out here to wait in the fresh air. It's pleasant here and comfortable." Then, after a few words of inquiry and reply, the veteran leaned back against the log and said:

"We have waited all day here for this train. It didn't used to be so before the railway came in here. I was born up there at the old trading post in 1849, and I have always lived there. When he wanted to go anywhere, we saddled our ponies and went. I remember that we used to think it an ordinary ride between breakfast and dinner from Post creek to Missoula. That was after I had grown up. I have made that ride more than once.

"But there are a lot of things that are no better now than they were then. I see now that it is fashionable for women in the cities to ride astride. Well, the Indian women have been riding that way ever since they rode at all. It was always the sensible way, but it was not fashionable, and so the poor Indian woman was decried and laughed at for riding the natural way. It is all the fashion that does it. That's all. Why, look at the way fashionable women wear their hair these days. Look at the front and then look at the front of an Indian's hair. You will see that it is the same, and the Indian has worn his hair that way for hundreds of years.

"Is Civilization a Failure?"

"I don't believe that the civilization, as it is called, "has helped things much. In the old days when the food of the Indian was what he collected and prepared himself, there was no sickness among the tribes. The camas root, the bitter root, the sarvice berry and all the roots and herbs that he gathered and dried and then ate with his meat kept him well. His teeth were good and his digestion was perfect. Now that the Indian has learned to eat like the white man his teeth

Duncan McDonald
Source: Photograph Archives, Montana Historical Society, Helena, Montana, photo 943-624

are getting bad, he has no digestion and he cannot be said to be in any such health as he was under the old conditions."

These followed a few minutes of silence as the speaker smoked and looked thoughtfully into the fire. The silence was broken by the guttural utterances of the Indians around the fire. One might close his eyes and imagine that time had turned back a generation and that he was a guest of the Indians around the camp fire. There was no sound of civilization to break the spell and nothing disturbed the silence but the almost inaudible conversation of the Indians. After a while Duncan McDonald resumed.

"This was a great country once. The old Indians tell me that these hills between here and Jocko used to swarm with mountain sheep. Even as late as I can remember there were hundreds and hundreds of white tail and black tail deer on these hills around here and in the valleys. This was a favorite hunting ground between the Jocko valley and Plains. The Bitter Root Indians and those of this valley used to meet at Plains the Indians from the coast and annually trade and gamble with them. These were great occasions.

Great Place for Sheep.

"Do you see that point of rocks across there?" asked Duncan, pointing to a spur of rocks that jut out boldly from the grassy hill, just at the mouth of a little draw. "That was the great place for killing the mountain sheep. The old Indians say that no matter where a band of sheep was scared up they would run for miles till they reached this point. There they would huddle behind the rocks while their leader mounted the top rock and looked up and down the valley. I have heard the old Indians tell many times about famous hunts that they had here. A party of hunters with their bows and arrows would conceal themselves in that draw and another party would go up or down the stream to start up the sheep. The animals always ran here and the hidden Indians killed them with their primitive weapons. It was one of the famous places of this part of the country among those old Indians. But you ask any of them about that point and they'll tell you some stories about their hunting experiences that will be good."

Duncan then spoke to old Isidor, a veteran Indian, near the fire, and told him what he had been talking about. The old fellow at once became interested and talked rapidly for a few minutes, gesticulating all the while. Duncan explained that Isidor had been telling one of the stories that he knew about when a lot of sheep had been driven up to the point and killed.

"Do you know," continued the speaker, as he looked out toward his handsome residence under the hills, surrounded with a big orchard and comfortable stables and sheds, "do you know that I believe that we're not as contented with all that we have these days as we used to be when all that we owned was a horse and a buffalo robe? You didn't hear of any such troubles as we have these days and the people were all the better and happier.

Recalls a Preacher.

"That may be contrary to your argument, but it's so just the same. It's with you like it is with a preacher who calls here sometimes. He always wants to hear some of the old Indian tales, and as long as they agree with some of his old Bible myths he thinks that they're good and says that that shows so and so. But when I told him a story the other day when he was here, he wouldn't hear to it at all because there was nothing like it in his list of myths. If I tell him something about the flood and those things he agrees with them, but if the stories are just the simple legends of the tribes, he laughs at them. So with you. If you don't reconcile my statements to your own arguments you don't think they're sound. But I speak from observation."

Then there was another pause. Thorndike found some old tin cans and set them up as marks. In a few minutes he was engaged in a warm contest with the old Indians who had been around the fire, throwing stones at the cans. Old Isidor and Paul, the young interpreter, were wonders. They could hit the mark with unerring accuracy and quite discounted the white contestants. It was a gay time for a while. The old Indians, who had hardly smiled all day, laughed heartily at the sport and entered into the contest with all the interest of a crowd of boys playing duck-on-a-rock.

When Isidor had clearly established his supremacy he posed for a photograph and wanted one sent to him.

Duncan watched the sport with amused interest. "There have been many games like that played here before," said he. "Such games as that are popular with the young Indians, and it is such practice that used to give them their skill with the bow and arrow. They were always playing something like that. They had different games for the different times of the year, just as the white children have. No, the Indian had no calendar. He knew the different seasons, of course, and his habits were governed by them. He, however, kept no account of the days and the months, and the calendar is still unknown to most of the Indians. They had no regular feast days or holidays. When they gathered for their hunting or their trading or their gambling they had their holidays and their dancing and their races and games. But there was no fixed calendar."

"There comes the train," said Duncan. His ear had caught the sound of the engine away down on the Jocko flat. The party broke up and crossed to the station. The wait at Selish was ended and it had not been an unpleasant one.

Document 19

Indian Prisoner Complains of Conditions at Missoula Jail November 20, 1901

Source: "Doesn't Like the Noise," *The Anaconda Standard*, November 20, 1901, page 12, col. 2.

Editors' note: Pascal was a prisoner at the Missoula jail during 1901. He was sentenced for attacking others in Plains, probably while drunk.

Doesn't Like the Noise
Pascele, the Indian, Complains About Prison Quarters.
Cellmates Talk Too Much
Has an Especial Antipathy for the "Sheeney Kid" and "Bum Mit" — Calls Upon Officer to Abate the Nuisances.

Missoula, Nov. 19. — Pascele, the Indian in the county jail on a six months' sentence for trying to make a slaughter pen out of the town of Plains, has been in the Hotel Prescott only a few days as a border, but he has become much dissatisfied with his quarters. The Sheeney Kid and the Bum Mit are the causes of his trouble and he wants a new boarding place. He confided his woes to Deputy Sheriff McCormick yesterday. The officer is an old friend of Pascele, having known him years ago on the reservation. Major McCormick was then Indian agent and "Dougal" was a small boy whom the reservation Indians liked very much. When they come to town they always hunt him up to confide in him their troubles and to seek his advice in their business and other transactions. Therefore, it was not considered strange by Mr. McCormick yesterday when Pascele called him.

"Willium, Willium, come here," was the summons of the Indian and the officer responded to the call. Pascele continued: "This house no good. Woman heap damn fool, all time talk. No good. Big Mouth no good. Heap noise. All time 'Yah, Y-a-a-h.'"

This description of the laugh of the Sheeney Kid left no doubt as to who was called Big Mouth by Pascele. The woman was the Bum Mit, who was in jail on the usual charge. Her conversation was thoroughly distasteful to Pascele and he had no hesitation in expressing his dislike of the conditions into which he had come. He found no fault with the officers for placing him behind the bars. All he wanted was somebody to keep off the Sheeney Kid and Bum Mit. The deputy promised to quell the disturbance and to make the jail as pleasant as possible during the six months that Pascele will linger there.

Document 20

White Boy in Nine Mile Described Visits of Flathead Hunting Parties 1902, ca.

Source: Dan Longpre, People and Places in the Frenchtown Valley, Frenchtown Historical Society Collection, OH 47-9, Toole Archives, Mansfield Library, University of Montana, Missoula.

Editors' note: Dan Longpre described his memories of Flathead Reservation hunting parties visiting the Nine Mile area at the start of the twentieth century. He mentioned the use of fish traps and traditional burning by hunting parties. He also remembered that alcohol was a problem.

Did your grandfather tell about how the Indians would come into the Nine Mile?

Yes, oh, yes, I remember when they did that. Oh, I remember that. I was just a little kid. When my dad first came he went to Scheffer, Uncle Euseb, it was Tom Scheffer's great grandfather, and I remember him when he died, the old fellow, because there was a Scheffer boy and I were little fellows, and he kept us in his bunkhouse all the time, we were only two or three years old, and I remember when he died, you know they didn't embalm him and then they covered him on a cot, and boy, we felt terrible because he was so good to us. And dad went to work for him, and in the fall, he noticed an awful smoke up the Nine Mile, and he says, "My god, the country's burning up." No, he says, "The Indians will be coming through tomorrow." And that's where he found out that when they left in the fall they fired the whole country, fired the old grass, and that's why the timber was so beautiful. We used to be able to drive with the wagon and there were 40-45 of those big pines to the acre. And then . . .

How far up the Nine Mile did they go?

They'd go about to where the Thisted ranch is. But they generally camped about, oh, on Stony Creek, now, that used to be 4-Mile Creek, and Butler Creek, that's about where their encampments were, and then they'd huckleberry & everything in the fall and sure enough, the next day the whole tribe was moving back and they'd come to Frenchtown, take Mill Creek, and go over the hill at Mill Creek — that was a shortcut to the reservation . . . . there was a trail.

. . From Arlee they crossed over Mill Creek. . . When they came to Frenchtown, they came down right by the graveyard up there now, by the creek, and then up the Nine Mile. They'd go by our place, and when they'd go up there . . . (how many?) Oh, gee whiz, there was quite a procession of them, I'll tell you there were a lot of them. I'd say a couple of hundred, three hundred. . . . they'd go right up the Six Mile, from Frenchtown, and on up the Nine Mile. . . . and one of their old encampments is where that cleared land is (Bladholm's) you were talking about. . . . that little old house on top there . . . they used to plow up there, and Edgar Scheffer had a cigar box or two completely full of the most beautiful arrowheads, because that cold deal? is all flint rock, different color, flint rock, like you used to make fires with, and that's what they liked, and Edgar had a walking plow, and he'd just pick them . . .

And when they went up, they'd stop in Frenchtown, there were about four saloons, those darn French would sell the Indians some whiskey, and they were drunk by the time they went by our place, singing and running races. . . . but the s...s was all coming behind, and they'd have all the guns . . . . they'd taken all the guns away from them. . . . but they'd want to trade horses with you and everything . . . . and crazy, you know . . . . and, of course, they were up there, and they had nothing to drink up there, and on their way home, oh, I suppose, maybe they liquored up again to go up the canyon, I don't know.

Did they go up there just for the berries, etc.?

Yes, hunting too, there was lots of game when they were there. . . . they didn't destroy the game, the just used what they needed. Dad says there was a deer every place you looked. And fish. . . . they made a trap. And they'd go up the creek for the fish, and everything under two pounds went through, and they had a big basket under there and the others would swim around. . . . and help themselves to the fish they wanted to eat. . . the large ones. . . and I remember my dad saying that he used to go there to check on his cattle and they'd say, well, "do you want some fish to bring to the s....?" You know, always the s...., so dad would say, "yeg, I'll take a mess." So they'd say, "take what you want, we're leaving tomorrow, take what you need." So he would.

Did you ever see these traps yourself?

No, but I know how they were made . . . I never seen them at work, is that what you mean? but I've seen them on the Flathead and stuff, they're made out of those little red willows like you have in Frenchtown a lot. . . . they go in one place but they can't come out . . . they leave the spaces, certain spaces, and then they take their traps, lifted it, emptied it, turned the fish loose, but my dad only wanted ten or twelve, you know, then they'd take it, three, four, five powerful bucks, and they'd take that trap and they'd go and put it under the brush. Well, then, the next year they went up to Lolo and did the same thing, then the following year they went up Fish Creek and did the same thing, then the next year they went back up Nine Mile so they burnt every place, it was always clean grass.

But they burnt more just the grass areas not the timber?

Oh, it didn't hurt the timber. All the bottoms of the big trees was all black, charred, but they were fast fires, just the old grass and pine grass, you see, so, if the tree was dead, of course they died, you know, then it would burn, and that's where we got up there we could cut a stump off those old dry trees and get those fine pitch posts that last forever. . . . but it was clean. . . . there was no disease, because the disease breeds in those little bushes. . . . currants, wild currants, well, there was none of that. . . . that was clean. . . . that timber was so healthy. It was beautiful. There was some sections of the Nine Miles that logged 17,000,000 feet.

Document 21

Pablo-Allard Buffalo Herd and Michel Pablo

1902

Source: Excerpts from J. B. Monroe, "Montana's Buffalo: The Pablo-Allard Herd," *Forest and Stream*, vol. 59, no. 2 (July 12, 1902), pages 24-26.

Editors' note: Monroe provided considerable information about the management of the Pablo-Allard buffalo herd on the Flathead Reservation in the early twentieth century. He also described Michel Pablo, his family, and his ranch. Monroe listed a number of sales of buffalo from the herd.

Montana's Buffalo.
The Pablo-Allard Herd.

The Pablo-Allard herd of buffalo consists this spring of about 360 individuals, divided as follows:

Full-blooded buffalo	300
Half-bred buffalo	60
Quarter buffalo	1
	361
In 1898 the calves produced were	48
In 1900	50
In 1901	50

It will thus be seen that the increase is very rapid, and by proper attention and the frequent renewing of blood the herd should last and grow. The heifer drops her first calf at three years and breeds thereafter for many years. The herd is now in charge of Michel Pablo. . . . .

Michel Pablo and His Home.

Michel Pablo is a half Blackfeet, half Spaniard, and was born on the Great Plains. When he was quite young his parents moved to the Colville Reservation. His early life was one of hardship and rustle, and he seems to be a man who knows every phrase of Western life.

About 6 ft. 2 in. in height, weighing about 240 pounds, without any spare flesh, active and pushing, he seems a man thoroughly awake and alive to all business ventures. His ranch is run like clockwork; a skilled Chinese chef runs the kitchen; two business-like men, a French-Canadian and a German, attend to the ranch and farm work; meals are had on time, horses curried night and morning, stables swept out, wagons, buggies and farm machinery under cover, fences and all buildings in good repair. Everything denotes push and progress. He has an elk park, and two cows, two bulls, and one last year's calf occupy a well fenced twenty-acre tract. I saw some wild geese, and some queer looking geese around the house. During our talk he told me he had some cross geese, between wild and tame. I forgot to examine them in my haste to catch the boat.

He told me of having had a white mountain goat which would get upon an ordinary rail fence and walk the top rail for a quarter of a mile. Some hounds one day caught it away from home and killed it. He is now negotiating with parties in the Northwest Territories for some antelope.

Large fine work horses are used on his ranch, and lighter horses for cow and driving purposes. In winter he runs a private school close to his ranch and pays the teacher. He has tried the mission schools, but they were too slow and worshipped the past. He wants his children to progress and look to the future. His wife is a full blood Flathead.

There are three children at home, a good-looking girl of about 16, who keeps books for her father and keeps account of all his many business transactions; a boy of about 12, who seemed to have his father's rustle and go. There was a younger boy; all could answer almost any kind of a business question.

The ranch contains some 450 acres of good farming and grass land. It is situated on the east side of the valley close to the belt of timber. He has large irrigating ditches. He has a barn that will shelter 100 head of stock. All kinds of improved harvesting and haying machinery are carefully housed. The broad level prairie rolls away to the west. Here is all a western man wants, plenty of fine timber, water and grass. His house is large and commodious, suitable for his business, and he is building an addition.

The cowboys or herders of the ranch are living about ten miles west, on the Pend d'Oreille River. They have a good ferry and a good house and stable.

I talked for about four hours with Mr. Pablo. His daughter got out the books and gave me the sales, which are kept as references. The Allard estate will some day have to be settled. Mr. Pablo, as I understand him, is guardian for the smaller children. Pablo owns half, and the Allard estate the other half interest in the buffalo. There is a great danger of the herd being divided and scattered (or one-half scattered), as one of the Allard boys insists on being a Wild West showman and is rapidly getting rid of his portion of the herd. I was given to understand that there must be some kind of a definite division this season. Herein lies the greatest menace to the herd.

Pablo told me of an exhibition they gave in Butte City some years ago. When they purchased the Buffalo Jones herd, or as they call them, the Winnepeg buffalo, Allard, who went east to ship them out, suggested that Pablo take a bunch of Flathead buffalo, drive them to Butte City and meet the herd from the east there. They would then give a show in the fair grounds at Butte. The buffalo were handled easily, and they arrived in Butte after a drive of about 150 miles. There were present bronco busters that could ride anything that walked on four legs; they were to ride the big bulls at the tail end of the show. The eastern herd came in by rail, and when they were turned loose with the others, there were many hard fights between the two herds.

The show was a success. Broncos were ridden to a finish, all kind of wild west roping was done with credit; then came the riding of the buffalo. This was "a new one" on cowboys. Wild Texas steers had been ridden for July 4 celebration for generations; there was no record of a man forking a buffalo.

Two of the best riders were singled out for this. Neither of the busters was anxious for the first ride, and they drew cuts to see who would have to climb the hump of the first bull. The first man to ride was a noted horse rider. He would crawl on the wildest cayuse as though it were pastime. A large husky bull, young and active, was roped by Pablo and heeled by another man; the rope was run through a hole in a post and bull's head was drawn up to the post. The buster complained of not feeling well, when he saw the rolling eye and fighting attitude of the bull.

"Don't weaken now," said Pablo to the cowboy. "Go and throw in a couple of glasses of the worst whisky you can find; we will have him saddled before you get back." The cinch had to be lengthened to fit the bull, and the saddle was on before the would-be buffalo buster had returned. After a look at the trembling and now thoroughly aroused bull, he again complained of not feeling well.

"Crawl him, son," said Pablo; "crawl him; see all these people here who have paid to see the wild son of the prairie ride the equally wild buffalo." The cowpuncher took a chew of Climax plug, drew a long breath, turned pale behind the ears, and climbed into the saddle. When the bull was turned loose it was a very tame performance. He could not twist a saddle, and the rider raked him with the spurs and rode him to a finish. They cannot jump high or land hard. The next rider rode his bareback, and said it was like riding work horses; a soft job. . . . .

Tame Buffalo at Home.

The herder, Jimmy Michel, is a very intelligent mixed blood, and took me out to see the buffalo. To him I am indebted for much information. We were riding for several hours, and he gave me a chance to see about two hundred buffalo. From a high butte a number of small bands could be seen, while close to us, stringing out in single file and coming to water, was a herd of about one hundred. The day was calm and warm, and we lay in the sun on the butte and watched the buffalo come in to water. Sometimes a cloud of dust would rise from around a water hole, and an old bull would be seen horning the ground and throwing up the dust in the air.

Jimmy told me of a cow and calf which stayed on the winter range until late. One morning she came to the river with a calf not over twenty-four hours old. They took the water without any hesitation. The river at this time is high; it runs like a millrace, and is a quarter of a mile wide. The calf swam easily under the lee of its mother, and landed without apparent exhaustion. The same swim is a hard job for a fat strong saddle horse.

With the herder I rode down off the butte, where we had lain watching the herd. There were about one hundred head close by, and they were slowly grazing away from the water. We approached, giving the buffalo the wind of us. When we were within 300 yards of them they threw up their heads and came for us on a gallop. They gathered around us, snuffing and looking, the yearlings bucking and playing like domestic calves. We stood still and watched them. Most of them were within 40 to 80 feet of us; a few old bulls were strung out behind, and they slowly came on, in our direction. There was no sign of fear or wildness; there was no indication of bad temper; just good-natured curiosity and playfulness. We rode off and left them standing, looking after us. The cows were commencing to shed. All looked in good flesh and thrifty. Not so with the range cattle close around, most of which were poor and had a distressed look after being fed hay for two months. . . . .

Cross-Breeding.

At one time a number of Galloway cows were purchased and conveyed to Wild Horse Island, in Flathead Lake. A number of young buffalo bulls that had been raised with, and as I understand, suckled by domestic cows, and kept with the milk stock until full grown, were put with the Galloway cows on Wild Horse Island. This island is about four miles square, or nearly square. It is called six miles by some. It rises about 1,000 feet above the level of the lake. On the north end it is covered by pines and other evergreens. Most of its surface is covered with good grass, with now and then a pine tree. It looks like a rolling prairie, sloping from the north end, where the hills are high and abrupt, in a gentle grade to the south end, where the prairie meets the lake. It is an ideal summer range.

These cows were kept there several years, but the venture was unprofitable, as a number of the cows died in giving birth to the first calf. After the first calf was born the cow seemed to have no further trouble in parturition. The experiment was discontinued, and since then there has been no effort made at cross breeding.

When the cows were taken off the island one or two of the buffalo refused to be driven or taken off. When the rutting season came on one bull swam off the island to the mainland, a distance of half a mile or more. The first herd he struck was a bunch of dairy cows belonging to a rancher. The cows seemed to be afraid of him, with his long beard and big black head, and they struck out for their home corral. The buffalo followed and insisted on being sociable. When the rancher came to milk, he also lost his nerve and would not go into the corral. He dispatched a boy to Pablo's and left his cows without milking for a couple of days. The rancher lived off the reserve, and it was a long way to Pablo's. When the herder reached the rancher's home he found that the bull could not be driven away, and herder threw him and castrated him, and he was then driven away without difficulty.

The general impression is that if left to themselves the buffalo will not cross with domestic cattle. The buffalo run in bands, and while occupying the same range, they herd together and act just as antelope, elk and buffalo would act when occupying the same range. In order to cross, they must be kept away from their own kind. What half-breeds are there run by themselves and with the buffalo, never with the domestic cattle. Half-breed bulls are castrated, and the heifers prefer the buffalo bulls and breed to them. There are number of three-quarter buffalo, but only one one-quarter buffalo.

There is no attempt made now to encourage them to cross-breed. The band is so large that with a few years of luck there will be all the buffalo the range will support. . . .

Sales from the Allard-Pablo Herd.

The following records of recent losses of buffalo from this herd by sale and accident are taken from the books of the concern. Many of them are without date, and other particulars, yet they are interesting so far as they go. From the dates given it probably would not be difficult to trace up many of these sales and to learn full particulars about them. It will be noted that almost all the sales are of bulls and steers. There is always a superabundance of males in the herd.

No date. Sold to a Mr. Adams, of Massachusetts, six yearling heifers and two two-year-old heifers; taken east for breeding purposes.

Sold to a Michigan banker named Hills, two two-year-old heifers, and one two-year-old bull.

Sold to Governor Young — and no one seems to be able to tell where he governed — two two-year-old heifers, one two-year-old bull; for breeding purposes.

Three head sold to C. C. Willis, Horse Plains, Mont. No record, but they were probably butchered.

The above undated sales were probably made by all parties interested in the herd.

1899 — Wilkins, of Bozeman, bought one old bull; butchered.

1899 — Five were sold to Meyers, of Helena, Mont. — bulls and steers; butchered. Record does not show by whom sold.

1899 — Sold by M. Pablo, to a butcher in Kalispell, Mont., one old bull. It is stated that the butcher sold buffalo meat at a high price all through the winter.

1899 — Sold by Michel Pablo, one old bull to Caspar Deschamps, of Missoula; butchered.

I find the following entries made without date:

Sold to Howard Eaton, one bull, one heifer. Went east for breeding purposes.

Dec. 14, 1901 — Jos. Allard sold one stag, very old. No record of purpose.

May, 1901 — Sold by Jos. Allard, four cows and calves. Went east for some park. No record as to buyer or locality.

May, 1901 — One cow and one yearling killed in round up. This was done while rounding up to take the Conrad purchase out, then made.

1901 — M. Pablo sold nine steers and stags to Morris, of Seattle, Wash. They were sold for butchering, but I heard that the city of Seattle bought them and put them in a park.

Nov. 23, 1900 — Michel Pablo killed one stag for beef for his home.

1902 — Sold to Wilkins, of Bozeman, by the firm Pablo & Allard, three head of old steers. The buyer came, butchered them on the range, took the heads and meat. Their hides were still hanging on the fence at the herders' camp.

January, 1902 — Jos. Allard sold eight head, sex not stated, buyer not known. (? Eaton and Talstrup. *Ed. Forest and Stream.*)

March 7, 1902 — Jos. Allard sold four head. There is no record of the sex of those sold, nor for what purpose.

Feb. 11, 1902 — Jos. Allard sold one cow, two bulls, to butcher at Horse Plains, Mont.

February, 1902 — Jos. Allard sold one steer to butcher at Horse Plains, Mont.

February, 1902 — Jos. Allard sold one half-breed to Sears, of Wallace, Idaho; butchered. . . .

J. B. Monroe.

Document 22

Flathead Buffalo and Wild West Show

May – September 1902

Source: "Buffalo and Wild Indians," *The Missoulian* (daily), May 4, 1902, page 1, col. 6; "Wild West Show Opens," *The Anaconda Standard*, July 3, 1902, page 14, col. 6; "Show Is Buffaloed," *The Missoulian* (daily), September 13, 1902, page 8, col. 3.

Editors' note: Charles Allard, Jr., organized a wild west show or rodeo to exhibit the Flathead Reservation buffalo. It played in a number of cities in 1902, but went broke in the Midwest.

Buffalo and Wild Indians
Missoula Will Send Out a Wild West Show.
It Will Be in Helena on July 4
George L. Hutchin Backed by Missoula Capitalists in Charge of the Organization.

About a band of 50 buffalo from the famous Allard herd of the Flathead reservation Missoula capitalists have organized an attraction that is promised will attain the magnitude of any of the big circuses and will tour the country in the manner of such attractions. This announcement was made by George L. Hutchin, a promoter of show attractions and well known all over the country as such, at the Florence hotel last night. He added:

"Our enterprise will be backed by Missoula capitalists to the extent of $100,000, and if capital and earnest management can make it a success it will be done. It will be an organization with Missoula as its home and winter quarters and of a magnitude to advertise the city over the land. It will be known as the Great Buffalo and Wild West Show, and will be essentially what its name implies. Features will be whatever goes to make up western life of an instructive nature. Our training will commence in Missoula June 1, and here will be mobilized the various attractions, of which the following are arranged for:

"Three cars of buffaloes — the pick of the Allard herd — 50 Indians, 40 cowboys, trainload of equipment including a canvas wall capable of holding 20,000 people, stage coaches. Features now contracted include fancy ropers from

Mexico and Texas, Conchos from Uruguay, Captain Pony May, "Yellowstone Bill," attack on pioneer's cabin, cataloes, broncho busting, lady and men riders, including Miss Austin, the most celebrated equestrienne of the county, two bands, one an organization among cowboys on horseback. Numerous other details are in process of arrangement to be added when deemed necessary to make of the show an event of historical reflection of Montana and western life, and its environments and resources. Stage coach and miner's cabin attacks by Indians will also be a feature.

W. A. and F. E. Simons are of the local people whose names are given out. These will accompany the show with Mr. Hutchin in direct management, and Charles Allard in charge of the buffalo. The opening performance will be July 4 at Helena on the occasion of the capital dedication and 3-day jubilee festival there, from where Mr. Hutchin yesterday returned after completing arrangements that are regarded as most favorable.

* * * * * * * * *

Wild West Show Opens
Large Crowds Witness Two Performances.
First Day Satisfactory
Life on the Frontier Depicted by Cowboys and Indians, and the Usual Stage Coach Episode Has a Place.

Mis[s]oula, July 2.—Two thousand people witnessed the first performance of the great Buffalo and Wild West shows here to-day, and this evening every reserved seat is taken and several hundred people are standing up to witness the performance. The first day's work was most satisfactory in every respect. The men and women in the show did their parts well. The Indians were much of the attraction and the special acts brought forth continued applause.

The drizzling rain interfered somewhat with the performance, but the riders did well notwithstanding. The buffaloes, too, were a big attraction, and although nothing wah [was] done with them, yet they were a splendid sight. The clowns did well and made everybody laugh, and the special acts of Mr. Barnes, Chamberlain, the rope man, the expert shooting of Miss Cody, and others deserved much praise.

The wild ride on the stage coach, brought back to the minds of many the exciting days of long ago, and the stealing of horses by Indians and white men was exceptionally well done. The riding by the women attracted much attention. The cowboys with this show are as good as there are on the continent, and the king of all, as it was announced this afternoon, is Charles Allard of the reservation. He did some extraordinary feats and his Missoula friends predict that he will gain a big reputation. The side shows and after concerts are without equal, the very best of attractions being secured for these departments.

There was a big crowd at the tents to-night to watch the loading of the shows onto the cars. It will play in Butte tomorrow. Manager Hutchins deserves much credit for being able to get up such a good show.

* * * * * * * * *

Show Is Buffaloed.
Wild West Enterprise Disbands at Marshalltown, Iowa.

That part of The Buffalo and Wild West show which has not been consumed in the expense of making up for bad business and other misfortunes will be in Missoula next Wednesday. Charles Allard, a feature and one of the promoters of the enterprise, came in from the east last night and brought word of the disbanding of the company at Marshaltown [sic], Iowa, on Monday. The canvas, horses, buffalo and other effects are loaded and in shipment to Missoula.

Mr. Allard does not come directly from the show, having been for a time in the east, but has word of the close. He repeats the accounts of bad show weather that ruined their business for weeks while touring Wisconsin and Illinois. In addition to this the life and travel was more than the buffalo and some of the horses could withstand, crippling the features of the show seriously.

Document 23

Bishop Brondel Visits for St. Ignatius Day Celebration August 6, 1902

Source: "Bishops at the Mission," *Helena Evening Herald*, August 6, 1902, page 5, col. 2.

Editors' note: In 1902 Montana Bishop John Brondel made his annual visit to St. Ignatius Mission to celebrate St. Ignatius Day. This was one of the major church and social celebrations on the reservation in the early twentieth century.

Bishops at the Mission
Assisted in the Celebration of the Feast of St. Ignatius.
Memorable Event on Flathead Reservation
How the Red Men Welcomed Dignitaries of the Church —
Bishop Brondel Said Mass.

In some respects the celebration of the feast of St. Ignatius at the mission of that name on the Flathead Indian reservation last week was the most memorable holiday the west side Indians have ever known. It was not alone the visit of the archbishop of Oregon and the bishops of Montana, Idaho and Washington that made the event a notable one, although St. Ignatius' mission had never before entertained so many dignitaries of the church. The Indians had anticipated an unusual feast and had assembled from every part of the reservation. With them were fifty scholastics of the Jesuit order, who are spending their vacations there. These young men are from all parts of the northwest, and they assisted very materially in the services at the mission.

Right Rev. John B. Brondel, bishop of Helena, has returned from the Flathead Indian reservation, where he went last week with his guests, Archbishop Alexander Christie of Oregon, Bishop O'Dea of Washington and Bishop Glorieux of Idaho, on their return from the Yellowstone National park.

The part[y] of bishops was met at the little station of Selish by a delegation of Indians on horseback, which grew as the cavalcade approached the mission. Before the white buildings of the mission came into sight the escort had grown to a party of 200 mounted red men. The first carriage contained the archbishop and Bishop Brondel, while the other bishops, including one of the Jesuit fathers of the mission, rode in the next carriage. The Indians kept in the rear, so that the dust from their horses' heels would not disturb their guests.

The march from Selish to the mission was one of the notable events of the sta[y] of the bishops. The Indians were dressed in gala attire and they shouted a welcome to their distinguished visitors. As the cavalcade approached the mission Archbishop Christie suggested that the Indians be permitted to go ahead. They wee rgiven [sic] the signal, and then the Indian braves, mounted on fleet ponies as they were, started in a grand race for the mission. Before they started the Indians fired their guns and their ponies danced up and down in their excitement. When the word was given the party ran madly past the carriages to the mission, where hundreds of Indians, all dressed in their gayest attire, the fifty scholastics and the priests and sisters of the mission were awaiting them. The brass band of the Indians played as the bishops came up.

That evening a ceremonial reception was given at the mission for the bishops. After the ceremony the four bishops, Archbishop Christie first, Bishop Bondel second and the other bishops next, were seated in the church, and the Indians given an opportunity to show their reverence for the church. As the devout Indians filed by each knelt and kissed the signet ring of the bishops in sign of love for the church. The ceremony took up an hour.

"The ceremony," said Bishop Brondel today, "means more to these Indians than to many of our white members of the faith. It is intended to show their devotion and love for the church and not for the wearer of the ring. I recall last year an instance which indicates very well how these Indians regard that particular ceremony. A chief of one of the tribes refused to recognized the oath of another person in a proceeding of some importance. 'I will believe him if he kissses the ring,' said the chief, 'but not unless he does.' It ended by the person kissing the ring and satisfying the chief that he meant what he said."

For twenty years Bishop Brondel has paid an annual visit to the Flathead mission. With the exception of two years he visited the mission on the feast of St. Ignatius, the founder of the Jesuit order. The Indians know him and have come to look for his visits. It was Bishop Brondel who made an address last Thursday, which was the feast day, to the Indians. He spoke through an interpreter, a priest who has resided on the reservation for forty years, and who has a mastery of the Selish tongue. In the presence of those hundreds of Indians the scholastics, sisters, priests and bishops, Bishop Brondel said pontifical high mass. The ceremon[y] was made the more impressive by the singing of the scholastics. Fifty trained voices sang the mass, and never before in the history of that old mission was it so beautifully sung.

In the evening a local society of Indians gave Bishop Brondel an entertainment, in which the band and an orchestra took part. There was other music, addresses and recitations and two or three scenes from a play. It was a very creditable performance.

After the main ceremonies of the day Archbishop Christie left for his home. Neither he nor the other bishops of Washington or Idaho had ever seen so many Indians before, and they counted their visit to the mission as one of the most pleasant features of their trip.

On the way to Ravalli to meet Bishop Brondel
Source: Image 120.4.13, Box 1.0292, St. Ignatius Mission, Montana, Oregon Province Archive, Jesuit Archives & Research Center, St. Louis, Missouri.

Document 24

Rich Michel Robbed of Thousands of Dollars

November 3, 1902

Source: "Robbed on Reservation," *The Anaconda Standard*, November 3, 1902, page 1, col. 4.

Editors' note: This Michel was considered to be one of the richest Indians in the United States in 1902. The robbery was even reported in the *New York Times*. The authorities searched for the robbers for months and arrested an Indian named John Deer in 1903.

Robbed on Reservation
Michel Loses Between $18,000 and $22,000.
S.... Was In on the Game
She Engaged Michel's Wife in Conversation While Two Men Enter an Outhouse and Make Off With Indian's Strong Box.

Special Dispatch to the Standard.

Missoula, Nov. 2. — William Reed returned to-night from Plains and brings the news of a big robbery on the reservation last night. Michel, a Kalispell Indian, is well known as one of the rich Indians of the reservation. His wealth is estimated all the way from $50,000 to $100,000, all in money and cattle. Some of his money he keeps on deposit at Plains. He has a considerable amount at his home, which is on the reservation about 25 miles from Plains. Last night while he was in Plains on a visit somebody broke into his house and raided his strong box, taking between $18,000 and $22,000. Of this sum $10,000 was in currency and the rest was gold coin.

Michel's wife brought the news to Plains, reaching there at 8:30 this morning. The old man took the matter very calmly. Mr. Reed says he was the most unconcerned of anybody at Plains when the news became known. In company with Colonel McGowan he at once started for his home. It is said that there are 30 Indians on the trail and that there is some prospect of their overhauling the thief.

C. C. Willis of Plains, who came in to-night, says that Michel kept his money in a box which was concealed in a small outhouse back of his dwelling. Mr. Willis says that Michel's wife later to-day told more about the robbery.

She says that about 10 o'clock last night a s.... called her out of her house and talked to her. The s.... was a stranger and could not talk Indian very much. While she was talking with her strange visitor she saw two men run from the outhouse with Michel's strong box in their arms. They ran to their horses and the supposed s.... joined them. They were all strangers to her.

Mr. Willis says suspicion points to three halfbreeds, but it is possible that the robbers were white men, as it was generally known about Plains that Michel had the money at his house.

Document 25

Flathead Indian Attacks Missoula Residence

November 27, 1902

Source: "A Murderous Indian," *The Missoulian* (daily), November 27, 1902, page 1, col. 6.

Editors' note: John McLain from the Flathead Reservation got drunk in Missoula and attacked a Missoula residence. He was arrested and jailed.

A Murderous Indian.
McLain, a Flathead Indian, Commits Depredations.

John McLain, a Flathead Indian from the reservation, now a prisoner at the county jail, owes his life to the fact that in the army they do not teach the art of pistol shooting.

McLain came to Missoula yesterday and filled up on whiskey. It was either a bad brand or else McLain is a bad Indian. For no sooner had his load been taken on than he made for the suburban districts. Reaching the residence and carpet factory of E. T. Dorsey on West Main street he asked for admittance in a surly manner. Corporal S. A. Lundy, an ex-soldier, was at work at the house and refused to permit him to enter. The "red" was determined and leaving the door he took a run and dashed head first through a front window, carrying the sash and shattering the glass.

Inside the Indian, now thoroughly enraged, commenced to demolish the place. Three sewing machines in crates were located and all broken to small bits, doing damage amounting to $300.

It was at this juncture that the fighting blood of Corporal Lundy was aroused and going to a closet he secured a heavy 45-claibre Colt's revolver. As the red did not stop his work of destruction at this the corporal fired a warning shot. The Indian took another whack at a machine so forcibly that broken bits filled the room. The corporal fired again, but this time not in fun. He meant to kill. But his aim was bad and until nine heavy packages of lead have been spattered about the room did the fusilade continue. Through the clearing smoke the corporal saw his man yet breaking furniture — and he out of ammunition. An alarm to police headquarters brought an officer who took the bad Indian to jail.

While the actions of Corporal Lundy availed of but little good results, his courage, coolness and bravery in so heroically defending the family of Mr. Dorsey overshadows his poor marksmanship.

Document 26

Special Indian Agent McNichols Has Problems Making Enrollment December 31, 1902

Source: Chas. S. McNichols to Commissioner of Indian Affairs, December 31, 1902, letter received 822/1903, administration division, RG 75, National Archives, Washington, D.C.

Editors' note: In this report McNichols, a Special Indian Agent compiling an enrollment of the Flathead Reservation Indians, outlined his problems in assembling his roll. See also his February 6, 1903, report on the same subject. McNichols' roll was not approved in Washington, D.C., and the government sent another agent, Thomas Downs, to compile another roll which was completed in 1905. Note what McNichols said about the Kalispel Indian community on Camas Prairie.

Department of the Interior,
United States Indian Service,
In the Field,
Jocko, Mont., Dec. 31, 1902.

The Honorable
Commissioner of Indian Affairs,
Washington, D.C.
Sir: —

I have the honor to report that there is no longer a prospect for the speedy completion of an *entirely satisfactory* roll of the Indians having rights on the Flathead reservation. I had hoped that this roll might be completed by Jan. 15, 1903, but this can not be done.

I have enrolled almost 1,000 names. To the best of my information there are about 215 full-bloods yet to enroll. In addition to these there are some 300 mixed-bloods, most of whom have sought enrollment, who are objected to by some of the Judges, Chiefs and head men. A large number of these, possibly one-half, are in my judgement entitled to enrollment, under the instructions I have received; but as a matter of good policy I have deferred a final decision on their cases until the work is nearer completed.

The full-bloods not enrolled are of two classes: (1) The "Cammas Prairie Indians," numbering about 110, who refuse to be enrolled, and (2) The band of full-blood Kootenais living at the extreme north-west edge of the reservation. They are supposed to number about 105, small-pox having greatly reduced their number during the past two years. They are Camp Nomads, speaking a different language and far behind the other Indians in civilization. I do not anticipate any difficulty in enrolling this band when I can reach them, as I have already enrolled their Chief, who was at first quite hostile, and two other families. Just now they are inaccissible [sic] on account of ice and snow-drifts. It is possible I may have to reach them from Kalispell.

The Camas Prairie Indians are a different proposition. They comprise not only those referred to in your letter of Sept. 30, Land 57496/1902, as "Michels band of Calispels," whose rights are not fully settled, but who now number only about 40, but also have more than 60 other Kalispels who have resided upon the reservation from the beginning. All these not only refuse to be enrolled but refuse even to talk to me. They were at the Mission last week, but have gone home. They live in a remote valley probably 80 miles from the Agency. There is not a white man or mixed blood among them and so far as I can learn no place where a man can stop among them or nearer to them than the village of Plains some eighteen miles away.

A few of these full-bloods are quite wealthy and have large herds of cattle. One of them, whose name is Michel (not the Chief of that name), was robbed of $22,000.00 in gold and currency which he had in a trunk in his house, the latter part of October. It is probable that these wealthy cattle owners are in part responsible for the Indians refusing to talk to me; but they are a peculiar, isolated lot and they claim that Government men have lied to them so often that they want nothing to do with any representative of the Government. They probably refer to the unratified treaty of Messrs. Wright, Daniels and Andrews made with them in 1887. They allow no whites or mixed bloods to live among them. I am told that they have never recognized the Agents, nor have they ever asked for any help or even medical assistance. Outside of drinking and gambling they are thrifty, industrious and entirely self-supporting, and conduct their own affairs.

As there are no mixed bloods or doubtful Indians among these Kalispels and as they have fixed habitations it will be possible to get a fairly accurate enrollment of them even if they continue to refuse to talk to me, not only from the 1900 Census and the Church (Mission) records, but from relatives living outside who have recently been among them. I still hope, however, that I can induce them to change their present attitude toward the enrollment.

In regard to the objected or doubtful mixed-bloods the judges and other head men oppose many who seem to be entitled to enrollment under my present instructions. It is a matter which I am compelled to handle very carefully until I have succeeded in enrolling all of the full bloods and those who claim adoption.

Some of the Chiefs and head men claim to have a letter "from Washington," written about 1880, which I have not seen, asserting the old Common law doctrine that the status of the child is that of its father. They assert that the letter declares that an Indian woman marrying a white man looses her rights and that the children of such union have no rights. They have, therefore, for years cherished the idea of ordering such families from the reservation and only look upon this roll as a step toward that end. Hence they do not see how I can enroll a wife and children where they expect to have the father removed from the reservation upon completion of the roll. I have told them that my instructions are to enroll all children whose mother's [sic] have undoubted rights by blood, but they go so far as to doubt the truth of my statements and the authenticity of them in the face of their oft quoted letter. I have not thought it best to press matters too hard until after I secured the full-bloods and those whom they claim by adoption.

These Indians are so suspicious of allotment that I do not dare explain anything definite about land rights. In fact they are so suspicious that I have been questioned a great deal about some recent surveys made for irrigation estimates, which they have demanded that I should cause to be stopped before proceeding further with the enrollment. They seem fully convinced that this irrigation surveying is done under my direction and is a part of some plan for their future undoing. Hence my work has been beset with difficulty all along.

In other communications I write more fully of these doubtful mixed bloods and ask for some further instructions.

Very respectfully,
Chas. S. McNichols
Special Indian Agent.

Chapter 2

Documents of Salish, Pend d'Oreille, and Kootenai History Between 1903-1904

Document 27

Livestock Owners on the Flathead Reservation in 1903
January 5, 1903

Source: Chas. S. McNichols to Commissioner of Indian Affairs, January 5, 1903, letter received 1,789/1903, land division, RG 75, National Archives, Washington, D.C.

Editors' note: McNichols provides a useful list of the largest cattle owners on the reservation in 1903 and land tenure practices. In 1903, the St. Ignatius Mission schools operated a major farm and livestock operation. He also explained his problems in assembling the enrollment of tribal members entitled to rights on the reservation.

Department of the Interior,
United States Indian Service,
In the Field,
Jocko, Mont., Jan. 5, 1903.

The Honorable
Commissioner Indian Affairs,
Washington, D.C.
Sir: —

I have the honor to reply, so far as practicable to your letter "Land 66436-1902, dated Nov. 15. This letter was forwarded to me after leaving this reservation on Nov. 18 for a month's trip, and not having the data for a reply until after my return, explains the delay in writing.

Even at this date and after considerable investigation entirely accurate information on some of the points can not be given. This is especially true of the amount of land fenced up by s.... men, mixed bloods and Indians, for the reason that there have been no surveys and the fenced up land is generally irregular in shape and any one is liable to make a very eroneous estimate. The estimate of cattle owned by each can not be made with much accuracy, for the reason that the owners, themselves, often have but a vague idea of the number they own. Then, too, the county authorities are trying to tax the s.... men, mixed bloods, etc., and each tries to make it appear that they have a smaller number than they really have. The following figures have been compiled after talking with several of the employes, traders, mixed bloods, etc.

	Acres fenced	Cattle & horses
Bateste Jette, s.... man	640	1500
Angus McDonald, single, mixed blood	1800	2000
Joe Morizeau, single, mxd b	860	1200
Edw. Lameraux, white, 1/2 b Blackf. wife	250	450
Wilson Markale, white (wife no rights)	150	250
Camille Dupuis, s.... man	300	1200
Joseph Ashley, s.... man	500	some
Josephine Revais, Widow, 1 child	—	500
Al Sloane, 1/4 b. Chippewa	1500	600
Ignace, full blood, wife but no children	640	some
Joe Allard, Mxd b, Doubt rights	400	400
Chas. Allard, mxd b. single Dbtf. rights	200	1200
Michel Pablo, (1/2 Mex., 1/2 Piegan) Adopted	300	5000
Michel, full blood, Camas prairie	some	2500
Joe Finley, mixed b.	640	1000
Henry Fellsman, s... man	800	some
Wm. Irvine, 1/8 b. (Adopted)	300	1600
Andrew Stinger, white, wifes' rights disputed	300	500
Duncan McDonald, mixed blood	300	800

Now please understand that the above is not authoritative, but only the best estimate that I can make without giving one or more days investigation to each case personally and even then the figures I could give would only be a *closer* estimate. An accurate statement of the number of cattle could not be had without rounding up the whole immense reservation. Neither do I claim that this list of large cattle owners or those having large tracts fenced is by any means complete. This is an immense reservation and it is doubtful if any one person is thoroughly familiar with it all.

Coroborative of the above and in ad[d]ition thereto, in speaking of a region I have not yet visited personally, I desire to call attention to the following extract from the report of Gen. Frank C. Armstrong, made to the Department under date of June 30, 1901:

> *** "The balance of this Country *west of the river*, probably 700,000 acres, is occupied and used by 14 French mixed bloods and their families and three s... men and mixed blood families, who are located at some of the best points, as mentioned in this report before, and have *immense herds of cattle, selling 1,000*

> *to 1500 beeves each year.* The remainder of the Indians on the east side secure no benefit whatever from this portion of the reservation." ***

As to "by what authority or sanction they have appropriated these lands?" I will state that in each instance where I have questioned these people they reply substantially that they were given permission by some old chief now dead (Michel, Arlee, etc.,) and in most cases they also claim the permission of Agent Ronan, now dead, who was agent here for almost twenty years. How much basis there is for such permission can not now be told. It is quite probable that one or more of the numerous old chiefs did sanction such settlement and, as is quite generally hinted, for a consideration. All such settlements date back from 12 to 25 years or more.

The "names of those having questionable rights on the reservation" can be more accurately submitted after I have completed the roll upon which I am now at work. Such list with full data will be submitted with the finished roll.

So far as I can learn the cattle are nearly all *owned* by the residents of the reservation. Very few outside cattle are grazed on the reservation, to the best of my information.

As to "whether or not these conditions were known to the Agent prior to my visit and what, if any, steps he took to remedy existing evils?" I will say that from the letters he has written your Office and from his annual reports, I judge that he not only knew these things but has tried to give your Office the facts as they exist. From the letter-press files of the Agent's office I note the following extract from a letter dated February 27, 1900, address to your Office, bearing directly and pointedly upon the matter under discussion:

> *** "Lands that will produce crops without irrigation, and those upon which water could be easily and cheaply carried, have long since been claimed, and are in the possession of white men and mixed bloods, principally, many of whom have no rights on the reservation, and others whose rights are in doubt.
>
> "Many of these people have large tracts inclosed, hundreds of acres in excess of what they would be entitled to, providing they have any rights at all, thus securing to themselves large tracts of land that should be in the possession of allottees."

Other letters dated Aug. 30, 1900, April 5, 1901 and June 21, 1902, bear upon these questions; also the annual reports of Agent Smead, particularly that of 1900, give information on these matters.

Agent Smead is also putting into force the permit system of pasturage at $1 per head to *resident* stock to which you refer as being in vogue on Pine Ridge and Rosebud reservations. He is increasing his collections from this source, under difficulties and strenuous opposition. Quite recently he collected $650.00 from Wm. Irvine for newly purchased cattle brought on the reservation. I believe from what I can learn that he is proceeding as rapidly in the matter as he well can do under all the circumstances.

In regard to the cattle owned and held by the Catholic mission I am convinced that in estimating the number at 6,000 I overestimated the number, which were variously stated to me at from 2,000 to 10,000. I recently talked with a mixed blood who has been employed in looking after their cattle. He says the Mission people, themselves, have only a vague idea of their number. He estimates that the Jesuit Fathers have 2000 head, the Sisters of Charity 1,400 head and the Usurline Sisters 150 head or about 3,500 in all. They are scattered over much of the reservation and receive very little attention and their losses by death and theft is considerable. I am told by many that their management of their cattle has been very poor and lacking both in business precautions and common humanity. Even the Indians complain that the Mission people do not care for their cattle in winter and predict large losses should there come a severe winter.

There is no way for me to ascertain, as you suggest "whether the proceeds from the herd are applied toward the support of the mission and school or whether they go to other uses." The Fathers in charge have treated me courteously but coldly. So far I have been unable to even get access to their records of births, marriages and deaths in the preparation of the roll, nor any information, whatever, to aid me. They have *not refused*, but bring up obstacles, such as want of time at present, etc. I was told that these records were in Latin and just now no one could translate them for me. I told them that I had a fair knowledge of Latin, enough for the purpose, I thought; but they said that it would be necessary to have some one familiar with the records, etc. At other Catholic Missions they have always seemed willing and anxious to give me any information, show me around, etc., but at St. Ignatius I see nothing of the interior beyond a cold ante-room and the business office. I hope yet to correct dates, etc., by means of their records, but if I succeed it will be because of insistant perseverance. The institution is not at all friendly with the Agent and employes.

It is the common belief of outsiders that the Mission is at least self=supporting. It is argued that the Mission (three schools, church, etc.,) has from 1500 to 2,000 acres under fence all or nearly all under irrigation. That the large boys do much of the farm work. They have orchards, gardens, dairies, etc. They have a custom grist-mill and a saw mill both operated by water power, own a threshing outfit, etc. They charge tuition whenever they can collect it and the children are expected to furnish their own clothing. As the greater part of their pupils are the children of well-to-do s... men and mixed bloods (many wealthy) who are adherents of the church, it can be readily seen they must get considerable in the way of tuition, fees for extras, [nuric?] etc. Still any assertion that the institution is self=supporting or that it yields a net revenue must necessarily be only guess=work.

You ask me to suggest a remedy for these abuses. The only feasible one, in my judgement, is allotment. In accordance with the old treaty (1856 I believe) these Indians can be allotted whenever the President deems best. After allotment the Indians will soon be reconciled to selling their surplus lands.

There are all grades of these Indians from the fully civilized, already owning costly houses with all modern country improvements down to a wild band of Nomadic Kootenais (numbering little more than 100) that live in movable camps, wholly uncivilized and whose children have never been in school and who spend most of their time off in the mountains, hunting and fishing. I have never seen a reservation affording such contrasts in civilization and wealth, although there seems to be little abject poverty. About 30 per cent appear to be blanket Indians, but all seem well dressed and, excepting the full-blood Kootenais, remarkably free from disease, compared with other Indians. All of the older Indians with few exceptions, occupy lands and have permanent homes. Although generally opposed to allotment 75 per cent of them are living as though allotted and allotment would bring little change in their abodes or method of living, beyond defining their rights, securing equality and depriving a few of the benefit of nearly the whole reservation for grazing purposes.

The wealthy mixed bloods, the Mission and those having no rights will all do what they can to stir up the ignorant full-bloods to oppose allotment for obvious reasons and for the additional purpose of escaping local taxation. One mixed-blood, Michel Pablo, recently showed me a tax-notice from the treasurer of Missoula County notifying him that his personal property tax for 1902 amounted to $1,686.00 and his poll tax was $2.00. He wished me to notify the County treasurer not to send him any more notices like that, as they made him feel bad. There has been considerable litigation over local taxation, the mixed bloods generally escaping. Thus you see the wealthy mixed bloods have many incentives to oppose allotment, but there is no reason why they should longer escape all the burthens of citizenship and be treated as wards when their wealth and paying powers are far above the average.

Very respectfully
Chas. S. McNichols,
Special Indian Agent.

Document 28

Special Indian Agent Reports Difficulties in Assembling Enrollment February 6, 1903

Source: Chas. S. McNichols to Commissioner of Indian Affairs, February 6, 1903, letter received 9,822/1903, land divison, RG 75, National Archives, Washington, D.C.

Editors' note: In this report McNichols detailed his problems in assembling an enrollment of Flathead Reservation Indians. See also McNichols' December 31, 1902 report which covers the same problems in a little more detail. The chiefs and head men were divided about enrolling some of the mixed blood families. The Kalispel Indian settlement at Camas Prairie refused to recognize the agency or government agents. The Indian Office did not approve McNichols' enrollment and later sent another agent, Thomas Downs, to do another roll, which was finally approved.

Department of the Interior,
United States Indian Service,
In the Field,
Jocko, Mont., Feb. 6, 1903.

The Honorable
Commissioner of Indian Affairs
Washington, D.C.
Sir: —

Before finally completing my work of securing a roll of the Indians entitled to rights on the Flathead reservation I desire as far as practicable some advice and instruction in the matter of adoptions.

Conditions are so different on this reservation than any other; there are so many complications and such a conflict of evidence, with an entire absence of any official records that I feel that no matter how well my work may be done there is sure to be more or less controversy over the result and some serious complications to be met and overcome by the Office or Department. I believe the sooner they are met and overcome the better.

There are perhaps forty families on this reservation possessed of some Indian blood, who have failed to satisfy me that they possess the blood of one of the five Confederated bands belonging on the reservation and whose claims to adoption are resisted by the more influential chiefs and headmen. These people have all lived on the reservation for periods varying from twelve to twenty=five or more years. They hold, as a rule choice, improved farms, the cost of the improvements varying from a few hundreds to several thousand dollars. None of these people, so far as I have learned came on the reservation later than 1890 or 1891.

Now all of these set up the claim that they were "adopted" either by Chief Michel or Chief Arlee, both now dead. They further claim to have settled on the land they now occupy with the approval of Agent Ronan, also deceased. None of them have any writing to show such alleged adoption and approval. Whatever record there may have been of such adoption or approval was of course destroyed when the Agency office was burned during Agent Carter's term of office.

Their claim of adoption is now stoutly resisted by Chief Charlo and "Judge" Lewison who did not come to the reservation until the Flatheads Composing Charlos band were removed here from "the Bitter Root Country" some seventeen years ago and quite generally by "Judge" Joseph, or Pati, who has always lived on the reservation. Some of these claims of adoption are supported by "Judge" Ki-Ka-she and practically all of them by Pierre the young Pend d'orieille Chief and Gusta the Kootenai Chief (Both of whom have been "Chiefs" less than two years) and the Kootenai band in general. Those who disclaim the adoptions have the most weight in the councils and, as will be shown, seem entitled to more respect.

It is my opinion after hearing and Considering many of these cases that a majority of these applicants were given permission to settle on the reservation by Agent Ronan, after they had been "adopted" by one or both of the above named deceased Chiefs for a consideration. In other words I believe that Chiefs Michel and Arlee, particularly the former, made a regular business of placing mixed bloods and whites on the reservation with the approval of an agent that was possibly easy=going rather than corrupt. Few of these applicants Allege such payment; but others whose adoption is conceded by all and still others having rights by blood, but whose parents had left the reservation and who returned during this period have told me that they made payments or presents to these chiefs — ponies, saddles, cattle, money and sometimes an annual tribute of one or two beeves.

There is also good reason for believing that many of the doubtful mixed bloods have continued to make "presents," "loans" and otherwise show favors to the younger chiefs of the Pend d'oreille and Kootenai tribes, and, according to reports, to "Judge" Kikashe, also. "Judges" Joseph (or Pati) and Lewison are wealthy full bloods, too proud to accept such "presents," unless very skillfully made in a general way and Chief Charlo is perhaps too proud, distant and ill=natured to be approachable on such lines. This in my opinion explains the attitude of the several head men on the subject of adoption.

However all of them are agreed as to the adoption of several families and these I have enrolled. They include Michel Pablo (1/2 Blackfeet and 1/2 Mexican) probably the wealthiest Indian in America, estimated to be worth a half=million, the McDonald brothers, half=breed Nez Perces and all wealthy or well-to-do, the Matts, half=breed Piegans and many others, most Nez Perces and Piegans. These people have all lived here for a generation and have large influence in the tribal councils.

On the other hand the large families of the Courvilles, the Clairmonts, the Coutures and those intermarried into these families as well as many others, nearly all wealthy or well-to-do, holding some of the finest farms in this or any other country have not been enrolled. Their status is as given above (i.e. they Claim adoption, but their claim is opposed by the more influential head men and stoutly championed by others.) In addition to the claim of adoption made by these families a number of them claim to be quarter=blood Kootenais and the Kootenai Chiefs admit the claim. But on inquiry I find the claims largely mythical or very hazy, as they involve the alleged capture of some prisoners, more than 100 years ago in the Canadian provinces.

I have enrolled no mixed=blood adoptions unless all the recognized head men have agreed that they were adopted, and will not do so unless otherwise advised by the Office. To enroll all that claim adoption and whose adoption is urged by the Kootenais would be practically enrolling all the mixed bloods on the reservation.

On the other hand the Office will doubtless realize that the mere fact of my not enrolling these mixed bloods is not going to put them off the reservation. They will not abandon homes that they had occupied for a generation — lands that for productiveness, beautiful surroundings and climate can hardly be equalled on earth, without invoking all the political and Church influence and sentiment of the Evangeline order, which they can call to their aid.

I want all the instructions and advice you can give me in the matter. I do not want to assume all the responsibility and blame. None of these people have any written evidence of adoption. If "Adopted" I am fully, convinced that the adoption was more or less purchased. Does the word of one or even two "Chiefs" Constitute adoption?

There are a number of other foreign mixed-bloods on the reservation, most of whom came here as employes of the large Mission at St Ignatius and a few as Agency employes. These only make slight Claims as to rights and are easily disposed of.

Finally I am anxious to close this work and get at something more congenial and where there is a better chance of doing work that will be acceptable. I can close very quickly after you have indicated what course I should take in these matters and have given decisions on some other cases that have been referred to you, but to which no reply has yet been made. There can be no roll prepared of these Indians that will not be subject to future attack and criticism. I am conscientiously trying to do my very best. But I have at all times labored under more disadvantages than you would care to have to read. The full bloods have been indifferent and often hostile and while I believe I have or will have them all, it is barely possible that some have escaped me. I am quite sure of having the Jocko (Agency) valley and the Kootenais complete. I have the names of all the Camas prairie Indians and a close approximation of their ages, but so far they have refused me all information and protested against enrollment. There are about 130 of these of which only about 45 belong to Michel's band of removals — the others having always lived here. These remote Indians deny the Agents' authority and seem in an ugly mood. They are all full bloods and there is no stoping place or whites living nearer than the town of Plains, 18 miles away. I have talked or tried to talk with them but they say they don't want anything to do with "government men." I would like to be instructed as to what future steps to pursue as to them.

There will be between 1450 and 1500 names on the roll exclusive of the 130 Camas prairie Kalispells, the number ranging as to the number of "doubtfuls" enrolled. There will be a considerable number to be rejected in any event.

Very respectfully,
Chas. S. McNichols
Special Indian Agent.

Document 29

Alcohol in Missoula and on the Reservation

February 21, 1903

Source: "Reds Causing Trouble," *The Anaconda Standard*, February 21, 1903, page 14, col. 5.

Editors' note: Alcohol fueled law and order problems in Missoula. Tribal members were accused of trying to bootleg alcohol on the reservation. Note that two prominent traders on the reservation put up the bail for Nenema.

Reds Causing Trouble
Flathead Indians Are in Town by Scores.
Have Money and Spend It
Mose Vandenberg Found Frozen to the Ground, but Revives Again.
Had Drunk Three Bottles of Whiskey.

Missoula, Feb. 20. — Flathead Indians were responsible for quite a little excitement in the city to-day. There are about a hundred of the Indians in the city at present, called here by the semi-annual payment on the Bitter Root preemptions. They all have a little money and most of them are spending it.

About 9 o'clock this morning Chief Larson was called up the Rattlesnake to care for an Indian brave who had literally fallen by the wayside. The redskin had lain down by the bank of the creek and had frozen solid to the ground. It was necessary for the chief to use considerable force to break the ice under him and get the brave to his feet. The fellow recovered sufficiently this afternoon to give his name as Mose Vandenberg and his residence as Arlee. He said he gave a hobo $4 for three bottles of whiskey and that the drank them all. Mose was laid up all day at the city jail as a result of the exposure he had been subjected to.

Chief of Police Cobell of the reservation found two runaway boys at the depot this morning who had evidently joined their elders in coming to the city for a good time. They spent the day in the county jail and were returned to the reservation this evening by the chief.

Several of the Indians were present at the preliminary hearing of Baptiste Nenema before Commissioner Brown this morning on the charge of carrying liquor upon the reservation. A little barrel of whiskey and the pasteboard valise it was in was produced by Constable "Chic" White and he testified that he found the liquor and valise cached behind a barn at Selish when he arrested Nenema for carrying the liquor there from Missoula.

Major Smead and Chief of Police Cobell of the reservation also testified against Nenema, who appeared in red blanket and Indian attire and smoked cigarettes. When Nenema was bound over to the United States court M. H. Prideaux and Alex Demers went on his bond for $200 and he was released from jail, where he had been since his arrest by Constable White several days ago. The defense produced no witnesses at the preliminary hearing.

Document 30

Indian Delegation to Washington Objects to New Grazing Tax March – May 1903

Source: "Indians Are Going East," *The Anaconda Standard*, March 28, 1903, page 14, col. 4; "They'll Have to Pay It," *The Anaconda Standard*, May 4, 1903, page 10, col. 1; excerpts from "They Who've Come Back," *The Anaconda Standard*, August 2, 1903, page 12, col. 3.

Editors' note: The 1903 Flathead Reservation delegation to Washington, D.C., objected to the one dollar grazing tax recently imposed on larger stock owners on the reservation. Most of the delegates were traditional chiefs and head men. The Washington officials refused to repeal the new tax. Duncan McDonald had some interesting comments on statues in the capital.

Indians Are Going East
Delegation from Flathead Reservation Will Travel.
To See the Great Father
Duncan McDonald will Conduct Party,
Which Will Present Grievances to President Roosevelt.
They Object to New Tax.

Missoula, March 27. — President Roosevelt will see some Indians before he comes west on his proposed spring trip. Judge Louison, Judge Baptiste, ex-Judge Cilo, all Flatheads, and Augustus, head chief of the Kootenais, and Judge Josephs and John Pierre, commonly known as Charley, head chief of the Pend d'Oreilles, accompanied by Alexander Matt and Duncan McDonald, as interpreter and guide respectively, departed to-night for Washington to lay before the great father a story of grievances.

The chief trouble has arisen over an order sent out by the Indian department to the effect that each Indian must pay $1 a head upon all cattle and horses over 100 in his possession. The order is to go into effect on April 1.

It is claimed that a great many of the Indians will not be affected by the order, but that it will head off their grazing of cattle for other people. It is also claimed that many "s.... men" have appeared in recent years upon the reservation and that a great many of them have taken advantage of owning stock interests in their Indian wives' and children's names and thus had the advantage of some of the finest grazing country in the Northwest. The Indians are greatly wrought up over the tax, and go to Washington to find if they cannot have it removed. They claim it will bring a hardship to a great many of their number.

The selection of counselors was made only after a great pow-wow upon the reservation, and the men selected were not the ones Chief Charlot had in mind for the honor. It is claimed Charlot favored the selection of a lot of young bucks, prominent among who was Pasquale. Charlot was ignored by the leading men and a meeting was held and a selection of ambassadors to Washington chosen as enumerated above. Then Charlot, it is claimed, sent word to Washington, which resulted in the receipt of a reply from the department that the Indians should not leave the reservation to come to Washington. McDonald set about having the order rescinded and was successful, receiving word yesterday that the braves might come on to the nation's capital.

It is claimed in favor of the decree of the Indian department that it makes the best sort of provision for the poorer Indians, providing that the $1-a-head tax shall be divided among the Indians who have little or no stock.

The Indians will present other grievances to the government besides the tax matter, but about them they are very secret. It is supposed they have something to do with Chief Charlot. It is stated that Charlot may himself go to Washington before the affair is straightened out, if it is possible for him to get a dispensation allowing him to leave the reservation. He was anxious to go when the commission was appointed. The affair may result in a quarrel among the Indians and the ultimate opening up of the reservation, and may be more far-reaching than is indicated at this time.

* * * * * * * * *

They'll Have to Pay It
Nothing to Be Done About the Stock Tax.
M'Donald Tells His Story
Says Secretary of Interior Would Not Yield,
but Settled Down Like a Mired Mule
and Refused to Answer Questions.

Missoula, May 3. — Duncan McDonald has been making Missoula a short visit from his home at Selish. Mr. McDonald returned a fortnight ago from Washington, where he went as guide and interpreter for the reservation delegation which went east to protest against the imposition of a stock tax upon the Indians of the reserve. It was on business connected with this matter that Mr. McDonald came to Missoula. He is not very hopeful regarding the outcome of the protest against the tax.

When asked regarding the eastern trip of the Indians, Mr. McDonald said: "Oh, it was a hard trip. I had all kinds of trouble with the Indians. It was the first time that most of them had ever been east or in any large city, and they wanted everything that they saw. They would simply rush at whatever pleased them, regardless of rules or laws. Twice I had to call upon the police for aid to prevent them from getting into trouble. It was interesting enough to watch them, but the trouble of keeping them out of mischief was too great and I didn't enjoy the trip.

"We called upon the secretary of the interior and upon Commissioner Jones of the Indian bureau. These gentlemen listened to the protest of the Indians, but they wouldn't do anything for us. When we asked the secretary of the interior what we could do with all the ponies, which are not worth paying taxes upon, he advised us to kill them. This, of course, the Indians will not do. Before we had finished our interview I told the secretary that he would never get a cent of taxes out of me. He looked hard at me, but didn't know what to say.

"Some of the Indians have paid their taxes under this new order of the bureau, but there are many who have not paid and who never will pay. I suppose the matter will have to settled by the courts, for we feel that the tax is not legal and that we should not be made to pay it. The treaties give us the absolute and exclusive right to the reservation and it does not seem right to make us pay this tax. The secretary of the interior would not yield an inch but simply settled down like a mired mule and wouldn't even answer us."

* * * * * * * * *

They Who've Come Back. Talks With People Who Have Returned to Their Homes. On Many Things They Saw

Missoula, Aug. 1. — . . . . .

Duncan McDonald has been visiting in town for a few days from his ranch at Selish. He has many interesting things to tell regarding his recent visit to the national capital and his interviews with the Indian commissioner. He saw many changes in Washington from the time when he was there before. "They have the greatest ideas of art" (Mr. McDonald pronounced "art" in capital letters) "that I ever saw. My ideas on this subject may not be up to date, but I don't want them to be if some of the things that I saw are art. There are some statues there that they call art that I don't think much of. In front of the congressional library there is a statue of Neptune, I think they called it, and I swear that statue wouldn't be allowed on the reservation. There was too much nude about it for even the Indians and those people down there call it a-r-t."

* * * * * * * * *

Mr. McDonald was discussing the game laws with Bob Martin, and was speaking of the new law, which forbids Indians from carrying firearms when off the reservation. "It is a bad law," said he. "The Indians have a right under their treaty to hunt wherever they want to. Some of them need to hunt. I don't care about it. In 25 years I haven't killed more than one deer. That was once when I had lived on beans and bacon for three weeks, and I wanted some fresh meat. But I do want to carry a gun when I travel in the mountains. A man needs one for protection. This law is passed to prevent game from being destroyed, they say. I tell you, it isn't the Indians who spoil the game as much as it is these hunters and trappers — white men — that spend so much time in the mountains. I have seen trappers slaughter moose and deer and elk and not touch the carcass at all, except to leave it for bait for their bear traps. That is what spoils the game."

Document 31

Tribal Member to Bring Sheep on Reserve

April 25, 1903

Source: W. H. Smead to Commissioner of Indian Affairs, April 25, 1903, letter received 27,676/1903, land division, RG 75, National Archives, Washington, D.C.

Editors' note: Cattlemen in Montana had long been sensitive to sharing the common range with sheep men. Agent W. H. Smead and probably many cattle owners were upset about Angus P. McDonald's plan to bring a large herd of sheep on the reservation common grazing land.

Department of the Interior,
United States Indian Service,
Jocko, Flathead Agency, Mont., Apr. 25, 1903

Hon. Commissioner Indian Affairs,
Washington, D.C.
Sir: —

I am in receipt of apparently reliable information that one Angus McDonald Sr. has or is about to place on the reservation a band of 3500 sheep. He has made no application for permission to bring them. Heretofore persons desiring to bring in stock from the outside have been in the habit (as required) of asking permission from this office before so doing. Sheep have always been refused admittance (except in small numbers and then under the conditions that they be kept within inclosures and not permitted to graze upon the common range.) The Indians have been and are opposed to the admittance of sheep.

Their presence on the ranges will in my opinion be very detrimental as it is well known that horses and cattle will not range where sheep graze. The proper care of sheep requires too close and constant attention to ever become an occupation at which the Indians will be successful, and I therefore deem it best to preserve the ranges for horses and cattle with which the Indians are successful.

Your instructions relative to the collecting of grazing tax on resident stock contains no provision for the taxing of sheep. Should you permit them on the reservation at all, I would recommend that the tax be made high, so high in fact that it would prohibit their introduction here. As this man lives nearly 100 miles from the agency, I desire definite and immediate instructions before taking same up with him.

For your further information you are advised that this man McDonald is a mixed blood, but I believe has no blood of any of the tribes of this reservation. I consider he has *no legal* rights here although Special Agent McNichols has placed his name upon the rolls. He (and sister) owns about 2000 head of horses and cattle. He has neglected so far to pay his grazing tax, and I believe will continue to do so. He is of the same stripe as William Irvine referred to in a letter of even date herewith. They are both men who seem to think the reservation maintained for their own selfish purposes. Both (and others also) are in the habit of parcelling out great tracts of grazing lands, — holding that *their* cattle *only* — have rights on such tracts, and enforcing such claims by chasing and running the cattle of other persons off such range, — much to the detriment of other owners. You may enquire why they are not punished for this, — in reply will say, — where these person live is very remote from the agency, and a very sparse settled section, and such acts are committed when no witnesses are present who will testify against them. In addition to the above McDonald is a man of bad repute, having been mixed up in a number of very serious scraps, and in a drunked [sic] brawl, is believed to have murdered a man, but escaped punishment through the influence of white friends. I have written somewhat fully of this man, as authority should be granted to remove him from the reservation unless he pays his grazing tax, and I want you to know the kind of man he is. Please give me instructions on matters involved immediately.

Very respectfully,
W. H. Smead
U.S. Indian Agent.

Document 32

Indian Arrested for Robbery of Rich Michel

June 1903

Source: "Supposed Leader of the Gang that Robbed Michel Is Caught," *The Anaconda Standard*, June 1, 1903, page 12, col. 1-2; "After Deer's S.... Now," *The Anaconda Standard*, June 3, 1903, page 14, col. 1-2.

Editors' note: An Indian named John Deer was arrested by the agent, the United States Marshal, and posse for the 1902 robbery of rich Michel on the west side of the reservation. This Michel was probably the richest Indian on the Flathead Reservation.

Supposed Leader of the Gang that Robbed Michel Is Caught
John Deer Taken in Cabin on Camas Prairie —
Concealed in Loft When Officers Run Him Down
— Starts to Make Resistance, but Is Overpowered.
Fruits of His Alleged Crime Is Twenty Thousand Dollars.

Missoula, May 31. — John Deer, an Indian, is in jail at the Jocko agency tonight, charged with being the principal in the robbery of Chief Michel last year, when the old chief was relieved of $20,000. Deer was captured just before sunrise this morning by a posse, led by Major Smead and Deputy United States Marshal Gage, after an exciting experience. As stated in the Standard a short time ago, the first attempt to capture Deer ended in failure, the Indian having received warning a few hours before the posse arrived at his house. At that time the members of the posse arrived at Plains in the evening and stayed at the McGowan hotel until 3 o'clock in the morning, when they started for the reservation. During the night, however, a horse was stolen from the hotel stables and a messenger sped to warn Deer of the approach of the officers. When they reached the house the officers found that Deer had been warned and had fled in haste.

Plans Are Success This Time.

Last night their plans were successfully carried out. Major Smead and Marshal Gage and their men followed the course that had been previously outlined, but care was taken that no messenger left Plains to give warning. An early start was made this morning, and Camas Prairie, just below the warm springs, was reached at daybreak. The posse reached the house where Deer was supposed to be in hiding just before sunrise. An examination was made of the premises, but there were no signs of any life about the place and the house had the appearance of being unoccupied. Thinking they had made a mistake, the officers rode on and would have missed their man had they not noticed a hobbled horse less than a mile beyond the house.

Hobbled Horse Causes Change.

Believing that there would not be a hobbled horse in that vicinity unless the house was occupied, the members of the posse returned to make another search. As they neared the house they saw a s.... splitting wood. The woman had been sent out to keep watch of the officers, for no s.... chops wood at that hour in the morning. She was questioned, but professed no knowledge of the English language and no information whatever regarding the man of whom the officers were in search.

A portion of the posse, however, entered the house and made a thorough search. In the loft, under the roof, they found their man. At first he attempted resistance, but before he could shoot he was covered and overpowered. As quickly as possible he was taken back to Plains and thence by train to Arlee, whence he was transferred to the Jocko agency. It was at first thought best to take him to Helena at once, but it was later decided to lock him up at Jocko, in the hope that he may divulge some of the particulars of the robbery of Chief Michel.

Facts of the Robbery.

Michel is one of the richest Indians on the reservation. His cash holdings have been estimated as high as $100,000, and he has big herds of cattle and horses. At the time he was robbed last year he had in an old tin can, which was concealed in an outbuilding on his farm, $20,000 in coin and currency.

While he was absent some Indians called at the ranch and talked to the women. While the attention of the women was diverted, some members of the party stole the can. Though every effort was made at the time to trace the identity of the thieves, it was not until lately that any clew was discovered.

There is no doubt that Deer is the man who planned the robbery. He will be tried at Helena.

* * * * * * * * *

After Deer's S.... Now
Supposed to Have Planned the Michel Robbery.
Located on Reservation
Officers Expect Her to Tell the Whole Thing When She Learns That Her Buck Is Under Arrest.

Missoula, June 2, — The s.... alleged to have been a party to the robbery of old Chief Michel, and who is credited with a prominent part in planning the theft for which Joe Deer [sic] was arrested on Sunday morning, has been located in the northern part of the reservation, near the Flathead county line. She will be taken into custody some time this week, according to the present plans of the officers. Now that the Indian, Joe Deer, has been placed in custody, it is believed that the whole story of the robbery of the old chief will be obtained, either from him or from the s..... The posse which captured Deer on Sunday morning would have ridden northward to where the woman has been located had it not been for the fact that they were few in numbers and did not care to leave a guard to hold Deer. It was out of the question to take him with them on a ride across the reservation and back, as he would certainly have been taken from them by some of his friends, or else there might have been a serious battle.

When the officers discovered the house where Deer was captured they at once entered it. The s.... whom they had seen outside on their second visit to the cabin was as fierce as her buck, Joe, and she brandished her knife at the officers who were near her, calling them "Heap bad, heap bad." It was thought a while ago that she was the one concerned in the robbery with her husband, but this has been learned since not to be the case. The woman who was with the robbers and who succeeded in diverting the attention of Chief Michel's wife at the time of the robbery is another one and will, as has been stated, be arrested as soon as possible. It is thought that she will be easy to pump, now that Deer is in custody, and if the man does not give up the secret it is believed that she will.

The search for these robbers has engaged the attention of nearly everybody on the reservation, as old Chief Michel is well known and is one of the oldest Indians on the reserve. Many of his friends have been searching for evidence or the thieves ever since the robbery was committed. Deer, however, has friends who kept him posted, and they have covered the trail for a long time. It was one of these who stole a horse at Plains when the first attempt at capture was made and gave warning of the approach of the officers.

When Deer received this warning he and his s.... fled hastily and remained in hiding until two days before the officers arrived the second time. They had been camped in tepees, it has since been learned, on a creek about 15 miles from the house. The s.... had been ostensibly digging camas and keeping watch of what went on. They had evidently made up their minds that the chase had been abandoned, as they returned to their house on Thursday. Deer is, as stated in the Standard on Monday, a western Indian, supposedly of the Colville nation. It is the belief of the officers that he is an Indian for whom the authorities of the state of Washington have been looking for some time. That Indian escaped from the state penitentiary while serving a long term there. It is doubtful, however, if he will be turned over to the Washington officers, as the present case against him is a strong one.

The pursuit of these thieves has developed new talent among the Indian police on the reservation. The new head of the reservation police, all of whom are Indians, is an Apache, Joe by name. He has been on this reservation for some time and has proved himself to be a good officer. Before he was placed on the force the members of the Indian police had talked to Major Smead about him and had all praised him for his courage and his skill. Finally, after they had touted him for long time, he was given a position on the force. He soon demonstrated the fact that he is a brave fellow and a skilled officer.

Not long ago he was sent over from the agency to the Mission valley to arrest an offender. The man he wanted was found easily, but he was surrounded by about 20 friends, who declared that they would not allow the Apache to take him. Apache Joe, however, was equal to the occasion. He drew his gun and backed against a tree. "The first one of you that moves will get his head blown off," he said, and they knew that he meant it. Then he commanded his prisoner to mount.

When the fellow was on his horse Joe backed to where his own horse stood and leaped to its back. Then, still covering the would-be rescuers with his revolver, he rode away with his prisoner. He has won his position at the head of the force by his good work, and he is respected by the good Indians and feared by the bad ones. His influence upon the reserve is said to be most salutary.

Document 33

Smead Requests Per Capita Payment from Grazing Tax July 2, 1903

Source: W. H. Smead to Commissioner of Indian Affairs, July 2, 1903, letter received 41,378/1903, land division, RG 75, National Archives, Washington, D.C.

Editors' note: The grazing tax on livestock owned by tribal members had been a very contentious proposal. It was largely initiated in order to encourage the sale of surplus horses from the range. Smead here proposed a per capita payment from the taxes he had succeeded in collecting in order to make the tax more palatable for the majority of tribal members.

Department of the Interior,
United States Indian Service,
Jocko, Flathead Agency, Mont., July 2, 1903.

Hon. Commissioner Indian Affairs,
Washington, D.C.
Sir: —

Referring to the matter of the collection of grazing taxes on the resident stock of this reservation, I beg to advise you that since my return from Washington, I have collected the first payment on some 7000 head of stock, and expect within a short time to collect on 3000 more. There are still two large cattle men who apparently are making no arrangement to meet this tax. The Catholic Mission have not paid on their stock. It is my understanding that they have appealed to the President to recind the order for collection of taxes on their cattle.

I have not collected much on the ponies of the full bloods, believing it better to collect from all breeds first, there has been however a very good sale of ponies as far this spring and summer and this is very desirable. In collection of these taxes from all, Indians white or breeds, I have tried to be as diplomatic as possible, desiring to avoid force so long as there was any possibility of succeeding in any other way. It has however been an up-hill task. The Indians returned from Washington disappointed and sulky over their failure to have the tax abolished, and consequently the tax has been and is now very unpopular.

W. H. Smead, Flathead Indian Agent, 1898-1904
Source: Photograph by W. H. Taylor Studio, Helena, Montana
Photograph Archives, Montana Historical Society, Helena, Montana,
photo PAc 99-36.67

The Indians themselves seem unable to realize that the money collected is to be distributed among them. Interested parties are largely responsible for this distrust. Therefore instead of having the people for whom this tax is intended as a benefit and source of revenue, favorable to and using their influence to assist the Government in its collection, we have their opposition.

Under these conditions I believe it would be desirable to make a per capita payment from the funds collected at an early date. I am of the opinion that there will then be a big change of sentiment among the full bloods, and that thereafter instead of their opposition we will have their assistance. The breeds and whites are afraid of the Indians and are anxious for their friendship. If we can make the tax a popular measure among the full bloods, I feel sure it will be of great assistance in carrying out the collection of this tax.

I now have on hand and deposited in Washington about $5600.00 proceeds of collections of grazing tax, I think it will be possible to collect another $2500.00 within a short time which with the amount now on hand will be sufficient to make a $5.00 per capita payment which I think advisable to make as soon as possible. I desire to have your views on this subject, and if possible your approval of the plan.

In this connection, will say, — In order to make a per capita payment it will be necessary to have a complete roll of the Indians. Special Agent McNichols has not yet returned to complete this roll. I think however if he could be here at the time a distribution of the funds is made that he would be able to complete the roll with little difficulty. All Indians entitled to receive payment will no doubt present themselves for same, when unless it has been heretofore done, they can be enrolled.

Please favor me with a prompt reply.

Very respectfully,
W. H. Smead
U.S. Indian Agent.

Document 34

Tribal Hunter Fights In Court for Hunting Rights September – December 1903

Source: "Alex Bigknife Loses His Gun," *The Missoulian* (daily), September 5, 1903, page 8, col. 2; "Will Test the Law," *The Missoulian* (daily), September 6, 1903, page 8, col. 2; "Indians on the Warpath," *The Anaconda Standard*, September 6, 1903, page 12, col. 4; "Indians Contest State Law," *The Missoulian* (daily), September 13, 1903, page 1, col 4, and page 8, col. 3; "To the Supreme Court," *The Anaconda Standard*, December 9, 1903, page 12, col. 3.

Editors' note: The most egregious example of white Montanans' efforts to obstruct Indian hunting rights was a 1903 law making it illegal for Indians to leave their reservation while armed. As related in these newspaper articles, in September 1903 deputy game warden Arthur Higgins confiscated Alex Bignife's guns when Bigknife was in Missoula shopping for his fall hunt. The newspaper reported Bigknife "was much surprised and put out." Bigknife returned to the reservation and he and the traditional chiefs immediately hired a Missoula lawyer, Harry H. Parsons, to sue the warden. On September 3, 1903, the Montana State Game Warden wrote to Agent Smead apologizing for the confiscation and instructed the Missoula warden to return Bigknife's gun. Bigknife refused to accept the return of his gun and he and chiefs raised $1,000 to pay the lawyer to pursue the lawsuit against Warden Higgins. The state dragged the Bigknife case out in the court on technicalities, but did stop enforcing the law against Indian hunters.

Alex Bigknife Loses His Gun
Had Started on His Annual Hunting Trip.
Is Disarmed by Game Warden
State Law Forbidding Carrying Arms by Indians
Off the Reservation Enforced.

Deputy Game Warden Arthur Higgins took a rifle and six-shooter away from Alex Bigknife, a Flathead buck, who, with his wife and their daughter and her two papooses, were passing through the city yesterday afternoon.

Alex Bigknife and his family were enroute from the Flathead reservation to the upper Bitter Root country on their annual hunting trip for deer. He was much surprised and put out when disarmed by the deputy warden.

At the last session of the legislature there was a law passed forbidding the Indians carrying firearms off the reservation. This act was passed in order to protect the game, as it is claimed that one Indian will slaughter more deer and other large game in one season while out on one of these hunting trips than twenty sportsmen would.

Tyler Worden, of this city, who is well acquainted with the Indians, stated last evening that Alex Bigknife was one of the best hunters on the reservation. He had talked with the Indian after he had been disarmed. Alex claimed that he was not aware that there was any law against his carrying arms off the reservation. He stated that Agent Smead never notified him of it when he granted him the leave of absence from the reservation that it was contrary to law to go hunting outside of the reservation, or to carry a gun.

This is the first instance in this section since the law was passed where an Indian has been disarmed.

* * * * * * * * *

Will Test the Law.

H. H. Parsons Has Been Retained by Alex Bigknife.

Attorney H. H. Parsons has been retained by Chief Carlos and several of the other chiefs and leading men of the Flathead tribe of Indians to make a test to ascertain if the law passed by the last legislature to the effect that no Indian can leave his reservation with fire arms or ammunition is constitutional.

Mr. Parsons departed last evening for the agency to meet with Carlos and other chiefs and leading men of the tribe, to arrange matters.

Under the new law no Indian is allowed to leave the reservation to go hunting. This, it is claimed is an unconstitutional step, in that it curtails the privileges of American people. All firearms and ammunition found on any Indian who is off his reservation can be taken by the game warden and are confiscated, the returns to go to the warden fund.

Alex Bigknife the Flathead buck who was relieved of his gun and six-shooter Friday evening by Deputy Game Warden Arthur Higgins, as reported in these columns yesterday morning, started back to the reservation yesterday. He took his pack animals, wife and daughter and her papooses with him, having given up making the trip into the upper Bitter Root valley.

* * * * * * * *

Alex Bigknife
Source: Toole Archives, Mansfield Library, University of Montana, Missoula, Montana, photo 78-248

Indians on the Warpath
Red Men Kick Because They May Not Carry Guns.
New Law Is to Be Tested
A Case Will Be Brought in the Federal Court to Have the Law Set Aside as Unconstitutional as It Violates Treaty Agreements.

Missoula, Sept. 5. — The Indians of the reservation have become greatly excited over the enforcement of the act of the last legislature which specifies that Indians cannot bear firearms when off the reservation. Several of them, including Nine Pipes, Joseph Lamoos, Antoine and Basil, arrived in the city to-day and placed the matter before Harry H. Parsons, with the instruction to begin suit in the federal court to test the constitutionality of the law.

Chief Charlot also took a hand in the matter, and sent a letter stating that it was his desire that the law be attacked. The act was passed last March, and is entitled "A regulation for the carrying of firearms by Indians when off the reservations."

The Indians claim that a strict enforcement of the law means that they cannot leave their reservation to hunt, and that the treaty made with them prescribed that they should have the right to hunt anywhere they please. Austa, the Indian who was disarmed yesterday by Deputy Game Warden Arthur Higgins, is a reservation policeman, and it is also claimed by the Indians that the enforcement of the law will prevent the Indian police from following outlaws off the reservation if occasion demands.

Deputy Higgins says attention was called to Austa yesterday and that he wore his six shooter in plain sight, and that under the law he had no other thing to do than to disarm him. Mr. Higgins himself, while enforcing the law, believes that its enforcement is an injustice to the Indians. The case will probably be begun in the federal court by application for an injunction restraining further interference with the Indians carrying firearms. It is almost a cinch that the law is unconstitutional, as it was passed in the interests of sportsmen, it is said, who desired to confine the Indians' hunting to the reservation.

* * * * * * * * *

Indians Contest State Law
Chiefs Raise Money With Which to Fight Act Prohibiting Hunting.

Attorney H. H. Parsons yesterday began a suit in the district court to test the validity of the law passed by the last legislature restraining Indians from leaving their reservations with arms and ammunition.

The law was passed in the interest of the sportsmen of the state to prevent the Indians from slaughtering the game ruthlessly.

The title of the case is Alex Bigknife against Arthur E. Higgins, as deputy game warden of the state of Montana.

Last week Deputy Game Warden Higgins found Alex Bigknife in this city carrying a rifle and a six-shooter. The Indian was enroute, with his s.... and their daughter and her papooses and several pack horses, to the upper Bitter Root valley on his annual hunting trip. The officer, in compliance with the law, disarmed the Indian. Alex Bigknife was compelled to return to the reservation without his annual hunt.

Chiefs Hold Meeting.

All of the leading chiefs of the reservation held a meeting and raised a purse of $1,000 and have employed Mr. Parsons to make a test of the law. Chief Moise and several of the other leading Indians of the Flathead reservation were in the city yesterday for that purpose.

In the complaint filed yesterday in the district court it is alleged that Alex Bigknife, on September 5, after securing a permit from Major Smead, Indian agent of the Flathead reservation, left for his annual hunting trip to the upper Bitter Root valley; that when he arrived in Missoula Deputy Game Warden Higgins took from him his rifle and ammunition, and he was compelled to return to the reservation without being allowed to hunt for deer and other wild game.

The complaint states that the action of Deputy Game Warden Higgins in disarming Alex Bigknife were performed officially, under and by virtue of a pretended authority as such public officer. The complaint further recites that Alex Bigknife is a mixed blood Indian; by birth and affiliation he is a member of the Flathead tribe.

Is Class Legislation.

The complaint then says that the act of the legislature of March 5, 1903, under which the officer was acting, is in violation of the treaty which was entered into between the United States and the Flathead and federated tribes of Indians, under the Stevens treaty of 1855, which was ratified by act of congress in 1859, which granted permission to the Indians to hunt and kill game on all public lands during the regular open season. The act of the legislature is also in violation of the 16th amendment to the Constitution.

The complaint goes on further to recite that this legislative act deprives the plaintiff of liberty and property without due process of law, and thereby is in violation of the Fifth amendment to the Constitution, as well as sections 3, 13 and 27, of Article III., of the Constitution of the State of Montana. The act is also in violation of Ordinance No. 1 of said constitution and that said act is class legislation.

Bigknife asks $100 damages and that the act be declared unconstitutional and null and void.

* * * * * * * * *

To the Supreme Court
Will Test Constitutionality of the Law.
In Alex Big Knife's Case
It Is Alleged That Game Warden Had No Right to Remove Gun From the Indian,
Though He Was Off Reservation.

Missoula, Dec. 8. — A bill of exceptions to the action of Judge Webster in overruling the motion to strike from the amended complaint in the case of Alex Big Knife against Arthur Higgins, as game warden, has been filed with the clerk of the court. The case is one of considerable interest and by this action it will be thrown into the supreme court.

It will be remembered that several months ago Arthur Higgins, acting in his capacity as game warden, took a gun from the Indian, Alex Big Knife, while Big Knife was off the reservation. Attorney Harry Parsons brought suit against Higgins as game warden for his action. The suit was an attempt to have declared unconstitutional the law which makes it a misdemeanor for an Indian to carry arms off the reservation.

Attorney Parsons claims that this law is not in accordance with the constitution of the United States or with the constitution of Montana, and that it is in direct violation of the treaty rights of the Indians. An amended complaint was filed some time ago. It was claimed then and there by the defense that the amended complaint changed the cause of action, as it was drawn against Higgins as an individual and not as an officer, as in the first complaint.

The defense moved on this ground that the court strike from the amended complaint. The motion was overruled and a bill of exceptions is now taken to this action. The attorneys for the defense are Attorney General Donovan and County Attorney Charles H. Hall. What the next move in the case will be is not known. However, it will be watched with interest, as it is a case which tests the law.

Document 35

Mixed Blood Accuses White Man of Robbery

October 1903

Source: "Because of a Scar on Neck," *The Anaconda Standard*, October 18, 1903, page 14, col. 3; "Man with Scar on His Neck Released," *The Anaconda Standard*, October 21, 1903, page 12, col. 5.

Editors' note: Missoula authorities were willing to arrest a white man accused of robbing a Flathead Reservation mixed blood in Butte. The white man was released when the Butte authorities declined to pay to have the prisoner transported to Butte for prosecution.

Because of a Scar on Neck
Young Man Arrested at Instance of Half-Breed,
Who Says He Tried to Rob Him.

Missoula, Oct. 17. — Because John Amer, alias John Crane, has a large scar on his neck he is in jail and will remain there for a few days unless he can pretty well establish the fact that he was not in Butte about the 1st of August, when a halfbreed from the reservation was there and was held up by a young man with a scar where John's is. The halfbreed's story is to the effect that he fell in with Amer on the street and the two entered an alleyway together, when Amer, who had seen him "flash" a roll of bills, attempted to waylay him. The halfbreed was struck in the head several blows by his assailant, but he managed to keep consciousness until he got to a saloon, where he fell on the floor. His assailant, however, had been unable to get his hands upon the roll of bills.

To-day the halfbreed saw the fellow on the street here and gave a description of him to Constable "Chick" White, who soon after locked up the man with the scar on his neck. The young fellow arrested denies that his name is Amer, says that his name is John Crane, that he was never in Butte in his life, and that he has been working in the lumber camps at Bonner and Nine Mile all the fall. He gives his age as 30. The halfbreed identified the fellow as his assailant.

* * * * * * * * *

Man With Scar on His Neck Released

Missoula, Oct. 20. — John Crane, the young man who was arrested Sunday by Officer "Chick" White on a description furnished by a half-breed who claimed he had attempted to hold him up in Butte, was released from jail tonight. The Butte authorities would not pay the cost of having Crane brought there. Crane has a scar on his neck, and by this the half-breed claimed to have recognized him.

Document 36

Whipping Returns to Reservation

October 27, 1903

Source: "A Whipping Post Used," *The Kalispell Bee*, October 27, 1903, page 8, col. 2.

Editors' note: The use of whipping as a punishment on the Flathead Reservation had been controversial in the late nineteenth century. In an 1889 council, Kootenai Chief Eneas complained that since he did not have a secure jail, he needed to use whipping to punish offenders. At that time white authorities objected to whipping on the reservation.

A Whipping Post Used
By Indians on Flathead Reservation to Punish Wrong Doers.
She Deserted Her Husband
And Eloped With Another Man — Was Captured,
Publicly Degraded, Severely Punished
and Then the Erring S.... Is Forgiven by Her Injured Husband.

Missoula, Oct. 24. — Whipping posts may be out of date, but the lash vigorously applied to the bare back as a punishment for wrong-doing is a practice still in vogue among the Indians at the Flathead reservation. The victim is laid flat upon a board floor, held in position by four brawny bucks, and publicly lashed.

The last wrong-doer to be publicly degraded and punished was Mrs. Lumphrey, who deserted her husband two months ago and eloped with John Charlie. They were captured a few weeks ago and brought back to the reservation to be tried. The trial was held recently, and John Charlie was sentenced to sixty days in the reservation jail. Mrs. Lumphrey, who is a half-breed s...., was publicly whipped for her transgression of the marital vow.

Laid face down, with her arms and legs held by four Indians, she was given twenty-five strokes of a horsewhip. The whip was wielded by Ustad, an Indian policeman, and with such muscular force that Indian stoicism could not withstand the pain inflicted. The woman's screams and the sight of her misery was even more than the wronged husband could withstand, and again the vanuted [sic] stoicism of the Indian suffered a downfall. Charley Lumphrey cried aloud in sympathy with his suffering spouse. He, who had swors [sic] that she should never again enter his wigwam, took his sobbing s.... to his breast, mingled his tears with hers and led her through the crowd of curious spectators to his home.

And there is another Mrs. Lumphrey for whom the lash is still in reserve. Louis Lumphrey, brother of Charley, was in town today looking for his mate. She left the reservation in company with a half-breed named Frank McClure, and Louis learned here that the couple had gone to Butte. When asked what he would do to McClure if he should find him, Louis answered:

"I can't do nothing. Frank, she's great big feller, and I'm afraid for him. But the policemans she'll fix him both, when she'll get him. Frank she'll have to get on jail and my woman she'll get licked good."

And Louis smiled broadly at the thought of what is in store for the couple. Then, with a more sober expression, he added:

"That's pretty bad thing, you know, when your woman'll gone 'way with 'nuther man."

Document 37

Joe Morrigeau Expelled from Reservation Over Tax Payments November 1903

Source: "Soldiers Leave for Reservation," *The Anaconda Standard*, November 27, 1903, page 12, col. 1-2; "It Was a Wierdly Garbled Account," *The Anaconda Standard*, November 29, 1903, page 12, col. 1-2; W. H. Smead to Commissioner of Indian Affairs, November 30, 1903, letter received 78,333/1903, land division, RG 75, National Archives, Washington, D.C.; W. H. Smead to Commissioner of Indian Affairs, December 31, 1903, letter received 711/1904, land division, RG 75, National Archives, Washington, D.C.

Editors' note: Joe Morrigeau had refused to pay his grazing tax, but Smead was backed up by the Interior Department. Soldiers were sent from Fort Missoula to arrest Morrigeau and expel him from the reservation until his grazing tax was paid.

Soldiers Leave for Reservation
General Opinion Is That It Is for the Purpose of Enforcing the Order of the Interior Department for Expulsion of All Cattle on Which Taxes Are Not Paid.

Missoula, Nov. 26. — Major Torrey, commanding the battalion of the 24th infantry at Fort Missoula, with Captain Maxey and Assistant Surgeon Merrick, left here to-night with 25 picked men for the Flathead reservation, presumably to enforce the order of the interior department for the expulsion of all cattle from the reserve on which the $1 per head tax had not been paid. The men have 100 rounds of ammunition each and rations for several days. Major Torrey was reticent as to the destination of the expedition and its purpose.

"We are going on a little hunt," he said, when asked regarding the movement, "and will probably be back tomorrow night. I cannot tell how far we are going, as I do not know."

Major Smead came down from the agency Saturday and said that he did not anticipate any trouble in getting the cattle from the reserve. Yesterday he made another trip to town, remaining only a few hours. He had a hurried consultation, it is said, with Major Torrey and returned to the Jocko agency on the delayed west-bound express last night. To-night the troops started, so it is presumed that his trip was in connection with the assistance which he found necessary to get the cattlemen to submit to his orders.

Some of the largest herds on the reserve are involved in this order, and despite the assurance of Major Smead that no trouble was in sight, it seems that difficulty is anticipated in removing the stock. Two or three of the interested cattlemen were in town to-day, but were not disposed to talk. The men in Major Torrey's detachment are the pick of the battalion. They are all sharpshooters and riflemen and have been chosen from the entire battalion for their expert marksmanship. They were all good-natured, but, having had a jolly Thanksgiving at the post to-day, they did not appear to relish the orders to-night to "hike" out in the cold.

"We're out on a pleasure trip — he, he, he," said one of them, "so it's all right."

It is not likely that there will be any resistance on the part of the cattlemen when the soldiers appear, but it is not probable that the removal of the cattle can be accomplished in a single day, and the stay of the command is apt to be prolonged beyond to-morrow night.

Major Torrey's command will go to Plains to-night and its special car will be set out there. It is certain that at least two days will be required for the work that is laid out for the troops, and possibly it will take even longer than that. The troops will occupy their car while at Plains and unless they have to camp on the reservation, will be comfortably quartered.

* * * * * * * * *

It Was Wierdly Garbled Account
Truth About Major Torrey's Trip to Reservation.
Morrigeau Pays His Taxes
Indian Says He Had Refused on What He Thought Was Good Advice — Comes and Goes a Free Man. No Idea of Opposition.

Missoula, Nov. 28. — Major Torrey's 25 sharpshooters are back at Fort Missoula. They arrived on No. 4 this morning and were at once taken to the post. Joe Morrigeau, who was the objective feature of the military expedition to the Indian reservation, was also a passenger on No. 4, but he came as a free man and not in irons. To-night he is on his way to his ranch on the Little Bitter Root with a receipt in his pocket for the amount of his cattle tax and thoroughly reinstated in his reservation privileges. The incident is closed, and the order of the government for the assessment of the $1 tax on reservation cattle has been enforced in this instance without bloodshed.

Seldom has an occurrence in this part of Montana been so exaggerated and misrepresented as has this one. Reporters and correspondents with a zeal greater than their knowledge of the conditions in this part of the state have represented the state of affairs at the Morrigeau ranch as something fearful. They had all the Morrigeau cowboys armed to the teeth and a bad lot of "Nez Perce outlaws" also on the path to resist the officers. Anybody who is in the least familiar with the conditions on the reserve will recognized the absurdity of these tales.

What Really Happened.

The conditions that really existed were very different. Major Torrey's soldiers left Plains as stated in the Standard at 3:30 o'clock yesterday morning. They reached the ranch without incident. When they got there Morrigeau was not at his house, so they waited. Morrigeau tells what followed:

"I was out after some cattle. I had rounded them up and in the middle of the afternoon drove them toward the ranch. As I came toward the place I noticed a lot of dark figures around the buildings, and wondered what they were. I did not suspect anything out of the way. When I got up to the corral several soldiers came out toward me and told me I was under arrest. I said, 'All right,' and got off my horse. As soon as I could get ready I went with the soldiers. When we were off the reservation I was told that I was not under arrest any longer, but that I must not go back to the reservation unless I received permission."

That was all there was to it. There was no resistance and no attempt at resistance. Morrigeau came to Missoula on the train that brought in the troops. Major Smead, Indian agent, was also a passenger. Immediately after the arrival of the train in Missoula Major Smead and Morrigeau had a conference in the Florence hotel. They afterwards adjourned to a lawyer's office and there affairs were straightened. After lunch Morrigeau paid to Major Smead $1,300, representing the amount of his taxes and the costs of his arrest and expulsion.

Morrigeau Is Reinstated.

Major Smead reinstated him and he took the next train for the west. To-morrow he will be back at his ranch. Morrigeau talked to-day to a Standard representative regarding his case. His statement follows, in substance:

"I had been advised that the tax was illegal and could not be collected. I was advised not to pay it. A few days ago I told the reservation authorities that I would come to Missoula in a few days and get more advice. If it was right to pay the tax, I was willing to pay it. If others paid it, I was ready to pay it. The first I knew that this was not satisfactory was when the soldiers came up to me at the ranch."

Major Smead, in response to an inquiry from the Standard, said:

"There is no disposition to work a hardship on anybody. The government has issued orders that this tax must be collected and that the collection must be strictly enforced. This is what we have been doing. That's all there is to it. Morrigeau has paid his tax and the costs of his arrest, and I have reinstated him."

Thus ends the fierce and bloody war prophesied by lurid writers who think more of head lines than they do of facts.

****

Department of the Interior,
United States Indian Service,
Jocko, Flathead Agency, Mont., Nov. 30, 1903.

Hon. Commissioner of Indian Affairs,
Washington, D.C.
Sir: —

Respectfully referring to my telegram of Nov. 19th. asking for assistance in removing Joseph Morrigeau from the reservation and your reply thereto of Nov. 21st. I have to advise you that in compliance with instructions from the War Department Major Torrey and 25 soldiers left Fort Missoula late on the night of Nov. 26th for Plains and thence to the reservation for the purpose of removing Morrigeau. The following morning they reached Morrigeau's place and placed him under arrest without difficulty. The visit of the troops was so secretly planned and executed that Morrigeau and outfit were completely surprised. He was removed from the reservation and warned that in case he returned he would be arrested under section 2149, R. S.

He thereupon very penitently appealed to me to be re-instated, faithfully promising to in future abide by the rules and regulations governing this reservation. Upon these pledges and the payment of $925.00 grazing tax and a fine of $250.00 (estimated cost to Government in removing him from the reservation) which I imposed upon him, all of which he not only promptly but willingly paid, I permitted him to return to his home on the reservation. I feel sure in saying that Morrigeau has had a lesson that he will remember a long time. Not only to Morrigeau will it be a lesson, but to this class of mixed bloods who have been attempting to defeat this resident grazing tax. They now *know* that the Government will enforce this tax, and I do not think any more of them will care for an experience like Morrigeau's.

This prompt and vigorous action is being applauded by the public generally and by many of the more intelligent Indians. I have yet to hear one word of criticism.

I desire to heartily thank you and the Department for this prompt support. It will be an object lesson long to be remembered and I am sure greatly assist in maintaining order in the future.

Very respectfully,
W. H. Smead
U.S. Indian Agent.

* * * * * * * *

Department of the Interior,
United States Indian Service,
Jocko, Flathead Agency, Mont., Dec. 31, 1903.

Hon. Commissioner Indian Affairs,
Washington, D.C.
Sir: —

. . . .

[On December 23, 1903, the Indian Office had written to Agent Smead that "The Office is very much surprised to learn from your letter and from Maj. Torrey's report that you did not accompany the military expedition in person, but sent your chief of police to represent you and to act as guide." This was Smead's reply in defense of his actions:]

We had discussed every detail of the proposed trip. I knew there would be no discussion or "council" held with the Indians. That in all probability he would see no Indians, save Morrigeau and his henchmen, and that they would be at Morrigeau's place, away from and detached from where any other Indians lived. That there would be no necessity, nor would it be desirable to "parley" with Morrigeau and his crowd, — such time having passed. I further knew that the troops would have no trouble or conflict with the Indians or Morrigeau and his crowd. That the latter seeing that they had soldiers to deal with would immediately submit. And this was the exact result. . . .

Very respectfully,
W. H. Smead
U.S. Indian Agent.

Document 38

White Man Convicted of Stealing Indian's Horse

December 1903

Source: "Charged with Theft of an Indian's Horse," *The Anaconda Standard*, December 13, 1903, page 14, col. 1; "Baird Found Guilty of Horse Stealing," *The Anaconda Standard*, December 14, 1903, page 10, col. 3.

Editors' note: In this case the Indian whose horse had been stolen in Plains seemed to have gotten some justice when Charles Baird was convicted of theft.

Charged with Theft of an Indian's Horse
Charles Baird on Trial in the District Court.
The Jury Cannot Agree
Antonio Bullhead Says He Left His Horse Tied at Plains and When He Returned It Was Gone — Found on the Defendant's Ranch.

Missoula, Dec. 12. — The case of the state against Charles Baird, charged with stealing a horse from an Indian, Antonio Bullhead, occupied the attention of the district court all day to-day. The entire morning was taken up in an effort to secure a jury, and it was not until about 2 o'clock in the afternoon that a suitable jury had been selected.

Bullhead was the first witness for the state. He said that on Sept. 5 he went to Plains from the Flathead reservation. He tied his horse to a fence near a livery stable there in the afternoon. When he returned in the evening the horse was gone. He immediately notified Constable Mosier that he had lost his horse.

Constable Mosier was called to the stand and testified to having learned from the Indian that he had lost his horse. He went to the ranch of Baird about a week after that time, he said, and there he found the horse in the possession of Baird. He took both Baird and the horse to Plains. Other witnesses were called who corroborated this testimony. Three witnesses were called by the defense.

The plea of the defense was that Baird had purchased the horse from an Indian whom he did not know for the sum of $10. These three witnesses testified to having seen Baird on the night of Sept. 5 with the Indian, Bullhead, and that the Indian was attempting to sell his horse to Baird for $10 worth of whiskey. Baird would not pay him in whiskey, but offered him $10 in cash. The attorney for the defense was W. F. Hughes, and Charles H. Hall prosecuted the case. The evidence was all taken in a short time, and the case went to the jury at 4 o'clock.

It is probable that the jury will have a difficult time in reaching a verdict. At 6 o'clock the deputy sheriff was called to the jury room and told to ask Judge Webster to excuse the members. The judge said he would give them until Monday noon to reach a verdict.

****

Baird Found Guilty of Horse Stealing

Missoula, Dec. 13. — At 3 o'clock this morning the jurors in the case of the state against Charles Baird, charged with horse stealing, announced that they had reached a verdict. Judge Webster was summoned to the courthouse at that unearthly hour and listened to the following verdict:

"We, the jury, find the prisoner guilty of grand larceny, and fix his punishment at one year at hard labor."

Antoine Bullhead, an Indian, was the complaining witness, he having lost his horse on Sept. 5 last. All the testimony in the case was taken yesterday, and it went to the jury at 4 o'clock in the afternoon. Judge Webster announced that he would pass sentence on Baird Tuesday at 5 o'clock.

Document 39

Joseph Dixon Introduces Bill to Open Flathead Reservation December 1903

Source: "To Open the Flathead Indian Reservation," *The Anaconda Standard*, December 19, 1903, page 2, col. 5; "Bill for Opening of the Reservation," *The Anaconda Standard*, December 26, 1903, page 12, col. 3-4; "Favorable Comment for Mr. Dixon's Bill," *The Anaconda Standard*, December 29, 1903, page 12, col. 1.

Editors' note: The allotment policy provided for the coerced sale of tribal land for far less than it was worth. Missoula and the surrounding white community saw this as a great chance to expand the local economy with a subsidy from the sale of tribal assets. The first article said that tribal members would get to vote on implementing the policy, but tribal consent was never obtained. Allotment did increase Dixon's popularity among white Montana voters.

To Open the Flathead Indian Reservation
Bill Introduced in Congress by Representative Dixon.

Special Dispatch to the Standard.

Washington, Dec. 18. — This afternoon Representative Dixon introduced a bill designed to open to settlement the Flathead Indian reservation, and there is reason to believe that the measure will have the approval of the department officials. Bills heretofore introduced provided that a treaty should be negotiated with the Indians, but the bill now being pressed for passage by the Montana congressman calls for the immediate survey of the reservation and an allotment of lands to the Indians.

An important provision of the bill is that all surplus land shall be disposed of by a commission composed of two members of the tribe, two citizens of Montana and a special agent of the interior department. It will be the duty of the commission to classify and appraise the surplus lands, dividing them into agricultural, first and second classes; timber lands, mineral and grazing lands. Appraisements will run from $1.25 to $5 per acre, open to homestead settlers only, payment to be made in five annual installments. Timber lands will be sold to the highest bidder for cash, and after five years all remaining land will be sold to the highest bidder. The bill will become effective when ratified by a majority of the adult members of the tribes. The proceeds of the sales are to be divided among the Indians.

* * * * * * * * * *

Bill for Opening of the Reservation
Much Interest in Representative Dixon's Plan.
The General Sentiment
Felt That Its Passage Would Be Beneficial to the Business Interests — Holding of Meeting Has Been Proposed to Indorse Measure.

Missoula, Dec. 25. — There is much interest in Missoula in the bill recently introduced in congress by Representative Dixon for the opening of the Flathead reservation. As has been stated, the bill makes an entirely different

Joseph M. Dixon in the 1920s
Source: "Governors of Montana" [poster]
(Historical Library of Montana, no date)

arrangement for the opening of the reserve from any suggestion that has heretofore been considered. The general sentiment in Missoula is that the bill is an excellent one and that Missoula businessmen should lend their assistance in every way possible to secure its passage. It has been suggested that a business men's meeting should pass resolutions indorsing the measure to show that it has the approval of the people out here.

The bill provides for the immediate survey of the reservation, and as soon as this has been completed an allotment is to be made to every person maintaining tribal relations with any of the confederated tribes. This is to be done under the provisions of the allotment laws already in force. When the allotment has been made the president is to appoint a commission of five, to consist of two persons holding tribal relations with the Indians, two resident citizens of Montana and a special agent of the interior department. This commission is to appraise the lands of the reservation after they have been examined and classified. Regarding the classification and appraisement of the lands the provisions of the bill are as follows:

"Section 5 — That said commissioners shall then proceed to personally inspect and classify and appraise all of the remaining lands embraced within said reservation. In making such classification and appraisement said lands shall be divided into the following classes: First, agricultural lands of the first class; second, agricultural land of the second of the second class; third, timber lands, the same to be lands more valuable for their timber than for any other purpose; fourth, mineral lands; and fifth, grazing lands.

"Sec. 6 — That when said lands are so classified they shall be appraised by said commission as follows: Lands of the first class, at a price not to exceed $5 per acre; lands of the second class, at a price not to exceed $2.50 per acre; lands of the fifth class, at a price not to exceed $1.25 per acre. Said commission shall in their report of lands of the third class determine as nearly as possible the amount of standing saw timber on each subdivision of 160 acres thereof and fix a minimum price for the value thereof and in determining the amount of merchantable timber growing thereon they shall be empowered to employ a timber cruiser at a salary of not more than $6 per day while so actually employed. Mineral lands shall not be appraised as to value.

"Sec. 9 — That said lands shall be opened to settlement and entry by proclamation of the president, which proclamation shall prescribe the manner in which these lands may be settled upon, occupied and entered by persons entitled to make entry thereof, and no person shall be permitted to settle upon, occupy or enter any of said lands, except as prescribed in such proclamation, until after the expiration of 60 days from the time when the same are opened to settlement and entry, provided, that the rights of honorably discharged

Cartoon celebrating Joseph Dixon's success in opening
Indian reservations and starting irrigation projects in Montana.
The Anaconda Standard, September 4, 1904, editorial section, page 1.

union soldiers and sailors of the late civil and the Spanish wars, as defined and described in section 2.304 and 2.305 of the revised statutes, as amended by the act of March 1, 1901, shall not be abridged; provided further, that the price of said lands shall be the appraised value thereof, as fixed by the said commission, but settlers under the homestead law who shall reside upon and cultivate the land entered in good faith for the period required by existing law shall pay the appraised value thereof in five annual payments annually in advance, and shall be entitled to a patent for the lands so entered upon the payment to the local land officers of said five annual payments in advance, and the usual and customary fee and commissions."

There are further provisions as to forfeiture of rights when there has been a default in payments, and certain reservations of land are made for the federal buildings now on the reserve and for the schools, hospitals and other institutions maintained by the Catholic missions.

All lands remaining, undisposed of in the first and second classes at the end of five years shall be sold at public auction to the highest bidder, conditions of sale being that the purchaser must be a citizen of the United States and that not more than 325 acres shall be sold to one person.

The proceeds of the sale of the reservation lands in conformity with this act and its provisions are to be paid into the treasury of the United States and from there to the Indians and other persons holding tribal rights. These payments are to be made as follows:

"At the end of one year from the date of the throwing open of said lands for entry such sums of money as have been expended by the United States government in the administration of the survey, classification of lands and such other incidental expenses as shall have been necessarily incurred in the administration of the trust hereby created by this act for the disposal of said lands, shall be deducted from the amount of moneys at that time received from the sale of said lands, and the remaining sum shall be divided among such persons holding tribal relations with said Indians, share and share alike. At the end of each succeeding year such sums of money as may then be in the treasury to the credit of said Indians arising from the sale of said lands shall be divided among all persons entitled to share in such distribution as aforesaid, share and share alike, for the period of four successive years. In each succeeding year after the expiration of the period of four years last mentioned there shall be divided among said Indians, as hereinbefore mentioned, all moneys then remaining in the treasury arising from the sales of said lands, such last-mentioned payments not to exceed, however, the sum of $30 per capita for any one year."

The bill is of much importance to Missoula. The citizens should take some means of showing that the proposition has their approval. Such action would doubtless have some weight, and every little helps.

* * * * * * * * *

Favorable Comment for Mr. Dixon's Bill
Talk of Holding a Business Men's Meeting.
Opening of Reservation
Measure Would Add Much to the Available Land of Western Montana — Plan Is Regarded as Eminently Practicable.

Missoula, Dec. 28. — Since the Standard published the terms of the bill introduced in congress by Representative Dixon for the opening of the Flathead reservation, there has been in Missoula a considerable amount of discussion of the measure, which meets with general approval. The suggestion which has been made that the business men and property owners of Missoula prepare and sign a statement indorsing the scheme has found favor, and it is likely that there will be prepared some document of this sort to be forwarded to Mr. Dixon.

The opening of the reservation would add to the available land in Western Montana a valley of incomparable agricultural possibilities and an immense area of fine grazing land. It is all well watered and is not remote from railway communication.

The plan suggested in the Dixon bill is regarded as eminently practicable, provided the men who are appointed on the commission to deal with the land question are men who are familiar with the conditions which exist and who are acquainted with the Indians. The chief trouble has been in the past, when efforts have been made to secure the opening of the reserve that men have been sent to treat with the Indians who had never seen a red man in a blanket and who knew less about the reservation than they did about Mars. Added to this, is the fact that the Indians have been so often deceived by the government's representatives that they are naturally suspicious of any new proposition, fearing that they will be robbed of the little that they have left.

The matter is of much importance to Missoula, and it would certainly do no harm to take it up locally. A statement from Missoula would serve to show that the measure has the indorsement of those who are best acquainted with the situation.

Document 40

Dixon Seeks Support for Allotment from Tribal Mixed Bloods
December 1903 — January 1904

Source: Joseph Dixon to Allen Sloane, December 19, 1903; Joseph Dixon to Angus P. McDonald, December 19, 1903; Joseph Dixon to Duncan McDonald, December 19, 1903; D. McDonald to Joseph Dixon, December 29, 1903; Joseph Dixon to Michael Pablo, December 19, 1903; Michael Pablo to Joseph Dixon, [December 1903]; Joseph Dixon to Joseph Allard, December 19, 1903; and Joseph Allard to Joseph Dixon, January 2, 1904, Joseph Dixon Papers, MSS 55, Toole Archives, Mansfield Library, University of Montana, Missoula.

Editors' note: Joseph Dixon did write selected Flathead Reservation mixed bloods about his bill to open the reservation, but he was also careful to point out that a recent U.S. Supreme Court decision meant that Congress could impose its will on Indians without tribal consent. Of those Dixon consulted, Michael Pablo was too busy with his cattle to consider the proposal; Duncan McDonald seemed to be resigned to the policy; and only Joseph Allard endorsed it. Typographical and spelling errors have not been corrected.

December 19, 1903

Allen Sloane
Ronan, Montana
My dear Sir:

I am sending you by this mail a copy of the bill introduced by me to open the Flathead Reservation. You people are the ones most directly interested and I want you after reading it to write me your views of the matter.

Under the decision of the Supreme Court in the Lone Wolf case, it is not longer necessary to have a treaty with the Indians before opening Reservations. I sent it better to open the Flathead while it is in the hands of it friends, than to wait longer and have it done by starngers. Under the terms of the bill the Commission will be composed of two persons holding tribal relations with the Flatheads, two white men and one Agent of the Indian Bureau here. I believe this bill will give the Flatheads four times as much money for their lands as other Indians in the Northwest have received.

Write me what your views are in the matter and any changes you think will improve the bill, and oblige.

Yours very truly,
[Joseph M. Dixon]

[No reply from Sloan in files.]

* * * * * * * * *
* * * * * * * * *

December 19, 1903

Angus P. McDonald
Plains, Montana
My dear Sir:

I am sending you under separate cover copy of the bill introduced by me to open the Reservation. I want you to read it and then write me fully your suggestions of the matter, fully and freely. The sentiment here is that all of the Indian Reservations must be thrown open to settlement in the near future and I have tried to prepare this bill, so as to give the Indian the say in the matter, the same as the Government.

You will notice that the Commission provides two indians, two white men and one Special Agent of the Indian Bureau to classify and appraise the lands. If the bill passes, I shall be glad to see the Chiefs and head men pick out two of your braniest men to act on the proposed Commission. I presume you would naturally be one of them. My own notion is that under the terms of this bill the indians will get three times and I think five times as much for their lands as on other Reservations in the west. The great difficulty with me is, what is the best way, for the indian, to dispose of his money. Should it be paid to him in a lump sum, as the lands are sold, or should it be held by the government in trust, at four per cent and the interest only, for the next few years be paid to them? Or should it be paid out in equal annuities extending over, say, twenty five years? You are the people interested in this matter and I wish that you would give me your conservative views in the case and make any suggestions that you think will be for the best. The only thing I wouldent want to hear you say is "That we dont want it opened at all." As I said in the first of this letter, it is only a question of a very short time until all of the Reservations will be opened and wouldent it be better to do so now, while you have the matter in the hands of yourself and friends than wait later on and take chances of strangers doing it. Under the decision in the Lone Wolf case, by the U.S. Supreme Court, you know that a treaty is no longer necessary with the indinas. Congress has the piwer to legislate as it sees fit.

Assuring you that I sahh appreciate any suggestions you may see fit to make in the matter. . . .

There has been a bill introduced in the Senate, here, to unload two hundred Chippewas on the Flathead Reservation. I have been opposing the move, as I dont think you will want them. I understand they are a band that have been roaming all over eastern Montana and are poor, starving and full of small pox etc.

Yours very truly,
[Joseph M. Dixon]

[No reply from Angus P. McDonald in files.]

* * * * * * * * *

* * * * * * * * *

December 19, 1903

Duncan McDonald,
Ravalli, Montana
Dear Sir:

I am senidng you by this mail copy of the bill introduced by me to open the Flathead Reservation.

After you have read it, kindly make any suggestions you think for the best in the matter. You will notice the provision making the commission compoed of two indians, two white men and one Agent of the Indian Bureau here. Under the terms of this bill I believe the Flatheads will received five times the amount of money that other indains are getting for their lands.

In the decision of the Supreme Court in the Lone Wolf case, you know that a treaty is no longer necessary to open Reservations. Is it not better to open the Flathead while it can be handled by friends than leave it to starngers in the future.

Yours very truly,
[Joseph M. Dixon]

* * * * * * * * *

Ravalli, Montana
Dec. 29, 1903

Jos. M. Dixon
Washington, D.C.
Dear Sir:

Yours is to hand & contents noted regarding the opening of the Flathead Indian Reserve. I must confess and say personally that I never was in favor of Indian Reserves it is only building up nests for Indian Agents. Indians would be better of if they got their lands years ago if honrest officials to look after them instead of having reserves for white people to fleece the poor Indian. It is for this reason I think is bad for the redman. Unless the Indian had exclusive right only the pure Indian under the jurisdiction of an honest man. To show what a bungling habit the Government way of appointed Indian Agents is nominated by Corporations or Society then they approve it. In stead of the tribes nominating by general council of their choice as their agent. Further more the policy of the government is not to allow any member of their own to be their agent no matter how honest he is. I think if they have one of their own things would be more satisfactory to the Indian & the people of the state. The government have inspectors to check or dismiss any man who would be dishonest both with the Govnet or Indians.

I have no suggestions to make only that I am dissatisfied and disgusted and have to take my medicine. You mention the decision of the U.S. Supreme Court in the Lone Wolf case. This affair is the last decision, but in former years the U.S. Supreme Court always decides that Indian reserves was an Indian Country. it always been that way for many years past I presume since the government started. I venture to say if three or four members of the Supreme Court should die. And others get in they are just as liable to decide as the decisions of former Courts. This puts me in mind of Uncle Salm planting troops in Columbia Soil to stop that government from stopping the revolution be cause she wants some one to make treaty as an excuse to gobble the Cannal them from there God only Knows where she will gobble until As poor Spain did about 400 years ago the grandest Empire at that time and where is she to day. pretty near out of existence. Of course as I said before longer it drags worse it will be for the Indian in case when time comes to take their allotments As it ~~will be that~~ is their best land is taken by some one who is about 1/8 or 1/16 Indian blood and from some portion of the Country. The Chipiwaes I think will be opposed as for myself I would do my best to oppose. Bye the way Chief Joseph was here with me for couple of days. I think figuring to come if permitted. This band I am satisfied would be permitted by the Indians if a general Council was called. It is too bad for him. He is in Colville reserve but the Colville Indians are like the dog in the manger will not allow Joseph people to select land to farm. As Joseph had enough war he would rather suffer with his band than raise a disturbance among the Indians who were there before him. Now my Hon Dear Sir you know your affairs and know us as well as any man in the State. give us justice. I notice all governments are stretching right and left on account of commerce for their people. The Red Man must stretch and follow suit to squeeze the last nickel from Uncle Salm for the benefit of his own race only in Smaller scale. In case you are opposed. Could you get the mineral land oppened this would be the wedge. . . .

Yours,
D. McDonald

P.S. White Indians are ~~the~~ opposing and influencing the Indian.

* * * * * * * * *
* * * * * * * * *

December 19, 1903

Michael Pablo
Ronan, Montana
Dear Sir:

I am sending you by this mail a copy of the bill introduced by me for the opening of the Flathead Reservation. I shall be glad to receive any suggestions that you may wish to make in the matter, as you are the ones interested.

By the tersm of the bill, you will notice, that the proposed Commission is to consist of two Indians, two white men and one agent of the Indian Bureau here. Under the tersm of the bill I believe the Flatheads will receive four times as much for their lands as the other indians of the Northwest have for theirs.

Under the decision of the Supreme Court in the Lone Wolf Case, it is no longer necessary to have a treaty with the indians before opening the Reservations. Congress no[w] has the power to act. Is it not better to open the Flathead while it is in the hands of its friends than wiat later for strangers to do so?

I shall be glad to have you write me any thing you wish regarding the matter.

Yours very truly,
[Joseph M. Dixon]

* * * * * * * * *

Ronan, Montana
[December 1903]

Joseph M. Dixon
Washington, D.C.
Dear Sir:

I have Received a Copy of the Bill Which you have introduced in the house. For the opening of the Flat Head Reservation and have Read with much Interest its Contents.

Being at the present time ve[r]y Busy With the Winter care of my cattle. I have Been unable to Consult my Friend With a View of Offering any suggestions with Regards To the Bill. In some future time I Will take much pleasure in addressing you on the subject I have the honor To Remain,

very truly yours,
Michael Pablo

* * * * * * * * *
* * * * * * * * *

December 19, 1903

Joseph Allard
Ronan, Montana
My dear Sir:

I am sending you by this mail copy of the bill intriduced by me to open the Reservation. Under its terms you will notice the Commission will be composed of two persons now holding tribal relations with the Flatheads, two white men and one agent of the Indian Bureau here.

I believe that under this bill the indians will receive four times as much for their lands as the other indians in the Northwest have for theirs. It is only a question of a few years until all the Reservations must be thrown open and is it not better to do so now while it is in the hands of its friends than wait later on for starngers to handle it?

Under the decision of the Supreme Court in the Lone Wolf case, you know it is no longer necessary to have a treaty with the Indians, as Congress now has the power to act direct.

I shall be glad to have you write me any suggestions that you see fit to make in the matter, for you are the ones most directly interested.

Yours very truly,
[Joseph M. Dixon]

* * * * * * * * *

St. Ignatius, Montana
Jan. 2, 1904

Joseph M. Dixon
Washington, D.C.
Dear Sir,

Yours of a few days at hand and must say I am glad to hear of the allotment scheme It could not take effect any too soon to suit me But I fear that the Indians will not give their consent at first and perhaps that Congress will finally have to act direct I have spoken to quiet a number of the leading members of the tribes and all they could say is that we don't want to open our reserve.

I have no suggestions in particular, only that we don't want those Chipiwais on here as we have already had a sample of them here and ~~it is~~ it was misery from the beginning to end. The only way the Government can unload these Indians here is by force that is without our consent for that would never be granted for such.

Well Jos, when the time comes for the appointment of commissioners I hope that you will not forget to drop in a word or two for me and as it stands I'll do my best to show the Indians the advantages of being alloted.

Yours,
Joseph Allard.

Document 41

White Men Fixated on Lewis and Clark

December 20, 1903

Source: "When the Flatheads First Saw White Men," *The Anaconda Standard*, December 20, 1903, part 3, page 2, col. 1-3.

Editors' note: White men felt that Salish tribal history revolved around the meeting between the Indians and the white explorers in Ross' Hole. This account recorded Salish Chief Victor's widow's memories of the encounter.

When the Flatheads First Saw White Men

One of the best known of the Flathead Indians, who lived so long in the Bitter Root valley, was Mother Victor, wife of the famous old chief of this tribe. Mother Victor had many warm friends among the whites, and the older residents of the valley speak with unstinted praise of this remarkable woman. The late Major McCormick was one of these friends and Maj. John B. Catlin of Missoula, who formerly resided at Stevensville, was another. Mother Victor was a woman of high intelligence and had great influence with her husband's people. This influence was always for their good and they regarded her with a degree of respect that is unusual among Indians toward a woman.

Just how old Mother Victor was when she died is not known, but it is said by those who knew her well that she was nearly 100. Her mind remained clear to the last and her reminiscences of the life of her people during her childhood have contributed largely to the knowledge that is possessed of this tribe. She had a wonderful memory and to those whom she trusted she talked freely.

Major Catlin relates one incident which is deeply interesting in connection with Mother Victor. In company with Major McCormick, who was then in the newspaper business, he visited Mother Victor at her home. They were accompanied by an interpreter, their purpose being to obtain from the old woman an account of her first sight of white men. Mother Victor was then more than 90 years old, but, as has been stated, she retained her mental faculties in her old age, and the story was one that she had told so often that she had the incidents well in mind and was able to give a clear statement.

"The face of the old woman brightened when we asked her if she remembered the first white men that she saw," said Major Catlin, in relating the incident. "She gave vigorous assent and was perfectly willing to tell us the story for which we asked. She talked rapidly and the interpreter was kept busy with his translation."

The first whites that the Flathead Indians saw were those in the Lewis and Clarke party, which passed through the Bitter Root in 1805. The meeting took place in Ross' Hole, where the Indians were camped on a hunting expedition. Mother Victor was then a child of 5 or 6 years and was with her people.

It was in the afternoon that the explorers and their party came down the hills from the Big Hole divide. The Indians saw them a long way off and at first thought they were a party of Indians from some of the Eastern Montana tribes. As the party neared the valley, however, they saw that its members were strange beings, the like of whom they had never seen before. The cry went up that the new arrivals were gods — their white skins and peculiar dress adding to the belief that the approaching visitors had come from another world.

Silently and reverently the Flatheads watched the approach of the whites. No hostile movement was thought of. Curiosity was the predominant feeling among the redmen and, with their s.... and children, they awaited developments. The movements of the whites convinced the watchers that no attack was to be made — the visitors must be emissaries from somewhere or somebody — who, they knew not. They could only wonder.

The white expedition made its way down the slope to the rich bottom land of the basin and proceeded to make camp. The site for the camp was selected near a watercourse, and not far away was some fallen timber, small trees mostly, which lay where the wind had dropped it. While the tents were being pitched the cook proceeded to prepare for his work. This cook was a coal-black negro, and the contrast between him and the white men added to the amazement of the Indians. This cook went to where a small tree lay on the ground, and, wrenching it from its stump, put it upon his shoulder and carried it to where he was to build his fire. This feat of strength added anew to the mystery surrounding the strangers. This black man of prodigious strength must be more than human. Long after they had become familiar with the white men the Indians retained their superstitious regard for the negro. At first they dared not approach him, and it required much argument on the part of the whites to convince them that this man was only a man.

Toward evening the Indian hunters returned to camp, and the formal meeting of the two races took place. The whites came to the Indian camp from their own, and, making the peace sign, accepted the invitation extended to them to sit beside the fire. Seated around the blazing logs with their Indian hosts, the whites produced tobacco which they shared with the Indians. This was the first tobacco that the Flatheads had ever seen. For the first time they placed it in their pipes, which had heretofore held the herbs which had been their "Lady Nicotine."

Convinced of the good intentions of their visitors, the Indians still regarded them with curiosity. They noted that their guests had no blankets and, discussing the matter among themselves, decided that the whites had been attacked and robbed in the hostile Indian country across the range. They must be destitute, they thought. At a word from their chief, Indian women advanced to where the white men sat and threw over their shoulders choice robes of buffalo and deer skin. It was an act characteristic of the kindly spirit that had almost invariably marked the Flathead Indians, except when they have been led away from their natural tendencies by malicious and meddling whites.

The whites and Indians exchanged visits for several days and became well acquainted. From this visit dates the friendship of the Flatheads for the whites, which has always continued. That the Indians made a good impression upon their visitors is shown by the reference contained in the journals of the expedition. Sergeant Gass, one of the members of the expedition, in his diary wrote: "To the honor of the Flatheads who live on the west side of the Rocky mountains we must mention them as an exception. They are the only nation on the whole route where anything like chastity is regarded."

Some accounts of the Flatheads state that they saw white men as early as 1742, when some French explorers reached the eastern slope of the Rocky mountains. This was near the headwaters of the Missouri. If these explorers met any of the Flatheads, it must have been a very small party of the tribe, as Mother Victor was positive in her assertion that the meeting in Ross' Hole was the first one between her people and the whites.

Document 42

Killing of Amelo Was in Self-Defense

December 31, 1903

Source: "Killing of Amelo Was in Self-Defense," *The Anaconda Standard*, December 31, 1903, page 12, col. 1.

Editors' note: Alcohol fueled violence on the reservation resulted in the death of Amelo in 1903. Louis Flying Bird, the young shooter, was freed on grounds of self-defense. Such news dominated newspaper coverage of the tribes because the cases were tried off the reservation in the white court system.

Killing of Amelo Was in Self-Defense
United States Commissioner Smith Listens to Facts.
Louis Flying Bird Is Free
Story of Witnesses Tends to Show That Boy Shot in Order to Save His Own Life — Believed Father Had Been Killed.

Missoula, Dec. 30. — Louis Flying Bird, the 14-year-old Indian lad who shot and killed John Amelo on the Flathead reservation, had a hearing before United States Commissioner Smith this morning and was acquitted of the charge of murder. The boy's father, John Deer, Petol, Aneas, Henry Matt and Major Smead were witnesses, and Matt also acted as interpreter. Attorneys W. F. Bailey and Carl Rice examined the witnesses, and Attorney Harry Parsons defended the prisoner. Commissioner Smith, after hearing the testimony, decided that Flying Bird had shot old man Amelo in self-defense and was justified. Flying Bird is once more a free Indian. The story of the affair as deduced from the testimony taken at the hearing is substantially as follows:

Louis Flying Bird, his father, Petol and Aneas were asleep in a cabin on Camas prairie on the reservation. About 11 o'clock at night Amelo broke into the house. He was drunk and had a bottle of whiskey with him. He asked old man Flying Bird to take a drink, and upon his refusal to do so Amelo pried the neck of the bottle between Flying Bird's teeth and poured whiskey down his throat. He then made his brag that he had killed one man that day and that old man Flying Bird would be the next victim. Amelo was ordered from the house. He went out and returned with a large club. He chased Flying Bird out of the house to an Indian tepee.

At the tepee Amelo grabbed hold of the old man's two braids of hair, taking a braid in each hand, and tried to twist his head off. At this stage of the game the boy Louis came up and tried to defend his father. Amelo grabbed for the boy, and the old man got loose. The old man ran to a barn near by. Louis ran toward the cabin with Amelo after him. They met Petol coming out of the cabin. Amelo picked up an axe and struck at Petol, hitting him with the handle on the back of the neck, knocking him unconscious, in which condition he remained for several hours.

Amelo ran into the house, where he found Louis Flying Bird, at the same time saying to him: "You are a dead kid now." Louis believing that his father had been killed and that Petol also had been killed, thought himself in immediate danger. He found a gun, took aim at Amelo and shot him in the head, the bullet taking effect just behind the ear.

Document 43

Two Flathead Indians Arrested in Death of Little Coyote January 1904

Source: "Charged with Murder of Indian," *The Anaconda Standard*, January 5, 1904, page 12, col. 1-2; "The Missoula River Gives Up Its Dead," *The Anaconda Standard*, January 7, 1904, page 12, col. 3; "Little Coyote Met Death by Drowning," *The Anaconda Standard*, January 12, 1904, page 12, col. 4-5.

Editors' note: Little Coyote or Louis Coyote came to Missoula, got drunk, and then either fell or was pushed off the bank into the river where he drowned. Two other reservation Indians, Joe Arlee and Eneas Granjoe, were originally arrested and charged with murder. Since conclusive evidence was lacking, the two Indians were released and the truth about the death was never discovered.

Charged with Murder of Indian
Joe Arlee and Eneas Granjoe Arrested and Lodged in the Jail at the Jocko Agency
— More Evidence of Foul Play Is Found — River Being Dragged.

Missoula, Jan. 4. — Joe Arlee and Eneas Granjoe are confined in the jail at the Jocko agency, charged with the murder of the Indian, Little Coyote, or, as he is known on the reservation, Louis Coyote, who disappeared near Missoula last week as already told in the Standard. Major Smead and the Indian friends of the missing man are satisfied that these two are the men who threw the Indian into the river. A searching party from the reservation is at work along the river below the spot where Coyote's trail led to the bank and disappeared, hoping to find his remains. In the party are a brother and a nephew of the missing man, and his wife also returned from the agency to watch the search.

The river has been partly dragged this afternoon, and the search will be continued to-morrow. The party this afternoon found Coyote's hat in some brush on the island near the point where his trail led to the steep bank over which he is supposed to have fallen or been thrown. His metal hat band was found near where the fight occurred at the Indian camp. On the river bank below the camp are blood stains in the snow, which the Indians found to-day by carefully sweeping off the fresh snow. These are all the clews that have been discovered to-day.

From the Indians who are in the searching party it was learned to-night that Coyote left the reservation alone. He is supposed to have had some money, and it has been learned that he fell in with Joe Arlee, Eneas Granjoe, Alex Finlay and others, with whom he drank considerable. On Tuesday night these Indians visited the Cree camp, above the old slaughter house, where they gambled with the Crees. Joe Arlee and Coyote had trouble, and a fight started in the tent. They went outside and the quarrel was renewed. Coyote was badly beaten, it is said, and was last seen going down the river to the lower camp with his companions. He has not been seen since. Acting upon this information, the searchers are at work.

The water is filled with slush ice and in some places is very swift; so the work of dragging is slow and tedious. Coyote's widow sits on the bank and watches every movement, rolling and smoking cigarettes in a nervous way, seldom speaking. John Daily says that a half-breed, who he learned afterward was Joe Blodgett, fell into the river Tuesday near the slaughterhouse and was nearly drowned. He was very drunk and was washed down the river a long distance before he could get out. He climbed up on the bank and came out to the road through the Mitchell ranch. Sidney Mitchell saw him and knew him. He had been sobered by his experience and came back toward town. It is possible that these incidents may have some connection with the Coyote affair.

* * * * * * * * *

The Missoula River Gives Up Its Dead
Body of Little Coyote Found by Searchers.
Nothing to Show Murder
Corpse Is Located in Still Water Below Place on Bank Where Blood Stains Were Found — Autopsy Reveals That Man Was Drowned.

Missoula, Jan. 6. — The body of Little Coyote, or Louie Coyote, the Indian who has been missing for a week, was found this forenoon in the Missoula river by the reservation searching party, which, under the direction of Joseph Pierre, a nephew of the dead man, has been dragging the stream for two days. The grappling hooks caught in the clothing of the body, which was drawn to the surface and laid upon the bank to await the arrival of the coroner. The body was found in some still water, about 100 feet below the place on the bank where blood stains were found and where, according to the theory, Little Coyote went into the river either by accident or through the criminal acts of his companions on the night that his carouse ended in a fight with Joe Arlee.

There were only slight scratches and bruises on the body and nothing to show that he had been murdered before being thrown into the river.

An autopsy performed by Drs. Buckley and Pixley revealed the fact that Little Coyote drowned, there being water in the lungs. Coroner Lucy brought the body to town, where it was viewed by a jury impaneled for an inquest. After the remains had been examined by the jury they were prepared for burial and were to-night shipped to Arlee, where the funeral will be held. The inquest will be continued Saturday, when it is expected witnesses will be present from the reservation.

The finding of the body has stopped a lot of talk that has been current here for several days. The Standard has been the subject of a good deal of joking since it published the news of the disappearance of Little Coyote and advanced the theory that he had been thrown into the river. None of the local officers paid any attention to the matter, evidently regarding it as a hoax, with the exception of Constable White, who has aided in the search for the body.

After the body had been found there was sudden activity on the part of some of these officers, and to-night they are not laughing at the Standard as much as they were. The fact that the body was found just below the place where blood stains were found in the snow leads to the conclusion that Coyote and Arlee renewed their fight there and Coyote either fell or was thrown into the river. The bank at this place is very steep and about 20 feet above the stream. The blood stains in the snow were found about four feet from the brink of the steep slope. Coroner Lucy has summoned witnesses and will investigate the matter thoroughly.

* * * * * * * * *

Little Coyote Met Death by Drowning
Verdict Rendered by the Coroner's Jury.
Indians Give Testimony
Physician Says Examination Showed That the Indian's Lungs Were Filled With Water — Joe Arlee and Eneas Granjoe Discharged.

Missoula, Jan. 11. — The coroner's jury that was inquiring into the cause of the death of Little Coyote, the Indian who was found in the Missoula river a few days ago, held a long session to-day. The town was filled with Flathead Indians, who came to attend the inquest and give what testimony they could. It was difficult work taking the testimony of the Indians, and County Attorney Hall and Coroner Lucy were very diligent in their search for facts which might lead to some conclusion throwing light upon the mysterious affair. The impression given by most of the Indian witnesses was that Little Coyote had come to his death through his own carelessness. At 4 o'clock this afternoon the jury rendered its verdict, finding that Little Coyote had come to his death by drowning by means unknown to the jury. The jury was composed of Dr. C. W. Lombard, L. F. Keim, Samuel Reed, C. Dinsmore, Charles Shellady and John Veeder. After the verdict of the jury the two Indians, Joe Arlee and Eneas Granjoe, who had been arrested and charged with the crime of killing Little Coyote, were discharged from jail.

Dr. Charles Pixley was one of the principal witnesses at the morning session. He told of having made an examination of the body after Little Coyote had been found in the river. He said that after making the post mortem examination he had concluded that Coyote came to his death by drowning, as the lungs were filled with water.

Harry [Henry] Matt, from the reservation, acted as interpreter for the Indian witnesses who could not talk English. Mary Finley testified to a fight that occurred in the Indian camp west of Missoula on the night of Dec. 27, between Little Coyote and Joe Arlee. She said she had assisted in separating the men and that after the fight they seemed to be friendly. Paul Lumphrey corroborated her testimony, and said he also assisted in separating the Indians. The night that this fight occurred was the night on which Little Coyote disappeared and a theory has been advanced by many who had made a study of the case that the fight was continued later and that possibly Arlee had pushed Coyote into the river.

Joe Arlee admitted having had the fight with Coyote, but said they were friends following the fight. He said that Coyote was under the influence of liquor. He said he and Coyote and a Cree Indian, Shot-Through-the-Ears, and Eneas Granjoe started west toward the Cree camp, walking together. After they had gone a few yards the Cree and Granjoe turned back to their tent, and later Arlee turned back also. He went to his tent and Coyote went on west. Arlee claims that he prepared to go to bed at that time and that about 10 minutes after he heard an Indian yelling, and he thought it was Coyote. That was the last he heard of Coyote. He said he did not know whether Coyote had any money. He had seen him gambling in the early part of the evening and he had lost a dollar. He said he did not believe the Cree and Granjoe joined Coyote after turning back to their tent. The next morning the Crees told him Coyote had disappeared.

Chief Antoine Moiese was one of the principal witnesses and advanced the theory that Coyote had been murdered. He said he came to Missoula the day after Coyote disappeared and made a search for the missing Indian. He testified to having found marks in the snow below the camp. which would indicate that there had been a struggle, and said he found at the same place a few blood stains. He said this place was about six yards from the river. He introduced a black felt hat as testimony, saying that he had found the hat some distance below this spot on the opposite side of the river. He found tracks leading into the river from the place where the struggle had been indicated, and on the opposite side where the hat was picked up he found the tracks of a man's shoe. He advanced the theory that the man who wore the black hat had thrown Coyote into the river and he then had entered the water and swam to the opposite shore, where he lost the hat.

Eneas Granjoe told practically the same story of the events of the night when Coyote disappeared as Arlee did, and advanced the theory that Coyote fell into the river on account of his being drunk.

Sam Vincent testified to having seen Eneas Granjoe the next morning, and Granjoe displayed a handful of money. Attorney Harry Parsons explained that he had loaned Eneas $4.50 the day before. Some witnesses were recalled, but nothing important was brought out in the testimony.

Document 44

Adolph Barnaby Charged with Bringing Whiskey on Reservation January 20, 1904

Source: "Firewater on Reservation," *The Missoulian* (daily), January 20, 1904, page 6, col. 3.

Editors' note: Adolph Barnaby was arrested by the Indian police and charged with bringing alcohol onto the Flathead Reservation. Barnaby claimed he was bringing the whiskey back to the reservation to share with his friends at a New Year's Day celebration, not to sell it.

Firewater on Reservation
Indian Held to Court for Introducing It on Prohibited District.
Is Captured with Difficulty
Mendes, Chief of Indian Police, Has a Desperate Struggle With the Suspected Red.

Adolph Barnaby, a Flathead Indian, was arraigned yesterday afternoon before United States Commissioner Wallace P. Smith on the two counts of introducing and attempting to introduce one gallon each of whisky and alcohol into the reservation on December 30, last. The defendant pleaded not guilty, but was held for the federal grand jury at Helena in default of $200 bail.

Only one witness testified at the brief trial, Joe Mesmes [Mestes], chief of the Indian police at the Jocko agency. His story, in substance was that on the day in question he had received a message from Major Smead instructing him to go to a point between Evaro and Arlee, on the reservation road, and there to await the coming of Adolph Barnaby and Louie Asherton [Ashley], who were expected to pass that way that night, with whisky in their possession. Joe deputized Clerk Holland of the agency, and together they proceeded to Evaro, where they took supper in plain view of the road.

Hear Horses Coming.

Within five minutes after they were through, Joe, who had gone outside heard horses approaching and proceeded to meet them. The first horse bore Asherton, who, on being commanded to halt and dismount by the chief, refused and put spurs to his animal, escaping in spite of the two shots sent after him. He was captured later. Chief Joe then seized the pommel of the saddle of Barnaby's animal and told him to dismount. For answer he received a hard kick in the face, which partly stunned him. He clubbed his rifle and at once struck Barnaby over the head with the stock, felling him to the ground. The whisky and alcohol was contained in two gallon jugs tied to the saddle. Barnaby was not badly stunned and rose up immediately, making for Chief Joe with a whisky flask, with which he struck him behind the ear. The officer then got his billy and hit Barnaby repeatedly until he got him down.

Barnaby is a very tall man, standing probably 6 feet, 2 inches, and gave the chief all kinds of trouble before he was finally jailed at Jocko. He was brought to Missoula yesterday.

Barnaby made no defense, and refused to engage a lawyer, merely remarking that he did not see why he was not allowed to have whisky in his possession when the government allowed a certain Chinaman to take it on the reservation. He further remarked that he intended to use the whisky on New Year's day for celebrating the advent of 1904 with some of his friends, and that he had no intention of selling it for cash. These were merely off-hand statements, however, the defendant making no effort to save himself and waiving all testimony in his own behalf. Ashley, who was later arrested by Gebo [Gebeau] and Holland, is now confined in jail at Helena, awaiting trial.

Editors' note: While in jail at Helena, Adolph Barnaby drew six drawings with crayon and pencil on paper. The image reproduced here appears to be the earliest depiction of an Arlee Fourth of July Powwow. Source: Untitled (Dance Arbor), Adolph Barnaby, crayon, paper & pencil on paper, ca. 1904, Courtesy of Montana Historical Society Museum, Helena, 1988.05.05. The original is in color.

Document 45

Laurence Finley Charged with Assaulting His Brother's Wife February 26, 1904

Source: "Finley Is Bound Over," *The Missoulian* (daily), February 26, 1904, page 8, col. 4.

Editors' note: Laurence or Larry Finley had a long history of trouble with law enforcement on the reservation. For more about Finley's legal problems see Peter Ronan, *"A Great Many of Us Have Good Farms": Agent Peter Ronan Reports on the Flathead Indian Reservation, Montana, 1877-1887,* ed. by Robert J. Bigart (Pablo, Mont.: Salish Kootenai College Press, 2014), page 400.

Finley Is Bound Over

Mrs. John Finley Swears That He Brutally Assaulted Her at Her Home.

Laurence Finley, the Flathead Indian, who stands charged with having committed an assault upon his brother's wife upon the night of January 31, had his preliminary hearing before United States Commissioner Wallace P. Smith yesterday and was bound over in the sum of $1,000 to answer to the United Stattes [sic] federal grand jury.

Major Smead, superintendent of the Flathead agency; George H. Bailey, United States District attorney; United States Deputy Marshal Elderkin and Chief of Indian Police Matts were present at the trial and there were a number of the Indians from the agency, witnesses and spectators interested in the case.

The story of the assault as told by the witnesses in the case was printed in the Missoulian at the time the crime was alleged to have been committed, and details are almost too revolting for belief.

Mrs. John R. Finley, the chief prosecuting witness, stated that on the night of January 31 her husband was absent from home, having been called to the mission in the afternoon and did not return until midnight. She had been entertaining company throughout the day, and when it came time to retire for the night, she drew the curtains and prepared to go to bed.

Woman Spurned Him.

Laurence Finley, the defendant, who occupied a room upstairs, came down and made advances to her which she repulsed. Her persisted and, finding that she spurned him, accomplished his purpose by force. Mrs. Finley was just recovering from a spell of sickness and was in no condition to make an effective resistance, and, as the house was in a sparsely settled neighborhood, there was no hope of arousing anyone to come to her aid.

Mrs. Finley further testified that about a year ago her brother-in-law had made a similar attempt on her and as a result of this her husband had driven him away from the house.

When the defendant was put upon the stand he endeavored to show that the charge was brought against him out of spite and revenge. According to his story, Mrs. Finley consented to his proposition, with the object of making the charge in order to be revenged on her husband, who, according to the defendant, was guilty of improper conduct with other women of the reservation.

After hearing the testimony, Commissioner Smith bound the defendant over to the Federal court for trial, fixing his bond at $1,000.

Finley is an ex-convict, having been recently released from Deer Lodge, after serving a ten years' sentence.

Lawrence Finley
Source: Montana State Prison Records, State Microfilm 36, reel 10, vol. 6, page 41, Archives, Montana Historical Society, Helena, Montana

Document 46

Compea Charged in Murder of Three Wood Cocks February 26, 1904

Source: "Compea Hearing on Murder Charge," *The Anaconda Standard*, February 26, 1904, page 12, col. 1-2.

Editors' note: William Compea was charged with killing Antoine Three Wood Cocks in a fight over alleged adultery. Compea was bound over to federal court. The case was alcohol fueled violence.

Compea Hearing on Murder Charge
Indian Appears Before Commissioner Smith to Answer to the Charge of Killing Antoine Three Wood Cocks and Is Bound Over to the Federal Court.
Changes His Story Told at First.

Missoula, Feb. 25. — William Compea, the Flathead Indian charged with the murder of Antoine Three Wood Cocks on Camas prairie on Wednesday night, Dec. 27, had a hearing before United States Commissioner Smith to-day and was bound over to await the action of the United States court. He will probably be tried in Helena some time during the month of May. At the trial to-day Attorney General George H. Bailey represented the government and Attorney Harry H. Parsons of Missoula appeared for Compea. The testimony of witnesses was very conflicting, and Compea did not stick to the story of the tragedy he had previously told to Chief Clerk Holland of the Indian agency. Henry Matt acted in the capacity of interpreter, and Major Smead of the reservation was present to testify as to whether the witnesses and those connected with the case were wards of the government. The trial was very interesting and the courtroom was filled with Indians of all descriptions.

Louis Sculnah was the first witness, and testified that before the crime was committed he and John Deer, William Compea and Eneas Downtree, were at Plains and started home together late in the evening in a semi-drunken condition. He and Louis left the other two some place on the prairie and went to a dance. About an hour after this he heard that Compea had killed Cheuck — as Three Wood Cocks was known among the Indians — and he went to the scene of the killing. He said he saw the body of Cheuck and told of seeing the bullet wound in the breast.

John Deer for Government.

John Deer was the principal witness for the government. He stated that he and Compea had gone to the house of Antoine Cheuck and as Compea was in a drunken condition and staggering Cheuck's wife ordered him out of the house. The witness said Compea went out and came back, saying: "Fire me out of the house again." Compea, after some coaxing, again left the place. The witness said he then arranged that himself and Cheuck would go for a ride, and they went away from the house, both on the same horse, Cheuck riding behind him.

Compea came out from the side of the road and met them, and when they were a short distance from the house of Flying Bird Compea said to Antoine: "I know you have been taking my wife right along for your intended wife." The witness further stated that Cheuck emphatically denied this allegation. Other words passed between the two, and Compea pulled his gun and shot at Cheuck, who then got off the horse. The witness said he went on a little and looked back and saw Compea shoot again, but did not know whether he killed Cheuck or not. A chase between Deer and Compea then ensued, and Compea took shots at Deer, but missed him. Both got off their horses and Compea started to chase Deer on foot. Deer said that when he arrived in front of Flying Bird's house he picked up a stick of wood and struck Compea, knocking him down. In conclusion the witness said: "I only struck the man once and then ran home to tell my friends of the affair. My wife went out to the scene of the fight and found Cheuck was dead."

Indian Woman Testifies.

Teresa Jerome, an Indian woman, who was riding horseback near the place the fighting occurred, said she heard a row and also gun reports, and the shooting took place about midnight. She said she recognized the voices of the men as those of Deer, Cheuck and Compea. She said the men had two horses. She also stated that Cheuck did not deny the statement that he had been using Compea's wife as his own, but when Compea charged him with this he admitted it and said he would stay by it like a man.

Magpie testified to seeing the dead body of Cheuck the next day after the fight, and said the bullet went into the breast and came out through the back and the shoulder muscles. She said John Deer was the man who beat Compea.

Eneas Downtree said that at a dance he heard of the quarrel and went to Magpie's place about 2 o'clock in the morning. He saw William lying in the snow near the house, with his head badly beaten up, and apparently unconscious. He made no efforts to help him, but rode home as fast as he could. He did not want to get mixed up in the murder affair.

Story of Defendant.

The defendant, William Compea, had a somewhat different story to tell about the affair. He said that while on the way home from Plains he had given his gun to John Deer, and Deer had kept it until after the time Cheuck was killed. Contrary to the story he told Clerk Holland at the agency, he denied having anything to do with the murder, and stated he did not know who killed Cheuck.

It is known that while confined in jail at the agency he had admitted that he killed Cheuck, and said he did it in self-defense, because Cheuck was the man who assaulted him with the club. On the stand to-day his story was entirely different. He said that John Deer assaulted him and knocked him down, and that shortly after that time he heard two gun reports. He learned Cheuck had been killed, but said he knew nothing whatever about who committed the crime.

The defendant was a pretty sorry looking spectacle in court do-day. One of his eyes was badly blackened and he wore a very noticeable scar on the left side of his mouth, which he said he had received at the time Deer assaulted him. He said the back of his head had been badly bruised. If his story is true he must have been struck more than once, as John Deer would have the court believe. The case was submitted without argument, and it did not take Commissioner Smith long to decide that Compea should stand trial in the United States court.

Document 47

Lawyer Recruits Enrollment Work in Saloon

February 1904

Source: A. L. Demers v. Fred Rouillier, February 6, 1914, Case 4261, Missoula County Court Cases, MS 82, Toole Archives, Mansfield Library, University of Montana, Missoula, box 11, folder 2, pages 13-14.

Editors' note: In early 1904, Fred Roullier was approached by William Q. Ranft, an attorney who was specializing in enrollment cases on the Flathead Reservation, who offered to represent Roullier in applying for enrollment on the reservation. Roullier signed a note agreeing to pay Ranft for getting him enrolled, and in 1914 A. L. Demers was suing Roullier for payment of the money promised Ranft on March 21, 1904.

Q [by Mr. Harry H. Parsons] What did [William Q.] Ranft say to you, in [Alex] Dow's presence, or what did Dow say?

A [Fred Rouillier] Dow talked to us to know if we were on the rolls and asked us if we were going to try to be on the rolls.

Q When was this conversation?

A That was . . .

Q How many conversations did you have with him?

A Two, before we made a bargain.

Q When were they?

A Well, it was about a couple of months before we signed the conracts.

Q Where were they held?

A Right in Missoula, in the saloon, and he told us, he says, "I know a man here that is the only man that can put you on the rolls," he says, "the agent has nothing to do with it," he says, "you give me a thousand dollars and I will put you on the rolls," so we didn't want to do that, we thought it was all "bugs"; we finally found out the agent wouldn't do nothing, — we found out that the agent wouldn't allot anyone, but that Ranft would do with work.

Q How did you find that out?

A By the agent.

Q What agent was that?

A Mr. Bellew. Well, finally we came to make arrangements, and thought we would decide to enroll and they told us that in order for our children and the women to get on the roll we would have to sign a note, you know, for Mr. Ranft and Mr. Dow.

Q How much did you give Ranft?

A $100.00 cash and a $600.00 note, and Alex Dow $350.00 for his work.

Q Well, was anything said, at the time you made the contract with them, was anything said to you about Ranft's being a government officer?

A Yes, he told me he was the only one that could put us on the rolls.

Document 48

Agent Smead to Remove Two Mixed Bloods from Reservation March 23, 1904

Source: W. H. Smead to Commissioner of Indian Affairs, March 23, 1904, letter received 21,470/1904, land division, RG 75, National Archives, Washington, D.C.

Editors' note: Since his appointment as Flathead agent in 1898, Smead had accumulated considerable opposition from tribal members. Some were upset about the resident grazing tax and others were unhappy about the pressure to sell the Indian ponies on the reserve. The Secretary of the Interior sent two inspectors to Flathead to investigate the charges against Smead. They ended up dismissing the charges, but decided Smead needed to be removed in July 1904 because of irregularities they discovered in his use of rations exchanged for building a telephone line between the Jocko Agency and the Ronan Sub-Agency.

Department of the Interior,
United States Indian Service,
Jocko, Flathead Agency, Mont., Mar. 23, 1904.

Hon. Commissioner Indian Affairs,
Washington, D.C.
Sirs: —

I have to request that authority be granted me to remove from the reservation, Mack Couture, and Louie Clairmont Jr.

In explination [sic] of this request will say that I am reliably informed that these two mixed bloods, neither of whose enrollment has been approved by the Department, are the leaders in a plot instigated by a disreputable attorney of Missoula named Parsons, for the purpose of having me removed as Agent of this reservation. From the information at hand, it appears that Parsons, desiring to secure an attorneys fee, has made representation to some of the cattle men, and some of the mixed bloods of class 4 whose enrollment was not approved by the Department, that I was responsible not only for the resident grazing tax, but also for their not having been placed upon the permanent rolls. That for $2000.00, or $2500.00 am not sure which, he would undertake the job, with their assistance, to furnish such evidence as would on presentation to the Department result in my removal from office. The two mixed bloods above named have acted as his agent in this disreputable business and as go-between, between him (Parsons) and some of the cattle men who are afraid to have their connection with this business known. They have raised a large corruption fund from this class of people it appears on Parsons representation that with my removal (of which he is sure) there will be no more grazing tax to pay, and that they can better afford to pay his fee than continue paying grazing tax.

Some time ago I warned Couture and Clairmont to desist from stirring up strife on the reservation and leave attorneys along [alone]. I am however informed that they are still at it, and for this reason I desire the above requested authority and further ask that same be *wired* to me. I feel that the discipline of the reservation demands this, and that the disreputable work in which they are engaged should be broken up immediately.

In view of the above outlined affair, I have to suggest that an inspecting official be sent here at once to look into any real or fancied grieviences [sic] of these mixed bloods. I regret exceedingly to trouble you about this matter, but I am unwilling to have an unprincipled attorney mixed in the affairs of this reservation and stirring up strife and discontent for the sole purpose of making a fat fee, and venting his spleen upon me personally.

Very respectfully,
W. H. Smead
U.S. Indian Agent.

Document 49

Joseph Dixon Gets Flathead Allotment Bill Approved April – May 1904

Source: Excerpt from "Opening of Flathead Reservation Marks End of Strenuous Endeavor," *The Daily Missoulian*, October 2, 1910, page 4, col. 1-3; "The Flathead Bill Passes the House," *The Anaconda Standard*, April 3, 1904, page 1, col. 3; "The Flathead Bill Is Signed by President," *The Anaconda Standard*, April 26, 1904, page 1, col. 6; "Hundreds Welcome Mr. Dixon Home," *The Anaconda Standard*, May 18, 1894, page 14, col. 1-2.

Editors' note: In a 1910 article in *The Daily Missoulian*, Congressman Joseph Dixon explained his political machinations to support the Flathead allotment bill. He was able to get his bill through congress and secure President Theodore Roosevelt's signature in 1904. He had failed to provide for tribal consent to the new policy, but received many accolades from the Missoula residents and businessmen who stood to gain from the forced bargain sale of Flathead Reservation land. Dixon used an obscure provision of the Hellgate Treaty, which probably had not been explained to the chiefs in 1855, to justify the opening. Dixon made no attempt to get the informed consent of the chiefs. Land sales to whites were under federal laws designed to convey public lands to white homesteaders for less than the real value of the land.

Opening of Flathead Reservation Marks End of Strenuous Endeavor Men Who Favored Change and Development of Big Valley Worked Hard and Long to Get the Bill Through Congress and Make Present Situation Possible.

Seven years ago this fall Joseph M. Dixon, then fresh in the lower house of congress, introduced the original bill which proposed to open the Flathead Indian reservation. A few days ago — on September 29, to be exact — the last names were called on the list of eligibles and the last selections of land made, and the last formality enacted in connection with the opening proclamation issued by President Taft. All of which goes to show that the opening of a reservation is not boys' play; that it is a man's job in the full sense of the term, and that it can not be accomplished in a day.

It was early in the session of the fifty-eighth congress that Congressman Dixon first took up the matter of the Flathead opening at Washington. He had drafted a bill and introduced it, and the same had been referred to the proper committee when he was one day called before it to give some information concerning the agreement or treaty that was in existence which might give the government a right to survey and open the Indian's domain. In discussing this and other early circumstances in connection with the opening bill, Senator Dixon talked interestingly a few days ago.

Up a Stump.

"I want to confess," said the senator, "that when I was called upon the first time to back up my eagerness to open the reservation with some authority which made it proper and lawful for the government to take such action, that I was simply up a stump. In my eagerness in planning the opening I had overlooked that important point.

"I have never told this before, but it is a fact that I had to ask more time from the committee and went back to study up the Indian treaties and find a plan of action. I finally got out the old treaty made with the confederated tribes at the time the Bitter Root reserve was exchanged for the Flathead. This was made by Governor Isaac I. Stevens on July 16, 1855. In reading through this I ran across a paragraph which gave me a peg to hang my hat on. I gathered this in with great glee and the next day carried the big book up to the committee, and read it off in as telling a manner as was possible. While there remained some question in my own mind as to whether it would be sufficient, it satisfied the committee and led to the passage of the original opening bill."

The Peg.

The article of the treaty is the sixth one, and reads as follows:

"Article 6 — The president may, from time to time, at his discretion cause the whole or such parts of such reservation as he may think proper, to be surveyed into lots, and assign the same to such individuals or families of said confederated tribes as are willing to avail themselves of the privilege, and will locate on the same as a permanent home, on the same terms and subject to the same regulations as the treaty with Omahas, so far as are provided in the sixth article of the same may be applicable."

The treaty with the Omahas contained the general opening provisions which were applicable in the case of the Flathead reservation in connection with the section quoted.

The Dixon bill was introduced in the fall of 1903. It passed the house on February 21 following and the senate some time in April. The original bill provided for the survey and classification of the land, and held the general opening provisions. It was a new departure in the plan of opening. It was fashioned after no other. It was simply forged in Congressman Dixon's own blacksmith shop. The provision relating to the personnel of the commission to appraise and classify the land put the work into the hands of two representatives from the Indians, a special agent from the Indian office, and two from the outside. This gave the red man better representation than he ever had before and made the bill popular with the Indian's supporters. Theodore Roosevelt said: "That is the fairest Indian bill I have ever seen." The Indian office liked its general make up so well that it was adopted as a standard form. . . .

* * * * * * * *

The Flathead Bill Passes the House
Mr. Dixon of Montana Scores a Neat Victory.
To Open the Reservation
Gentleman From Treasure State Experiences a Strenuous Half-Hour, but in the End Is Successful. Measure an Important One.

Special Dispatch to the Standard.

Washington, April 2. — Representative Dixon scored a brilliant parliamentary victory to-day in obtaining recognition under the unanimous consent rule and securing the immediate passage, despite objections, of his bill designed to open to settlement the Flathead Indian reservation. It was an anxious and strenuous half hour that advocates of the Montana measure experienced after Speaker Cannon determined to recognize about a score of members who were urging the passage of bills. Very soon after the speaker arrived at this decision Representative Madox made the point of no quorum, but subsequently announced, under pressure from several of his colleagues, that he would withhold his motion for half an hour, until a sufficient number of members could be brought back from the Benning race track to complete the quorum.

Mr. Dixon Gets Busy.

Then Representative Fitzgerald, who had raised a dissenting voice while the Flathead bill was under consideration in committee, threatened to object, with the consequence that Mr. Dixon had to cross to the minority side and spend a season of close communion with that gentleman. Mr. Fitzgerald objected to one of the Indians bills introduced by a New York member, but had nothing to say when the Flathead bill was reached. The half hour had almost expired when the Montana bill was reached and, as it was of some length and had to be read, it was not known what would happen, until Minority Leader Williams exercised his good offices and reassured the Montana congressman by saying that the democrats would interpose no obstacles until the vote could be taken on his bill.

Has Smooth Sailing.

The Dixon bill has fared well since its introduction, and its progress through the house had been unusually smooth. The measure had from the beginning commended itself to those interested in the development of the West, and it has also received the support of the Indian Rights association people by reason of the eminently fair manner in which it deals with the allotment of lands to the wards of the government who have rights upon the Flathead reservation. The Standard's correspondent is informed that there are good prospects for the passage of the bill by the senate at this session if Montana people interest themselves in the matter with their senators.

* * * * * * * * *

The Flathead Bill Is Signed by President.

Special Dispatch to the Standard.

Washington, April 25. — While Representative Dixon was at the white house to-day, President Roosevelt affixed his signature to the Flathead bill and that measure is now law. The Montana member asked the president to give him the pen with which the bill was signed and the president assented. Mr. Dixon will send the pen to the state university at Missoula. The Crow bill will, in all probability, receive executive approval to-morrow, when the pen with which it is signed will be sent to the Commercial club at Billings. This club will also get the pen used by President Pro Tem. Frye in signing the bill. This pen was procured to-day by Mr. Gilliland.

* * * * * * * * *

Hundreds Welcome Mr. Dixon Home

Montana's Congressman and Missoula's Citizen Accorded a Royal Welcome in Which Citizens of All Western Montana Join — "Dixon Day" One Long to Be Remembered.

Missoula, May 17. — That Joseph M. Dixon, Montana's representative in the national congress, is dear to the hearts of the people of this state and especially to those of the city and county of Missoula, who gave him to the state, was truly proved by the demonstration accorded him on his arrival home to-day. This day, in remembrance of what Mr. Dixon has done for the state during his brief incumbency, was "Dixon day" in every sense of the phrase. With hearts that were buoyant, spirits that were patriotic and words that rang with earnestness, people from all sections welcomed Mr. Dixon home. Surely no congressman ever before received a more royal reception upon his return to his home state and city.

The committee on reception and arrangements appointed by the chamber of commerce carried out its plans to the letter and the programme from beginning to end was one complete success. Banners were flying in all parts of the city, and hundreds of people walked the streets wearing badges, bespeaking their welcome to the homecoming congressman.

It was 3:15 this afternoon when Montana's congressman stepped from the train to the depot platform, accompanied by his family, and greeted the hundreds of people who had gathered there. Missoula is credited with having a large depot, but there was not space enough on the extensive platform to accommodate the expectant and patriotic crowd. Mr. Dixon was rushed to a carriage as quickly as possible, but must have shaken hands with a hundred people before his arrival there.

The committee to meet Mr. Dixon at the depot was composed of Col. Thomas C. Marshall, Will P. Fisher, E. A. Winstanley, B. E. Palmer, J. Lauzier, J. M. Keith, H. Kohn, P. H. Gerber, H. T. Wilkinson and P. M. Reilly. Mr. Dixon was driven down Higgins avenue and thence to his home. He was accompanied in the carriage by Mayor M. R. C. Smith, Judge Hiram Knowles and Thomas C. Marshall. Mrs. Dixon and children, accompanied by friends, were also driven in an open carriage to the Dixon home.

A public welcome was accorded the home-coming congressman in the courthouse yard, beginning at 8 o'clock this evening, and the demonstration on this occasion was something long to be remembered. The new Missoula band was on hand and rendered several selections. The spacious yard was crowded almost its entire length with people who had gathered from all portions of the western part of the state. All the Deer Lodge delegation was here and the Bitter Root valley was well represented. Many of the reception committee from the various towns were given places of honor on the speakers' platform. The platform and, in fact, all portions of the yard had been decorated in red, white and blue. The decorations were never more noticeable for artistic beauty. All in all, with the decorations, the expectant crowd of people, the music of the band and Mr. Dixon on the platform surrounded by prominent men of the state, the scene was a brilliant one.

Col. Thomas C. Marshall was chairman of the ceremonies and was feeling at his best. He delivered a brief and stirring address in calling the meeting to order and explaining its purpose. He said the people were here from every county to accord a welcome to Mr. Dixon and listen to whatever he had to say to them. Speaking of Montana's congressman, Colonel Marshall said: "Judged by the results of his works, he stands without a parallel in the history of the state of Montana, and his name is a household word."

Colonel Marshall first introduced Mayor M. R. C. Smith, who delivered a brief and earnest address of welcome. "In the name and on behalf of the good people of this commonwealth," said the mayor in closing, "I desire to extend to you, Congressman Dixon, a cordial welcome home."

Colonel Marshall, following the address of the mayor, introduced Congressman Dixon. The cheers that greeted the introduction were deafening, and it was some time after Mr. Dixon had taken the stand before he attempted to speak.

"Friends and neighbors," said Congressman Dixon. "I want to say first that I am mighty glad to be home. Red blood would not run in my veins if I failed to appreciate the reception you have accorded me." Mr. Dixon then told of what he had believed to be his duty while in congress and of the measures he had supported and the way their passage had been secured. "I did not see a town in the East," he said, "which impressed me as favorably as Missoula does now. I am glad Missoula people are pushing the wheel and all working together. I feel mighty proud that I am from Missoula and Montana. I'm glad to come home again and be among my own people, and I thank you, one and all, sincerely for this testimonial of your friendly and neighborly feeling. As one of your fellow citizens, I thank you."

The meeting was adjourned following the address of Mr. Dixon. Later in the evening a formal reception was held in the rooms of the Missoula club, and many people were accorded the pleasure of meeting the congressman personally.

Document 50

Horse Roundup on the Reservation

May 21, 1904

Source: "Roundup Is On in Flathead," *The Missoulian* (daily), May 21, 1904, page 5, col. 3-4.

Editors' note: Sales of Flathead horses to off-reservation buyers were a big business in the early twentieth century. Income from the sales supported many Indian families, and cattle owners were happy to have less competition for the grass on the open range.

Roundup Is On in Flathead
Indians Are Gathering Ponies to Sell to Dealers from Eastern States.

One of the Flathead Indians, who can talk as good English as the majority of the residents of the United States, was a visitor to the city yesterday and informed the Missoulian that for the past few weeks there has been a horse roundup on the reservation. This roundup is being made for the purpose of selling a number of Indians ponies to a couple of buyers who are on the reservation from the east and who will probably purchase a large number of horses from the Indians before the summer is over.

Thursday the roundup crew, which is composed of twenty or thirty riders, finished the Moose creek section and moved to another part of the reservation which is being ridden at present.

The ponies are gaining flesh rapidly, although they came through the winter in rather poor condition. Now that they have an abundance of green grass and no snow to contend with, they have nearly all lost their long winter coats and they come into the roundup corrals as sleek as moles and are fast assuming the plump condition which is characteristic of the Flathead ponies.

The men who are purchasing these ponies, whose names could not be learned, make a business of the enterprise every year. They pick out the most likely looking animals and ship them from Selish to different points in the middle west where they are shaped up for market. A few years ago the best pony on the reservation, unless he should be some race horse, could be purchased for $2 or $3, but of late years there has been a decided advance in the price of horseflesh and now these buyers are compelled to pay from $10 upwards if they buy a pony worth the having. Once these horses arrive at their destination they are thoroughly broken and trimmed up for the market, which is, for the greater part among the children of people of the east who can afford to keep a pony. In order to be sold for this purpose they have to be thoroughly broken and trustworthy. Many of the Indians horses are handled from the time they are colts, the red men believing in the old saying among horsemen that it is a good idea to begin the education of a horse when it is young, and as soon as the pony reaches an age which will permit him to carry a buck on his back he is generally broken. The youngsters of a tribe are natural horsemen and they are always anxious to try their skill as "broncho busters" and the result is that nearly every horse on the reservation knows the ways of his red master. It takes some time after the white buyers get their ponies to learn the ways of their new owners, but they are naturally intelligent and soon adapt themselves to their new conditions and get on famously in their new homes.

One of the most interesting events during the entire year in a horse raising country are the roundups, which generally occur twice a year. A big bunch of riders assemble at some rallying point where a mess wagon is provided and all from there start together to drive all of the horses in some certain section to a corral where they can be "worked" — that is, the colts branded and the horses which are wanted, either for sale or for other purposes, are cut out of the main bunch and placed in a separate herd to be taken to the home ranch at the end of the roundup.

This is done day after day until the roundup is finished, the horses which have been rounded up one day being "thrown back" the following day on the ranges from which they came. There is no stopping for weather or unfavorable conditions of any kind; a rain or a snow storm is accepted as a matter of course and every one in the entire horse raising section considers the event as one of the holidays of the year and are willing to undergo any hardship in order to be allowed the privilege of riding in the bunch and mayhaps be given an opportunity of riding some "outlaw" "straight up," without "pulling leather."

Document 51

Jocko Government School Closing Ceremonies

June 19, 1904

Source: "Indians Like Idea of Schools," *The Missoulian* (daily), June 19, 1904, page 2, col. 4-5.

Editors' note: The school described in this article was the government school at Jocko Agency, despite the attribution to St. Ignatius. According to the report, Chief Charlo attended the closing ceremonies. See also Agent Samuel Bellew's letter of October 20, 1905, relative to Superintendent William A. Root.

Indians Like Idea of Schools
Interesting Notes on Commencement Day at Flathead School on Reservation.

Special to The Missoulian.

St. Ignatius, June 18. — On Thursday afternoon about two hundred Indians, parents of the pupils and friends of the school, assembled on the campus of the Flathead Indian boarding school to witness the closing exercises. The large attendance bears evidence that the attitude of the Indians toward the school has changed materially since it was opened about three years ago.

At 5 o'clock dinner was served to all of the guests. As they left the table one could see they were satisfied, not only with a feeling of fullnes [sic], but also with a feeling that the larger girls had been taught to prepare food in large quantities.

After dinner the guests were seated on the campus while Superintendent Root gave them a practical talk on the value of an education to the Indians of the reservation. At the close of his talk Mr. Root asked how many would like to have the government erect new and larger school buildings and how many would do all they could to maintain such a school. When the vote was taken nearly all voted in the affirmative.

Before 7:30, the time appointed for the literary entertainment, the assembly room, windows, hall and porches were crowded to their utmost capacity and many were unable to get near enough to hear the program, which was as follows:

Recitation, "Welcome," Octave Couture.
Song, "Stars and Stripes," School.
Recitation, "Six Little Maids," Jane Bousquet.
Sing, "Linden Tree," Nora Cobell, Collette Lamoose.
Recitation, "Counting the Eggs," Matilda Gebeau.
Recitation, "Somebody's Mother," Frank Roeder.
Song, "Red, White and Blue," School.
Dialogue, "The Tramp," John Hunter, Nora Cobell, Jane Bousquet.
Song, "Sweet Afton," Collette Lamoose.
March and dumb bell drill, twelve boys.
Song, "The Tin Soldier," Jane Bousquet, Nora Cobdell.
Recitation, "Breaking the News," Charles Hunter.
Dialogue, "When the Cat's Away," Seven girls and five boys.
Song, "Indian Home," School.
Tableau, "Reapers and Flowers."

The program was well rendered and greatly appreciated by the audience.

Chief Carlos, who was bitterly opposed to the school when first organized, was present and gave his approving smile to all the proceedings of the day, except the heat caused by the crowded condition of the assembly room.

Document 52

Three Mixed Blood Cattlemen Ordered Off the Reservation June – August 1904

Source: W. H. Smead to Commissioner of Indian Affairs, June 25, 1904, letter received 43,029/1904, land division, RG 75, National Archives, Washington, D.C.; "Must Pay Grazing Tax or Leave the Reserve," *The Anaconda Standard*, August 11, 1904, page 12, col. 2; "Trouble May Be Settled," *The Anaconda Standard*, August 12, 1904, page 12, col. 4.

Editors' note: Agent W. H. Smead moved to force the collection of the reservation grazing tax, despite its questionable legality. Poor market conditions made it hard for many stockmen to pay the money. In August 1904, the new agent, Samuel Bellew, ordered three mixed blood cattlemen off the reservation for failure to pay up, but, faced with eviction, they found a way to raise the funds.

Department of the Interior,
United States Indian Service,
Jocko Flathead Agency, Mont. June 25th, 1904.

Hon. Commissioner of Indian Affairs,
Washington, D.C.
Sir:

Respectfully referring to the matter of the collection of the resident grazing tax on this Reservation, I desire to call your attention to the following named persons who are now the principal delinquents on last year's taxes, and ask that immediate instructions be given me relative to same.

Angus McDonald and his sister Maggie, own approximately 1800 head of cattle and 300 head of horses. McDonald has been repeatedly notified to pay these taxes, and on several occasions, he has led me to believe that he would do so, however, he still neglects to pay same. I am now of the opinion that it is McDonald's purpose to refuse to pay these taxes, and if any effort is made by the Government to collect it he will undertake to get it into the courts.

I might add that during the Winter, McDonald told me that I could come and take cattle in payment of the grazing tax; however, in this he was perfectly safe, as the ranges were then covered with snow, and it would have been utterly impossible for the Government to have cared for such cattle, had I been authorized to receive them for the grazing tax.

Both McDonald's and his sister's names appear upon the roll as follows: Maggie McDonald, Class One, No. 663; her enrollment was not approved by the Secretary, pending her supplying evidence of her rights to be enrolled. Angus McDonald, Class Four, No. 1701, his right to enrollment not approved by the Secretary, pending his furnishing such evidence as would entitle him to be enrolled.

I might add that in my judgment, both McDonald and his sister will be able to supply such evidence as will be required by the Honorable Secretary, to secure their enrollment.

McDonald, while possessed of a large amount of property, is in debt to probably the amount of $14,000 or $15,000, and under the present depressed condition of the cattle market, I am of the opinion that it will be hard for him to raise cash to pay the grazing tax.

Arthur Larrivie is delinquent on about 335 head of cattle, which he purchased from the outside after his regular permit had been granted; payment on these cattle has been demanded on a number of occasions without any satisfactory response. Larrivie is a resident of the Reservation, and has been for a number of years; his name does not appear on the rolls, although he has a small amount of Indian blood; possibly he may be entitled to enrollment, as I find the children of a deceased sister, who was married to a white man, are enrolled. It is generally believed that a white man is interested in these cattle, with Larrivie, although he claims the ownership.

Mike Matte is delinquent on approximately 600 head that were purchased from the outside after his regular permit had been granted. Payment on this additional number has on a number of occasions been demanded, and he has apparently been willing to pay same, but claims to be unable to raise the funds with which to do it. Matte is an enrolled mixed blood, and is considered an exceptionally intelligent and responsible person. It is my opinion that he would pay, had he the money with which to do so.

There are two or three delinquents on the second payment of last year's taxes, but I think I will be able to collect these within a very short time. In this connection I wish to say that since the resident grazing tax was authorized to be enforced on April 1st, 1903, that I have constantly borne in mind the injunction that was given me in Washington to "collect this tax diplomatically; keep it out of the courts[.]"

As perhaps you will recall, this matter was very thoroughly discussed, when I was there in April, 1903, and I was advised that it was questionable as to whether the collection of this tax, although entirely reasonable and just and for the benefit of the Indians generally, would stand the test of the courts. For this reason I have been exceptionally careful, and have used practically every means available to collect same without resort to the courts. And I might further add that on a number of occasions I have been informally advised that should this question go before the Honorable Hiram Knowles, U.S. Judge for this District, (now retired) he would have decided against the Government. I might also add that he has held in the past, that where a person (white) had interests upon the Reservation, he might return and look after and protect same, although he had been ejected from the Reservation by the order of the Department.

You will thus see that the ejecting of persons from the Reservation who neglected or refused to pay their grazing tax, would probably have resulted in an order from the court, permitting of their immediate return.

I have thus been handicapped in the collection of this tax, the legality of which is questionable, and the attitude of the court, which I had good reason to believe, and had been informed by persons who were in a position to know, would be unfavorable to the Government.

You will perhaps recall that I requested, when in Washington that the legality of this question be submitted to the Attorney General for a decision, and it was my understanding that this would be done; however, several months later, when I asked to be informed if a decision had been returned by the Attorney General, you replied that it had not.

A new judge has been appointed to fill the vacancy caused by the retirement of Judge Knowles, and possibly his views upon the grazing tax, should it be submitted to him, may be different from those of his predecessor.

I am now in receipt of your "Land 38928-1904" authorizing the change of dates in collection of the grazing tax from April 1st and October 1st of each year, to July 1st and January 1st. In this you deem it advisable that the present leases be issued from April 1st, 1904 to July 1st, 1905, 1¼ years, and that on July 1st, I collect 75 cents per head and on January 1st, 50 cents per head, and this will be done as far as practicable.

It seems proper that I should state in this connection that the cattle industry in this country is practically in a state of collapse. I think it safe to say that cattle have depreciated in the last fifteen months, 33⅓%; last Fall practically no beef at all was sold from this Reservation, and stock owners were consequently forced to carry over a large number of cattle, which ordinarily would have been sold during the Fall. The long Winter required a large outlay by them in the purchase of feed, to carry them through, and as a result, nearly every stock man on the Reservation is now more or less in debt, some deeply. It was hoped there would be some market for cattle on the June round up, which has just been finished; however, in this the stock men were again disappointed, and the result is that they are still carrying over last year's beef, with no immediate prospect of disposing of same.

With this condition of affairs, I can hardly see how it will be possible for cattle men (who are willing) to pay their cattle tax on July 1st.

With this condition of affairs in view, I deemed it essential and necessary that I should be called into Washington for conference, before attempting to collect the tax which falls due on July 1st, and requested that such authority be granted; however, I am now in receipt of a telegram which reads as follows: "Department denies your request to come to this city and directs that you carry out existing instructions." I had hoped that by a personal discussion of this matter, some plan might be devised that would relieve to a great extent, this vexatious problem; it had occurred to me that possibly it might be wise to perfect some scheme whereby the Government might take cattle in lieu of money in the payment of this grazing tax, from parties who are unable to pay the cash, and to carry such cattle until after such time as the present depression in the cattle business may have passed away, and then place them upon the market. It now seems almost certain to me that unless there should be an immediate change in the condition of the cattle market in this country, that it is going to be utterly impossible for a considerable number of the cattle men to meet this grazing tax, and if the Government should take any extreme course in collecting same, it would be so vigorously resisted that it would end in failure in collecting these taxes.

I am unwilling to allow, in the future, the payment of this grazing tax to be dragged out to meet the convenience of the cattle men, as was done during the past year, for it seems hardly fair that one man should pay when the tax falls due and another by pleading some excuses, should be allowed to perhaps defer his payment for several months. This, however, seemd [sic] to be necessary last year, to collect these taxes "diplomatically."

This year is [it] is my purpose to allow 20 days from the dates on which the tax falls due, for payment, and if same is not paid at the expiration of this 20 days, to proceed [sic] in some manner to collect same.

After a year's experience with this problem, I had deemed it desirable that I should meet you and have a full and complete discussion of the matter, and that definite arrangements for the future be provided; however, in view of your denial for me to go to Washington, I have written you as best I could on this subject, and I have to request that you give me immediately a full response with your advice and suggestions in this matter.

I assure you that the collection of this tax is most unpleasant and vexatious, and seems to being [bring] on me personally the spleen, malice and hatred of those having to pay same.

That it will be resisted goes without saying, and to add to my annoyance and embarrassment, the Office has just notified me that three positions at this Agency, filled by whites, and four policemen will be abolished July 1st. With probably as hard a reservation to properly manage as any in the U.S. it will be impossible for me to enforce law and order unless at least two of these positions be restored.

Very respectfully,
W. H. Smead
U.S. Indian Agent.

* * * * * * * * *

Must Pay Grazing Tax or Leave the Reserve
Much Interest in Order Affecting Cattle Owners.
Few Days of Grace Remain
Major Bellew Carries Out the Instructions of the Department and Notifies Three of the Leading Residents to Go.

Missoula, Aug. 10. — As a result of trouble over the payment of grazing tax on the Flathead reservation, Arthur Larravie, Angus McDonald and Mike Matt, owners of hundreds of head of horses and cattle, have been ordered to take their belongings and leave the reservation. The order for the men to leave was issued just after Maj. Samuel Bellew stepped into the office on the 1st of the month, according to instructions received from the commissioner of Indian affairs at Washington.

Major Bellew found the duty of having these men leave their homes on the reservation one of the first tasks for him to perform, and he attended to it immediately. He issued the order as received from Washington and told the cattle owners he would give them just 15 days to leave the reservation peaceably. The men yet have a few days of grace in which to leave, and in this city great interest centers in the outcome of the affair. It will be no small task to round up all the horses and cattle belonging to these men and drive them from the reservation lands. This was the reason the newly appointed Indian agent gave them ample time in which to make their departure.

The order to remove the cattlemen comes from the interior department as a result of the refusal of the cattle owners to pay the $1 a head grazing tax. It will be remebered [sic] that last year the interior department instructed Major Smead to collect a tax of $1 per head from every family on the reservation owning more than 100 head of horses and cattle. When an attempt was made to place the order into execution the Indians objected strenuously to the action.

The rich cattle owners believe they have been imposed upon, and will carry their cases to the highest tribunal.

* * * * * * * *

Trouble May Be Settled
Mike Matt Pays His Grazing Tax as Required.
Expected That Other Cattle Owners on the Reservation Will Do Likewise and Will Be Allowed to Remain.

Missoula, Aug. 11. — According to reports from the Flathead reservation to-day, the trouble there with three men over the non-payment of grazing tax is going to be adjusted. As stated in to-day's Standard, Arthur Larravie, Angus McDonald and Mike Matt were ordered from the reservation because they refused to pay their grazing tax on several hundred head of horses and cattle. This order was issued on the 6th, and the men were given 15 days in which to leave.

Yesterday Matt paid his tax, and the order respecting him has been rescinded. When he was ordered from the reserve, there was a disposition on his part to settle the trouble, and it was recommended to the interior department that the order expelling him be rescinded, providing he would agree to pay the tax. The department agreed to this recommendation, and yesterday Matt paid nearly $700 to the government as his share of the tax on horses and cattle.

It is believed McDonald and Larravie, who are large cattle-owners, will be allowed to settle their trouble in the same manner Matt did. Mr. McDonald is very ill at his home just at the present time as the result of being kicked by a horse and is not able to make his preparations to move, although this will have nothing to do, of course, with an adjustment, if one is made. The government does not anticipate any trouble in settling the matter and believes that in the future the grazing tax will be paid according to the rule of the department. It is not known for a positive fact whether McDonald and Larravie will take their grievances to the courts.

Document 53

Killing of Antille Tom Ruled Self-defense

July 22, 1904

Source: "Indians Are Not Held on Charge of Murder," *The Anaconda Standard*, July 22, 1904, page 12, col. 1.

Editors' note: Another murder charge dismissed on grounds of self-defense during a drunken quarrel near Polson. Johnnie Couture and Cayo were released and returned to the reservation.

Indians Are Not Held on Charge of Murder
Little Evidence Against Johnnie Couture and Cayo.
Antille Tom the Aggressor
Testimony of Eyewitnesses Differs and Commissioner Smith Decides Not to Bind the Red Men Over. Self-Defense Pleaded.

Missoula, July 21, — Johnnie Couture and Cayo, the two Indians charged with the murder of Antille Tom, another Indian, at the foot of Flathead lake near Polson, on the night of July 1, had a hearing before United States Commissioner Smith here to-day. This evening they were free men and rode back to their homes on the reservation. The Indians had been confined in the Missoula county jail for a couple of weeks past and were alleged to have killed Antille Tom late at night during a drunken quarrel in the Indian camp. The evidence was of a circumstantial nature.

Abraham, an Indian eyewitness to part of the trouble, was one of the principal witnesses for the state. Commissioner Smith did not consider the uncorrobrated [sic] evidence of Abraham sufficient as against the testimony of the defense, which was corroborated, and therefore did not consider it advisable to bind the Indians over to the federal court. Harry H. Parsons represented the defendant and made a good fight on behalf of his clients. Testimony was introduced for the state to show that there was a drunken brawl while the Indians were camped near the lake.

The defendants met Antille Tom, who started towards Couture with a knife in a threatening manner. Cayo hit Antille Tom in the head with a rock and knocked him down, and Couture hit Antille Tom again with a club three times. The next morning Antille Tom was found dead. Testimony for the defense was introduced to show that Couture had not hit Antille Tom with a club, and the witnesses were uncertain at whose hands he met death. The defense also showed that Antille Tom had been the aggressor in the quarrel and, if the defendants did kill him, they committed the deed in self-defense.

Document 54

Full Blood Indian Purchases Piano for Daughter

July 22, 1904

Source: "Reservation Indian Buys a Piano," *The Missoulian* (daily), July 22, 1904, page 8, col. 2.

Editors' note: A full blood Flathead Indian purchased a piano for his daughter who had learned to play the instrument in Carlisle Indian School in Pennsylvania.

Reservation Indian Buys a Piano

Believed to be First Instance of a Similar Sale Among the Flathead Braves.

That the Flathead Indians are becoming more and more civilized each year is shown by a deal which Orton & Tait made yesterday when they sold one of the finest pianos in stock to a Flathead reservation Indian. The Indian did not give his name, but as soon as the deal was made he planked down his money, all of it in shining gold pieces, and ordered the instrument shipped to Arlee, from where it will be freighted to Ronan. The Indian explained that he had a daughter who is attending Carlisle Indian school in Pennsylvania, and as she had been given a good education there he wanted to have a music box that would please her when she returned home.

This is believed to be the first time that a piano has ever been sold to a full-blooded Flathead, although a large number of the mixed bloods have instruments in their homes.

Document 55

Chiefs and Judges Rule on Tribal Adoptions

September 1, 1904

Source: "Proceedings of a Council of the Flathead and Confederated Tribes, Held at the Flathead Agency, Jocko, Montana, September First, 1904," U.S. Bureau of Indian Affairs, "Selected Records of the Bureau of Indian Affairs Relating to Enrollment of Indians on the Flathead Reservation, 1903-08," National Archives Microfilm Publication M1350, reel 1, frames 358-364.

Editors' note: The allotment policy provided for traditional chiefs and tribal judges to decide on adoptions of Indians from other tribes. The adoptions allowed the new members to get allotments of land before the reservation was opened to white homesteaders. Only two of the many proceedings of such councils are reproduced here. The other council occurred on September 19, 1904.

Proceedings of a Council of the Flathead and Confederated Tribes Held at the Flathead Agency, Jocko, Montana, September First, 1904.

Agent Bellew: Micheal, I want you to tell the Chiefs and Judges that the Agent by instructions from Washington desires to hold a council with them; that there are some people here who claim rights with the tribes of this reservation, and that they have at some time been adopted by these tribes, but we have no record to show that this is true, and Washington wants them, if they desire to adopt these people, to say so now, and we will put it in writing, so it will be kept forever, and we can always refer to it and know what has happened at this time. Now, that is the object of the council. We want the names of the Chiefs, Judges and headmen of the tribes, who are present to appear here:

Chief Charlo, of the Flatheads
Chief Michel of the Kalispells
Chief Koos-ta-ta of the Kootenais
Judges Batiste Ka-ka-shee and Joseph Standing Bear, and
Judges Antoine Moiese and Louison of the Flatheads
Judge Selah of the Pend d'Oreilles
Louie, Headman of the Kootenais.
also

Michael Revais, Official Interpreter, Samuel Bellew, U.S. Indian Agent, and John L. Sloane, Financial Clerk.

****

Agent: Batiste Marengo says that on the 26th and 27th of December 1902, there was held a council, and the following Chiefs were present: Chief Charlo, Chief Koos-ta-ta, Judge Ka-ka-shee, Joseph and Louison, and at that council Tony Cobell and Frank McLeod were adopted. Now we have no writing to show this, and if it is true Washington wants this council to ratify it. We are ready now, and would like to hear from the Chiefs, Judges and Headmen.

Micheal: Judge Ka-ka-shee says all the people here now were there at the council and all know that they adopted these two men at that time, Tony Cobell and Frank McLeod. Judge Louison says he heard Judge Joseph say that the did not want Tony Cobell to leave the reservation, that he is a good man. Chief Charlo objects to his staying. Chief Michel was not at the council when they adopted him, but he says it will be all right as far as he is concerned for Tony to stay, and Frank McLeod too. Koos-ta-ta says that he heard Judge Batiste say that Tony Cobell has been working for the Indians here and that we had better keep him here with us. Chief Michel says when you started to adopt people here, I told you then not to begin adopting outsiders, but you would adopt them, so I will go with you now that you have started to adopt them, but I wanted to stop this the first time it happened. Louie says he does not know any thing about Tony Cobell, whether he is good man or not. Selah says I object to it, I know him myself. Moiese says I dont know the man myself, but I have heard he is a good man, working for his living.

Agent: You tell these people, Micheal, that Tony Cobell has rights on the Blackfeet Reservation, he says he has never tried to obtain his rights there, as he does not like the country. They want to consider that he is a good blacksmith, a very useful man in a community. We are now going to ask them to vote just as we do in a big council of white men. I am going to ask that all those in favor of Tony Cobell remaining upon the reservation, and being adopted into the tribes, raise their hands to vote yes.

Micheal: Judge Joseph, Judge Ka-ka-shee and Chief Michel say yes. Charlo, Koos-ta-ta, Louie, Selah and Louison say no. Moiese refuses to vote one way or the other. In regard to the adoption of Frank McLeod, the vote is unanimous in his favor, all being willing that he should become a member of the tribes.

Agent: Pierre Lucier, whose wife is a Flathead Indian woman, and who is himself a half blood Chinook, has made application to be enrolled here on the reservation, and says he has given up any rights that he may have had as a Chinook. Now it is for this council to say whether they want to adopt him or not.

Miche[a]l: They all say yes, except Chief Koos-ta-ta. He objects.

Agent: Mary Finley Gingras, 76 years old, whose mother was a sister of Chief Eneas, desires to make application to become enrolled. Mary was born on the Little Bitter Root, and has lived here all her life. Now it rests with the council.

Micheal: Koos-ta-ta says she is a fully blood Kootenai and that she is the mother of Adelaide Gingras Ledoux, and Koos-ta-ta told his children to go to McNichols and have her put on the roll. She is very feeble and cannot walk well, being a very stout woman, weighing over 300 pounds, and he thinks that is the reason she did not go to see McNichols when he was here, and he now aks [sic] that she be enrolled, and makes ap[p]lication on her behalf, and the whole council ask that her name be enrolled among the other members of the Kootenai tribe.

* * * * * * * * *

Theodore and Isaac Tellier appeared before the council, claiming to have rights as members of the Flathead tribe, through their mother, Angelique Tellier (Ka-ka-tsee) a full blood Flathead Indian woman, whose husband was Louis Tellier (now deceased) a Frenchman.

The council recognized the rights of these men as members of the Flathead tribe, but as Isaac is a married man, having married a Nez Perce woman, who has rights and has an allotment on the Nez Perce, and as Theodore, a single man, has resided for some little time upon the Nez Perce Reservation, the council would request that care be taken and that the claims of these parties be closely scrutinized, as to whether they have received any rights or allotments upon the Nez Perce reservation.

* * * * * * * * *

Mrs. Eugenia Wild-shoe, a full blood Flathead woman, appeared before the council and asked to be recognized as a member of the Flathead tribe. Her father was a full blood Flathead, and her mother a full blood Pend d'Oreille (both now deceased) She married Philip Wild-shoe, a full blood Coeur D'Alene Indian.

The council recognized the woman as a member of the Flathead tribe, the majority of them having known her as a child, and all urge that her enrollment be recommended.

The council then adjourned.

Witnesses to mark: Jno. L. Sloane, Charlo, his x mark.

Olive E. Groves, Jno. L. Sloane, Michel, his x mark.

Olive E. Groves, Jno. L. Sloane, Koos ta ta, his x mark.

Olive E. Groves, Jno. L. Sloane, Baptiste Ka ka shee, his x mark.

Olive E. Groves, Jno. L. Sloane, Joseph Standing Bear, his x mark.

Olive E. Groves, Jno. L. Sloane, Antoine Moiese, his x mark.
Olive E. Groves, Jno. L. Sloane, Louison, his x mark.
Olive E. Groves, Jno. L. Sloane, Selah, his x mark.
Olive E. Groves, Jno. L. Sloane, Louie, his x mark.

I certify on honor, that the proceedings of the Council, held at Flathead Agency, Sept. 1, 1904, as hereinbefore transcribed, were by me explained to the several Chiefs, Judges and Headmen present, after being transcribed and I am satisfied that they understand the same and that I witnessed the signing by each of his name thereto.

Micheal Revais, his x mark.
Interpreter.

Witnesses to mark:
Jno. L. Sloane
O. E. Groves.

I certify on honor, that the foregoing transcript of the proceedings of a Council held at Flathead Agency, Sept 1, 1904, was made from my stenographic notes taken during the progress of the Council and that the same is true and correct.

Olive E. Groves
Stenographer

I certify on honor, that I was present at and acted as Clerk of a Council of the Flathead and Confederated Tribes, held at Flathead Agency, Montana, Sept 1, 1904, and that foregoing transcript is a true and correct account of the proceedings had.

Jno. L. Sloane
Financial Clerk.

I certify on honor, that I was present at the Council held at Flathead Agency, Montana, and that the foregoing transcript of the proceedings is true and correct.

Samuel Bellew
U.S. Indian Agent

Dated Flathead Agency, Montana
September First, 1904.

Document 56

Markets for Reservation Cattle Depressed

September 1904

Source: "Cattle Market Looks Blue," *The Missoulian* (daily), September 2, 1904, page 3, col. 1; "Beef Market Is Depressed," *The Missoulian* (daily), September 10, 1904, page 3, col. 3.

Editors' note: The poor market for reservation cattle in 1904 made it difficult for many cattlemen to raise the money for the new grazing tax.

Cattle Market Looks Blue

Duncan M'Donald Says Hay Will Be Scarce the Coming Winter.

Duncan McDonald, one of the well known residents of the reservation, who has spent all of his fifty odd years in western Montana, is in the city attending to business matters. Mr. McDonald is one of the large cattle owners of the reservation and a member of the Flathead tribe. He states that the range is poor on the reserve this year, and that it has been the driest season that he can remember in many years. There will be a general shortage of hay and the outlook for cattlemen is most discouraging. Some of them will be compeled [sic] to sell off their cattle before winter sets in, as there is little winter feed in the pastures and a smaller amount of hay than usual in the stockyards at the ranches.

Mr. McDonald does not take kindly to the ruling of the interior department compelling all Indian stockmen who own more than 100 head of cattle to pay a range tax of $1 per head. He says that white men feed cattle on the ranges at a cost of about 17 cents per head per year — the cost of their taxes. He thinks the scheme will discourage thrift among the Indians, who are following the advice given at the time Chief Charles, Mr. McDonald and a number of other members of the tribe went to Washington, when Secretary Hitchcock told them that the solution of the Indian problem was to raise cattle and kill off the ponies, if need be.

On Mr. McDonald's range matters are a long ways from being encouraging. He stated yesterday that it was his intention to sell off as many of his cattle as there is a good market for, saving what stock cattle he can carry through the winter in good shape. With the Chicago strike still on and a lessening of demand from coast markets owing to general drouth crowding a large number of immature stock on the market, the cattle situation is anything but encouraging in western Montana.

* * * * * * * * *

Beef Market Is Depressed
Reservation Shippers Realize Low Values from a Recent Consignment.

Mr. and Mrs. Francis Dupuis, well known residents of the reservation, spent yesterday in the city. Mr. Dupuis is a member of the firm of Dupuis Brothers, among the leading cattle growers of the reservation. The firm has just made an extensive shipment of cattle, and Camille Dupuis returned but a few days ago from Chicago, at which point the cattle had been marketed. Yesterday Mr. Dupuis stated that they found the market very indifferent. There were nearly twenty carloads of cattle in the shipment, and they averaged better than 1,220 pounds. They found a poor market, selling from $3.35 to $3.40 per hundred weight, which would give the cattle growers little more than $41.50 per head for the beeves. One year ago and two years ago the same cattle would have sold for $60 per head. This slump in the price is attributed to a considerable extent, according to Mr. Dupuis, to the packing house strike. There was little demand while the Dupuis cattle were in the yards, and they had to take what was offered and be glad to get that. The Fathers at the mission also had several carloads of cattle in the shipment.

Mr. Dupuis said that the cattle were all native Montana stock and when they left the reservation they were in excellent shape, the fact that they averaged over 1,200 pounds when they arrived in Chicago being proof of that fact. The run they had to market was not of the best and the cattle must have weighed at least 1,400 pounds when they left the ranges.

The outlook for the cattlemen on the Flathead this year is not very bright. There has been an unprecedented drought and a considerable amount of the ranges have been burned over by timber and the prairie fires started, so a number of the reservation residents aver, by the carelessness of white men who have trespassed on the reservation. The feed problem in consequence has become one of vital importance to the stockmen of that section.

The settlement of the Chicago packing house strike is hailed with pleasure by the stockmen of that section. It will be undoubtedly necessary to sell of a large number of cattle this season in western Montana and the resumption of work on an extended scale in the packing houses will mean that a practically unlimited market will be available.

Within the next few weeks it is expected that there will be a large number of cars ordered for the shipping points on the reservation, and that every fat cow or steer that is in good flesh and that will justify shipping will be "cut" into the "beef herd" during the roundups and later shipped to the stock markets in the east.

Document 57

Charles Buckman Charged with Selling Liquor to Indians October 6, 1904

Source: "Is Held for Grand Jury," *The Missoulian* (daily), October 6, 1904, page 3, col. 2.

Editors' note: Charles Buckman, a mixed blood, was charged with selling liquor to a Flathead Indian. Not all tribal entrepreneurs operated legally.

Is Held for Federal Grand Jury
Charles Buckman Has Proven a Pest to Reservation Police by Selling Liquor.

Charles Buckman, the breed, accused of selling whisky to a Flathead Indian, was given a hearing before Commissioner W. P. Smith yesterday and bound over to await the action of the United States grand jury, bonds being fixed at $200. Yesterday afternoon in company with Marshal Young he looked over the town in an effort to raise a bail bond, but was unsuccessful and will be taken to Helena this morning.

Buckman is said to be a Pocatello Indian and has spent some little time during the past summer in the reservation jail. He has been ordered off the reservation a number of times and the Indian police have received strict orders to keep him off. However, there are only five policemen on the entire reservation and Buckman dodged between lines and returned to the territory which had been forbidden him.

Antoine Paulouse is the name of the Flathead brave to whom Buckman is alleged to have sold the whisky and the evidence of yesterday brought out a very strong case against the accused.

Buckman is supposed to be the same fellow who arrived in this section about the Fourth of July and supplied some of the Indians with the liquor to help them celebrate. He was detected by Sheriff Thompson while he was attempting to negotiate for a supply of fire-water and given such a scare that he took to the hills and remained away from Missoula for several weeks. Buckman has proved a disturbing element on the reservation and the Indian police are not a bit sorry that he has been placed where he will not bother them for awhile.

Document 58

Indian Hunters Get Bounty for Bears

October 12, 1904

Source: "Big Knife Maintains Reputation," *The Missoulian* (daily), October 12, 1904, page 7, col. 1.

Editors' note: Alex Bigknife and Victor Vanderberg brought in bear pelts for the bounty.

Big Knife Maintains Reputation
Flathead Brave, Who Captured a Bear this Summer With a Lasso, Brings in Another Pelt.

Alex. Big Knife, a Flathead brave, brought one of the finest bear hides ever seen in Missoula to town yesterday and sold it to Otis Worden. The hide came from an immense silver tip which was killed at the head of the west fork of the Bitter Root. Bounty upon the hide was secured in Hamilton, the bear having been killed in Ravalli county. Victor Vanderberg, another Flathead, also brought in a hide from a black cub and this was also sold to Mr. Worden.

The bear killed by Alex. Big Knife weighed at least 700 pounds. Both of the animals had been killed with rifles, the Indians shooting from safe distances and getting their meat with the first shot.

Mr. Big Knife has made quite a reputation for himself in killing bear during the past summer. Some few weeks ago while the huckleberries were ripe, he and his s.... were berrying. Big Knife was sleeping while his wife did the work. While she was berrying a big black bear came to help her. She screamed in alarm and ran to her husband for aid. Alex grabbed up his lariat rope in place of a gun and took after the bear. He lassoed it, wound it round and round with coils of rope and when he had poor old Bruin helpless he beat him to death with a club.

Since then Alex. has posed as the champion bear killer of the Flathead tribe.

Document 59

White Businessmen Move to Claim Dam Site

October 15, 1904

Source: A. C. Tonner to J. M. Dixon, October 15, 1904, from file 74,927/1907, Flathead 371, Central Classified Files, RG 75, National Archives, Washington, D.C.

Editors' note: The ink was barely dry on the Flathead Allotment Act before white businessmen tried to claim the Flathead Lake dam site for their personal profit and development. Fortunately, the government decided the site was tribal property.

Department of the Interior,
Office of Indian Affairs,
Washington.
October 15, 1904.

Hon. J. M. Dixon,
Missoula, Montana.
Sir:

The Office is in receipt of your communication, dated September 24, 1904, stating that Frank R. Miles, C. B. Roberts, C. E. Shoemaker, W. J. Johnson, and G. W. Stapleton, have written you that they had filed application with this office asking to be allowed to construct a dam across the Pend d'Oreille River on the Flathead Reservation and asking for land for power house etc. You state that they are desirous that no action be taken in the matter one way or the other at the present time.

Replying thereto, you are advised the Office is unable to locate the application referred to by you from the names supplied. There is an application, however, submitted to this office by one Jeremiah Miller, Kalispell, Montana; in the communication submitting the same it being stated that he "together with a number of other parties" were forming a company for the purpose of developing water power in the Flathead Valley and County and that they desired to secure a permit to construct a dam across the Flathead River, which is sometimes known as the Boundary River, at a point three miles south of the outlet of Flathead Lake in the said reservation.

It is requested that you will advise this office whether or not this application is the one referred to by you.

Very respectfully,
A. C. Tonner,
Acting Commissioner.

Document 60

Another Council to Consider Tribal Enrollment Adoptions October 19, 1904

Source: "Proceedings of a Council of the Flathead and Confederated Tribes Held at the Flathead Agency, Jocko, Montana, October Nineteenth, 1904," U.S. Bureau of Indian Affairs, "Selected Records of the Bureau of Indian Affairs Relating to Enrollment of Indians on the Flathead Reservation, 1903-08," National Archives Microfilm Publication M1350, reel 1, frames 373-387.

Editors' note: This was another of a series of councils of traditional chiefs, government judges, and tribal headmen to consider adoptions of Indians from other tribes. See also September 1, 1904, council proceedings.

Proceedings of a Council of the Flathead and Confederated Tribes Held at the Flathead Agency, Jocko, Montana, October Nineteenth, 1904.

A Council of the Flathead and Confederated Tribes of Indians of the Flathead or Jocko Indian Reservation, was this, the nineteenth day of October, 1904, convened for the purpose of considering the adoption of certain persons into the respective tribes, and such other business as may properly come before the Council for consideration, Samuel Bellew, United States Indian Agent, calling the Council to order and stating the reason for the convening of said Council and at which the following proceedings were had, to wit:

Agent Bellew: Micheal tell these Chiefs, Judges and Headmen that I have called them together in Council, by instructions from Washington, to pass upon the claims of some people who have lived here among them for a great number of years and who claim rights with the tribes of this reservation, but Washington has no evidence that they have ever been recognized by the Chiefs and Headmen as entitled to such rights; now, Washington wants you to say what you know about these people and if you desire them to remain with you and be part of your people, to say so, and adopt them, and we will put it in writing so that it may be kept and we can always know what you did at this time. This is the reason why I have called you in General Council. We will now have the names of all the Chiefs, Judges and Headmen, who are present, appear here:

Charlo — Chief of the Flatheads.
Koostah-tah — Chief of the Kootenais.
Charley Michel — Chief of the Pend d'Oreilles.
Judges Louison and Baptiste Ka-ka-shee — of the Flatheads.
Judge Joseph Standing Bear — of the Kalispells.
Paul Cah-Cah-she — Headman of the Kalispells.
Batiste Tell-poo — Headman of the Pend d'Oreilles.
Paul Andre — Headman of the Pend d'Oreilles.
Martin Sin-pi-nah — Headman of the Pend d'Oreilles.
Big Sam — Headman of the Flatheads.
Judge See-lah — Headman of the Flatheads.
Louis Vandeberg — Headman of the Flatheads.

Also

Michael Revais, Officer Interpreter, Samuel Bellew, U.S. Indian Agent and John L. Sloane, Financial Clerk.

* * * * * * * * *

Agent Bellew — Now, Micheal, Philomene Dumontier Hustin, is a woman who is one-quarter blood Indian, she claims she was born in the Bitter Root Valley when the Flatheads lived there, that she was raised among them and knows no other than an Indian life; her brother and other relatives are now on the Rolls. Now, we want to submit to this Council, for them to consider the matter of her adoption by them[.]

If she should be adopted by this Council, she will have to relinquish all her rights as Piegan; now we want this Council to discuss this matter and then we will take a vote as to whether they want to adopt her.

Louis Vanderberg, says that Chief Victor, the father of Chief Charlo regarded this woman as one of his children, and he therefore votes to adopt her.

Judge See-lah says he does not know the woman and will not vote at present, but ask the others first.

Martin Sin-pi-nah says that he will stand by what his old Chief has done, and he will therefore vote for the adoption of this person.

Paul Andre says that he thinks as Martin-sin-pi-nah does, my old Chief regarded her as one of the tribe, and I vote for her adoption.

Batiste Teel-poo votes for the adoption of Philomene Dumontier Hustin because she is my relation.

Paul Cah-Cah-She says: She belongs to us and is one of our children and I vote for her adoption.

Judge Joseph Standing Bear says: I vote to adopt her

Judge Ka-ka-shee says: Our Old Chief Victor adopted her and I will go with him and vote for her adoption.

Judge Louison says: She is a poor woman, all of her relations are on the reservation and I want her to stay here and I vote for her adoption.

Chief Charley Michel says: I am very glad to hear what Chief Charlo says; that is that every one who has Indian blood and has stayed with the Indians so long, should stay here, and I vote to adopt her.

Chief Koos-tah-tah says: She has been here a long time, raised with the Indians and I vote to adopt her.

Chief Charlo says: I vote to adopt her.

Judge See-lah says: I see that all of these people want to adopt her, so I vote for her adoption.

Big Sam says: All right, she is a poor woman, and I vote to adopt her.

All of the members of the Council were unanimous in favoring the adoption of Philomene Dumontier Hustin.

* * * * * * * * *

Agent Bellew: Now Michael tell the Council that I have a letter here from Washington in regard to Joseph Brooks and his application for enrollment; he swears that his mother was named Therse, she was a woman belonging to the Flathead Tribe of Indians; that he was born in the Bitter Root; that he is a half blood; that his sister Sophie, is enrolled, Number 357; now Washington wants to know from this Council if they recognize his claim to be a member of the Flathead Tribe.

Louis Vanderberg — Votes for adoption.
Judge See-lah — Votes to adopt.
Big Sam — Votes to adopt.
Martin Sin-pi-nah — Votes for adoption.
Paul Andre — Votes to adopt him.
Batiste Teel-poo — Votes to adopt.
Paul Cah-Cah-She — Votes to adopt.
Judge Standing Bear — Votes to adopt.
Judge Batiste Ka-ka-shee — Votes to adopt him.
Judge Louison — Votes for adoption.
Chief Charley Michel — Votes to adopt him.
Chief Koos-tah-tah — Votes for adoption.
Chief Charlo — Votes to adopt him.

Chief Charlo, speaking for the Council, says: That this man is personally known to all members of the Council and that he belongs here and he was unanimously adopted.

* * * * * * * * *

Agent Bellew: Now, Micheal, you tell the Council that there are some other people here who want to present their claims to the Council; they will come before the Council themselves and state their own cases, and we want the Council here to hear them and decide whether they want to adopt them as members of the tribe, and whatever the Council does, will be put down in writing and go to Washington, so that Washington will know what they have done here to-day, just the same as if Washington were here itself.

Fred Normandin appeared before the Council and said: I am a quarter breed Colville Indian; I was born on the Colville Indian Reservation, and have lived among the Indians all of my life. I came to this reservation and married a member of your tribes, Josephine Lucier, with whom I am living on the reservation and have lived ever since I came here. I am willing to relinquish all of my right to the Colville or any other reservation and ask that this Council adopt me as one of their members, or as a member of their tribes.

I am a poor man and am willing to live up to all of the laws of the Chiefs, Judges and Headmen and do as they order.

Agent Bellew — You have heard the statement of Fred Normandin, and have discussed the matter among yourselves, and I will ask you now to vote yes or no upon the matter of his adoption.

Louis Vanderberg — I don't know him.
See-lah — I don't [know] him, either.
Big Sam — I don't know him.
Martin Sin-pi-nah — No.
Paul Andre — No.
Batiste Teel-poo — No.
Paul Cah-Cah-She — I don't know him.
Judge Joseph Standing Bear — No.
Judge Batiste Ka-ka-shee — No.
Judge Louison — No.
Chief Charley Michel — No.
Chief Koos-tah-tah — No.
Chief Charlo — No.

Chief Charlo, speaking for the Council, declares that Fred Normandin has been unanimously rejected.

* * * * * * * * *

Joe Matt then presented himself to the Council and said: That he is a full one-half breed Chinook Indian, has lived among the Indians all of his life, knows no other than an Indian life and has lived continuously on the Flathead Indian Reservation for more than twenty years and every member of this Council knows him. He asks that he be adopted, he being willing to relinquish all of his right to any other Indian Reservation and to abide by the laws of this Reservation and of all the Chiefs, Judges and Headmen and the Agent.

Agent Bellew — After discussing this matter of the adoption of Joe Matt, I will now ask you to vote yes or no on the matter of his adoption.

Louis Vanderberg — Yes.
Judge See-lah — Yes.
Big Sam — Yes.
Martin Sin-pi-nah — Half Yes and Half No.
Paul Andre — Yes.
Batiste Teel-poo — Yes.
Paul Cah-Cah-She — Yes.
Judge Joseph Satanding [sic] Bear — Yes.
Judge Batiste Ka-ka-shee — Yes.
Judge Louison — No.
Chief Charley Michel — Yes.
Chief Koss-tah-tah — Yes.
Chief Charlo — Don't want to vote.

Chief Charley Michel, speaking for the Council said that majority voting for the adoption of Joe Matt, he is considered as adopted.

* * * * * * * * *

Agent Bellew — On the first of September, last month, you were asked to act in regard to the adoption of Tony Cabell, his wife and her daughter by her first husband, and for each one to say just what you knew about them and what you[r] reasons you may have for either accepting or rejecting them as members of your tribes; now, I would like you to tell me, so that it can be put in writing and sent to Washington, just what you know about these people and whether you wan[t] them to remain among you as part of your people.

Agent Bellew — Micheal ask Chief Charlo what he knows about Tony Cabell, his wife and her daughter.

Chief Charlo — I don't know them at all. I don't want him to s[t]ay because he is a Blackfeet.

Chief Koos-tah-tah — Judge Joseph and Judge Ka-ka-shee say he is a blacksmith there; that he always helps the Indians; and I am willing that they be adopted. I know Tony Cabell and his wife and two children and that they are good people and I am willing that they be adopted and want to stand by the Judges.

Chief Charley Michel — I know Tony Cabell and I like him; we have no blacksmith in our neighborhood, and whenever I have anything to fix he fixes it. I have a relation on the Blackfeet reservation who is a cripple; and they help him up there, and I think we should help Tony Cabell and his wife and children and I want to adopt him and them and I vote for their adoption. I want to see Tony Cabell and his wife and her daughter adopted.

Judge Louison — I have nothing to say against this man here. I want to adopt him, but I want him to be good to the Indians. I am also in favor of adopting him and his wife and her daughter.

Judge Ka-ka-shee — Yes, I know him very well; he is a good man; he has nothing, only one horse, and has to work for his living; he is a good blacksmith, works well and we need him on the reservation and I want to adopt him; and I also want his wife and her daughter adopted.

Judge Joseph Standing Bear — I am very glad to have Tony Cabell adopted, because he is a good blacksmith; he has been here a good many years and I have never seen him do anything wrong and we need him on the reservation; I also want to see adopted his wife and her daughter.

Paul Cah-Cah-She — I know Tony Cabell and his wife and their children very well; he is a good blacksmith; and the Indians need him. I am in favor of adopting him and his wife and her daughter.

Batiste Teel-poo — I am in favor of adopting Tony Cabell and his wife and her daughter. I think he is a good man, a good blacksmith and I want to adopt him and his wife and children.

Paul Andre — I am very glad to adopt Tony Cabell; he is a good man; I have known him a long time; and I want to adopt his wife and children.

Martin Sin-pi-nah — I want to talk to Tony Cabell myself. Do you want to leave your country and live on this reservation? By Tony Cabell — Yes, I want to live here. By Martin — And you promise to abide by the laws and treat the Indians well. By Tony Cabell — Yes. By Martin — I am very glad then to adopt Tony Cabell and his children. I am blind; I can't see, but I have heard that Tony Cabell is a good man and I want him and his wife and children adopted.

Big Sam — I am in favor of adopting Tony Cabell and his wife and children; they all say he is a good man and I want to see him and his [wife] and daughter by her first husband adopted, as also his other chil[dren].

Judge See-lah — All right, I am in favor of adopting Tony Cabell his wife and her daughter, for the reason that the rest of the Council want to adopt him and his wife and children.

Louis Vanderberg — I can't say anything about Tony Cabell; I don't know him, so I can't say anything about him; and I don't care to vote.

Agent Bellew — Ask Chief Koos-tah-tah, Micheal, whether he understands now that this Council has now adopted Tony Cabell, his wife and children and whether he is now willing to speak for the Council and say that he and his children have been adopted.

Chief Koos-tah-tah — Yes, we want Tony Cabell and his wife and children adopted; he is a good man and a good man for the Indians, and we want them adopted.

* * * * * * * * *

Mary Lameroux, then presented herself to the Council, and states that she is a half-breed Piegan; that she has lived on this reservation twenty-eight years; that she lived with the Flatheads in the Bitter Root before coming to this reservation; that she lived under Victor when he was the Chief of the Flatheads in the Bitter Root; and she now asks that her right to be recognized as a member of these tribes be acted upon by this Council and that she be formally adopted. That all of her immediate relatives are on the Roll and residents of this reservation.

Agent Bellew — Now, you have heard her statements, Members of the Council, and you all, or nearly all, appear to know her, and I now want you to say whether you want to adopt her. And also give your reasons why you want to adopt her.

Chief Charlo — I have known her in the Bitter Root and here for a number of years.

Chief Koos-tah-tah — She has been here a long time and we ought to adopt her.

Chief Charley Michel — I will take her for one of our children; all of her relations are here; adopt her.

Judge Louison — I have known her for a long time in the Bitter Root and on this reservation and she has been here all that time; I am in favor of adopting her

Judge Ka-ka-shee — The old chiefs adopted her and took her as one of their children; and I want her adopted.

Judge Standing Bear — I am in favor of her adoption.

Paul Cah-Cah-she — I take her for one of our children; I adopt her.

Batiste Teel-poo — All right; she is a very good woman and I adopt her

Paul Andre — I am glad to adopt her as I think she will stay here until she dies.

Martin Sin-pi-nah — My old Chief took her for one of his children; she stopped here all the time; and I am glad they are going to adopt her. I adopt her.

Big Sam — All the chiefs want to have only one heart and I want to adopt her.

Judge See-lah — I adopt her, she is a good woman.

Louis Vanderberg — She was a child of Chief Victor a long time ago and I can't go back on that, so I adopt her.

Chief Charlo, now speaking for the Council says that Mary Lameroux has been unanimously adopted.

* * * * * * * * *

Mary Rodgers Deschamps, presenting the name of her daughter-in-law, the daughter-in-law, being present in person, and being the wife of Mary Rodgers Deschamp's son Edward Deschamps, who is enrolled as No. 332; she is a white woman, but has lived among the Indians and says she has adopted the habits and customs of the Indians; that her said daughter-in-law desires to present herself and her name for the consideration of the Council and asks that she be adopted. That she, Mary Rodgers Deschamps, is a first cousin of Chief Charlo.

Agent Bellew — Now, Micheal, you tell the Council that this young woman Ora Deschamps, is the wife of Edward Deschamps; he is a five eighths blood Flathead, born in the Bitter [Root] and removed here on this reservation eighteen years ago; now, it remains with the Council to say whether they want to adopt this man's wife. As her husband is a relative of Chief Charlo, I am going to ask that the other chiefs and headmen speak first.

Chief Koos-tah-tah — I am favor able to her adoption because she is Ed Deschamps wife.

Chief Charley Michel — I am in favor of her daoption [sic]; she belongs here.

Judge Louison — I want to say that when Garfield was here he told me that when an Indian married a white woman she became a member of the tribe; but that when a white man married an Indian woman, he was not a member. I am in favor of adopting her.

Judge Ka-ka-shee — I want to adopt her.

Judge Standing Bear — I vote for her adoption.

Paul Cah-cah-she — She is the wife of one of our children and I adopt her.

Batiste Teel-poo — I adopt her.

Paul Andre — I adopt her; she belongs to us.

Martin Sin-pi-nah — That woman belongs to us; it was a law we made many years ago; I adopt her.

Big Sam — I adopt her; she is one of our children.

Judge See-lah — I adopt her; she belongs here.

Louis Vanderberg — She belongs to Charlo, Judge Louison and I adopt her.

Chief Charlo — She belongs to us; I adopt her as one of my children.

Chief Charley Michel, expressing the voice of the Council, declares that Ora Deschamps, the wife of Ed. Deschamps is unanimously adopted.

* * * * * * * * *

The Council then adjourned.

Witnesses to marks:

R. J. Holland, Jno. L. Sloane, Charlo, his x mark.

R. J. Holland, Jno. L. Sloane, Koos tah tah, his x mark.

R. J. Holland, Jno. L. Sloane, Charley Michel, his x mark.
R. J. Holland, Jno. L. Sloane, Louison, his x mark.
R. J. Holland, Jno. L. Sloane, Baptiste Ka ka shee, his x mark.
R. J. Holland, Jno. L. Sloane, Joseph Standing Bear, his x mark.
R. J. Holland, Jno. L. Sloane, Paul Cah cah she, his x mark.
R. J. Holland, Jno. L. Sloane, Baptiste Teel-poo, his x mark.
R. J. Holland, Jno. L. Sloane, Paul Andre, his x mark.
R. J. Holland, Jno. L. Sloane, Martin Sin pi nah, his x mark.
R. J. Holland, Jno. L. Sloane, Big Sam, his x mark.
R. J. Holland, Jno. L. Sloane, Seelah, his x mark.
R. J. Holland, Jno. L. Sloane, Louis Vanderburg, his x mark.

I certify on honor that the proceedings of the Council held at Flathead Agency, October 19, 1904, as hereinbefore transcribed, were by me explained to the several chiefs, Judges and Headmen present, after being transcribed and I am satisfied that they understand the same and that I witnessed the signing by each of his name thereto.

Micheal Revais, his x mark
Interpreter.

Witnesses to mark:
Jno. L Sloane
R. J. Holland

I certify on honor, that I was present at and acted as Clerk of a Council of the Flathead and Confederated Tribes, held at the Flathead Agency, Montana, October 19, 1904, and that the foregoing transcript is a true and correct account of the proceedings had.

Jno. L. Sloane
Financial Clerk.

I certify on honor, that I was present at the Council held at Flathead Agency, Montana, and that the foregoing transcript of the proceedings is true and correct.

Samuel Bellew
U.S. Indian Agent.

Dated, Flathead Agency, Montana,
October Nineteenth, 1904.

Document 61

Flathead Wrestlers, Henry and William Matt and Two Feathers November 1904 – June 1905

Source: "'Two Feathers' to Meet M'Millan," *The Missoulian* (daily), November 21, 1904, page 8, col. 2; "Two Feathers Is Ferninst 'Gym,'" *Spokesman-Review* (Spokane, Wash.), March 19, 1905; "Will Matt Defeats Jack Curran," *The Daily Missoulian*, April 22, 1905, page 8, col. 2-3; "Will Matt Leaves for North," *The Daily Missoulian*, April 23, 1905, page 2, col. 1; "Wrestlers Arrive for Match," *The Daily Missoulian*, May 7, 1905, page 6, col. 1; "Two Feathers Goes in Training," *The Daily Missoulian*, May 8, 1905, page 6, col. 5; "Two Feathers Wins Wrestling Bout," *The Daily Missoulian*, May 13, 1905, page 5, col. 2; "Union Opera House," *The Daily Missoulian*, May 23, 1905, page 6, col. 6-7; "O'Neill Is Defeated by Wm. Matt," *The Daily Missoulian*, May 27, 1905, page 8, col. 4; "Curran Is Winner of Match," *The Daily Missoulian*, June 9, 1905, page 8, col. 5.

Editors' note: In 1904 and 1905, Two Feathers (Kootenai), William Matt, and Henry Matt wrestled professionally in Missoula, Spokane, and other venues. Wagers on the matches made the wrestling matches a significant economic event. This section only includes a sample of the available articles about the matches. The April 22, 1905, account of the Will Matt – Jack Curran fight was garbled in the original *Daily Missoulian* article and has been left as it was printed.

"Two Feathers" to Meet M'Millan

Indian Wrestler Has Ambition to be Champion of World.

"Two Feathers," the great Indian wrestler of the Flathead reservation, has signed the articles of agreement for a match with Duncan McMillan, the celebrated athlete, who is well known in this city and over Montana. In sporting circles yesterday it was learned that the match would be pulled off at Spokane within the next three weeks. Jack O'Neil of Kalispell is at present acting as manager of "Two Feathers," and he has put up $100 as forfeit money. The contest will be for the gate receipts and a side bet of $250.

McMillan, for a number of years, has been the champion of the west and has probably been one of the most successful wrestlers in the country. He won considerable distinction some three years ago when he wrestled with the "Terrible Turk," who bet $1,000 that he would throw him three times within an hour. It was one of the fiercest encounters that he has ever had, and resulted in a victory for McMillan, the "Terrible Turk" being able to throw him only once in the hour.

"Two Feathers" is a strapping fellow, over six feet tall, and has been thrown but once since he has been on the mat. That was by Gotch in Seattle last December. He is one of the most powerful men in all of the west and has an ambition to become champion of the world. He states that he will throw McMillan three times within an hour and backs up his statement by putting up the actual cash.

"Two Feathers," who is one of the best known men on the reservation, and who has a large number of friends in Missoula, has been figuring with New York managers for some time and it is likely that after his combat with McMillan he will go direct east and sign contracts for a number of engagements.

* * * * * * * * *

Two Feathers Is Ferninst "Gym"
Indian Wrestler Eschews Civilization at Athletic Club.
Hits the Country to Train
Shirks Steamheated Hotel at Early Hours —
M'Millan in Fine Fettle for Match.

Two Feathers refuses to train for his wrestling match with D. A. McMillan on the mechanical devices of civilization. McMillan, on the other hand, is the daily center of admiration at the athletic club. Both men are in fine fettle.

By decree of Dan L. Deaver, manager of the Spokane theater, there will be no 15-round preliminary boxing bout between Barney Mullin and "Indian" Joe Gregg at the Spokane theater Wednesday night preceding the wrestling match.

Long and earnest powwow was had between Manager Weaver and the representatives of the fighting men yesterday, and at 4 o'clock the manager said he had decided to permit no more boxing bouts in the theater. Accordingly the Mullin-Gregg folks were up in the air last night; but were still hoping to fulfil the engagement at some other point.

Two Feathers and D. A. McMillan, who are to do the wrestling best three out of five falls, Wednesday night are the wonder of Spokane sports who have studied their methods of training. They are as opposite in methods as two athletes could be.

Henry Matt in wrestling outfit
Source: Virginia Matt Brazill, Arlee, Montana

McMillan is the center of admiration each afternoon at the gymnasium of the Spokane Amateur Athletic club, where he is doing most of his training. Two Feathers, on the other hand, refuses absolutely to have anything to do with the gymnasium. All efforts to get him to come down to the gymnasium and "show off" have been unsuccessful. His nearest approach at civilization is to sleep in a hotel on Riverside avenue near Browne street. Shortly after daybreak Two Feathers is up and away from the steam heated sleeping room. His trainer and friend, Jack O'Neil, grumbles and sputters, but ends by meekly rubbing his eyes and hiking after the noble Two Feathers.

Two Feathers takes a hot pace for the open country, and begins real live training by the time he reaches the eastern city limits. His favorite diversion is to run 10 or 15 miles. O'Neil as a rule, goes part way and then stoically waits for the man with the feathers to make the home run. Some time, Two Feathers makes a line for the hill district toward Manito park. He skoots over the hills like a man after a runaway horse; and these hill "stunts" are the real sore spot in O'Neil's merry life of trainer to the redskin.

With all the strenuousness, O'Neil says he is becoming as hard as the Indian, and expects to be able to carry out his contract for bouts with six different men preliminary to the Two Feathers–McMillan go. Among the six men whom he contracted to meet and throw during the hour preceding the main event are Joe Heinrich and C. A. Johnson. Wrestlers from Fort Wright are likely to finish out the list of six men. Those who have seen the soldiers say they are sturdy fellows, and will keep O'Neil busy. O'Neil has $100 forfeit up to carry out the contract.

McMillan is in better condition than ever before, and he is confident of throwing Two Feathers. He is doing country road work in the morning and "gym" work in the afternoons. He is six feet one inch and a half tall and weighs 205 pounds. The Indian is six feet six inches tall and weighs about 225 pounds.

* * * * * * * * *

Will Matt Defeats Jack Curran

Indian From Reservation Is Only Thrown Once by White Man.

Will Matt was the winner of the wrestling match at the Union opera house last evening, throwing Jack Curran three times in one of the best bouts ever seen in Montana. Curran took the first bout, but after that he was unable to do anything with the sturdy boy from the reservation, and though he wrestled for every minute he was on the mat, he was beaten decisively.

The crowd was wild with enthusiasm throughout the evening, and both men as they wrestled on the mat for the mastery were cheered to the echo upon every good play in the game. At first the sympathy of the audience was with Curran, but as the other man began showing the remarkable strength he possesses, his friends began to grow in number in the crowd, and he was soon an equal favorite with the Missoula man.

Betting was brisk throughout the preliminary and while the crowd was gathering and several hundred dollars were wagered by the thorough sports of the town, the Matt family of the reservation covered all of the money as fast as it came in sight.

After the match came to an end Mr. Matt stepped to the front of the stage and made a brief speech to the audience. He paid a tribute to Mr. Curran and said he was the gamest and most scientific man he had ever met. However, he would be willing to wrestle him again tonight or Monday night for a bet of $100, and would agree to throw him three times in an hour of wrestling.

There was a big crowd present when William Wyman called time for the preliminary, which was between "Big Henry" Matt and D. A. McMillan. Mr. McMillan was to throw his opponent twice in twenty minutes of wrestling. Big Henry showed that he was an adept at the game, and kept away from Champion McMillan for 11 minutes and 8 seconds, before he was pinned to the mat. The second bout ended without a fall, although Henry was in a dangerous position just before the end, which found him on his feet, and the match went to "Big Henry."

In the main event Mr. McMillan refereed, and when he called the men to the center of the mat he told them that he was going to referee it square and make them wrestle during all of the time they were on the mat. And he kept his word.

First Bout. — The men shook hands in the center and, almost before the spectators could realize it, Curran had secured a body hold and threw his opponent through the chairs on the outside of the mat. There was no scuffling around when they returned. Matt was almost immediately in danger, but he wriggled out and turned the tables on Curran, who, when it was thought certain that his shoulders would touch, sprang free from the strong arms of his opnonent [sic] and was on his feet. They went together with Matt having the best of the hold. Jack squirmed out of the grip were tried time and again as either put Matt down [sic]. Matt, however, got to his feet, and in the next clash Jack had one of the shoulders of his opponent touching, but Matt was game and strong and he wiggled away. For twenty minutes this work was kept up, Curran doing the hardest of the work. Finally Jack got Matt in a hammerlock and a half Nelson, and inch by inch he pressed his shoulders down until finally they touched, in 20 minutes and 34 seconds.

Second Bout. — Matt was back at the edge of the mat within five minutes, ready and anxious for the second bout. Curran, however, stayed in the room until time was called, and when he came out the men went after it with vigor. Without waiting for a minute of sparring for the best hold. Jack again rushed Matt over the chairs, and when they came to the center of the ring Matt remonstrated to the referee and Jack tackled him. Matt claimed a foul, but it was not allowed, and they went after it again. Half Nelsons, hammerlocks, crotch holds and every other part of the game in catch-as-catch-can wrestling were tried time and gaain [sic] as either men had the best of the struggle, but it was 34 minutes and 25 seconds before Matt secured the scissors and half Nelson hold and Curran was forced to the mat.

Third Bout. — The men locked and backed one another around and around on the mat, Curran finally being thrown. He broke away immediately and got a half Nelson, which would hold Matt for only a minute. Matt was still strong, but the pace was telling on Curran, but he was still game, and put up a pretty exhibition of wrestling. He had the more science, but the other man had the strength, and the result, after they had struggled for twenty minutes and five seconds, was that Curran was caught in a crotch and arm around neck hold and borne to the mat.

Fourth bout. — Matt sat unconcerned beside the mat during the rest between the bouts, while Curran took all the time of his assistants in preparing for the final struggle, which for a while seemed to have been postponed indefinitely, as Curran wanted the full advantage of the twenty minutes allowed by the rules, although the men had verbally agreed to wrestle with ten minutes' rest. Matt declared that he wanted Curran on the mat at once or else he wanted the match. When the time was up Mr. Curran appeared and went at the game vigorously, but Matt had the best of it. He was apparently as strong as he was the minute the men went on the mat, and he finally secured a crotch hold on Curran and, raising him up off the floor, jammed his shoulders fast to the mat and the match was won in 8 minutes and 9 seconds.

Dougal McCormick and A. W. Woodworth were timekeepers for the bouts.

* * * * * * * * *

Will Matt Leaves for North

Wrestler Says He Herds Cattle, But Others Think Differently.

William Matt, accompanied by Henry and John Matt, returned to the reservation last evening more than pleased with the result of the match Friday evening. Will Matt states that he will soon leave for the Canadian side of the line, having in charge a number of cattle owned by his father, which will be summered across the border and afterwards be brought back to Montana points. According to his story, he has spent eight years at the Carlisle school in Pennsylvania and it was from the athletic instructor at that place that he learned the wrestling game as well as he knows it. He stated to The Missoulian yesterday morning that it would cost him at least $100 to return from Canada to make a return match with Mr. Curran, in case the challenge at the opera house should not be taken up at once. He asserted that he could not afford to wait longer than Monday night as it was imperative that he be on the reservation following the occupation of a cattle herder by the middle of the week.

However, there were a number of people in Missoula yesterday who were of the opinion that Mr. Matt was a "ringer"; that he is a professional wrestler; that he knows very little about the cowboy business and that he was brought to Missoula for the express purpose of defeating Mr. Curran. No matter what may be the truth in the matter, he is a wrestler, every inch of him, and plainly showed that he was a master of the game. Too much credit can not be given Jack Curran for the excellent contest he put up Friday night. In the face of certain defeat he appeared on the mat gamely and aggressively during every minute of the contest and made a heroic effort to save the money of his friends which had been wagered upon him. In the final bout it was plain that it was all off with him, still he fought against odds and when the end came he was jammed against the mat with a violence that would have put many a man out of business permanently. Still he recovered in an instant and walked off the man [mat], defeated, but still retaining the honor and admiration of every man in the house for the excellent contest he put up.

Competent judges say that the bout was one of the best ever pulled off in any country and Referee McMillan, old stager though he is, said that the match was the best and most interesting that he had ever witnessed.

* * * * * * * * *

Wrestlers Arrive For Match

Two Feathers and Jack O'Neill Came in From West Last Night.

Chief Two Feathers, the champion Indian wrestler arrived in the city last evening, accompanied by his manager, Jack O'Neill, and will begin his training in this city for his match with D. A. McMillan at the Union opera house Friday evening. Two Feathers is fresh from his match with Ole Marsh, which took place in Spokane Friday evening and which resulted in the defeat of Two Feathers.

The Indian is a member of one of the tribes on the Flathead reservation and is a splendid specimen of humanity, towering several inches above his manager, who is nearly six feet tall. This is Two Feathers' first visit to Missoula since he attained prominence as a wrestler, and his appearance on the street is a matter of much interest.

The contest Friday night, when he and McMillan meet on the mat, promises to be one of the best that has ever been seen in Montana. The men will wrestle catch-as-catch-can, two out of three falls, to a finish. Mr. McMillan, who has been in Spokane for the past several days, is expected to arrive in Missoula this evening to finish his training for the contest.

Mr. O'Neill met many of his old time friends in the city last evening and was kept busy for a considerable time shaking hands and renewing old time acquaintances.

Another interesting bout will be the one between Mr. O'Neill and Jack Curran, which will also take place in the Union Friday evening. This contest will also be catch-as-catch-can and by the terms of the agreement Mr. O'Neill is to pin Mr. Curran to the mat three times in an hour of actual wrestling. Both men are confident that they will win the contest and the liveliest of bouts is promised.

****

Two Feathers Goes in Training

Big Indian Expects to Put Up Good Match with M'Millan May 12.

Throughout yesterday, Two Feathers, the big Indian wrestler, found happy repose within his tepee or in some other secluded place, for it was impossible to get any trace of him during the day. In his striking regalia, however, he put in his appearance on Higgins avenue during the early evening and was soon the cynosure of all eyes. The big fellow is a fine specimen of an Indian and although he talks but little English, he is a good observer, and through an interpreter yesterday expressed great confidence in his ability to throw McMillan.

Two Feathers with his manager O'Neill will go into active training this morning and will not let up until Friday evening, May 12, when the big match will be pulled off at the Union opera house here. O'Neill is also training for his match with Jack Curran, and the latter has been training, it may be said from the time that he held his last match in this city with Indian Matt. McMillan arrived in Missoula yesterday.

According to the Spokane Review the match between Two Feathers and Marsh there on Thursday evening was the fiercest that ever took place in that city, and that the people who witnessed it got their money's worth. Marsh took three falls from the Indian, winning the first, third and fourth. The Indian won the second. The Review says:

"At times both would throw science to the winds and match strength and speed against strength and speed. As in his other matches at Spokane, the Indian was a marvel at quick recovery, and struggled on the defensive most of the time. Marsh was the aggressor, leading the struggle all the way. The terrible strain and bruising told more on Jack O'Neill's protege than it did on the hardy Norseman, who was in much better shape than in his previous matches here.

Marsh won the first fall on a half Nelson and a crouch, and using the crouch again in the third bout, forced his opponent's shoulders to the mat with the half Nelson. He won the last bout after a most exciting struggle, forcing the Indian back with the scissors hold and then pinning him down with the reverse arm lock. The Indian won his only fall by catching Marsh unaw[ar]es with an arm roll.

Jack O'Neill, the Indian's trainer, was to throw five men in an hour, but only had four on hand at the beginning of the match. He threw them easily in 33 1-2 minutes. Joe Heinrich, the athletic club champion, then gave O'Neill the prettiest struggle of the evening. The men went on for a 10 minute bout, and O'Neill failed to put Heinrich down in that time. It did not affect his agreement to put down five men in an hour, however.

O'Neill threw Dan Martin in 10 1-2 minutes, Charles Gugat in 9 1-2 minutes, Washtucnan, an Indian, in 9 minutes, and D. H. Flanders, a big 210 pound fellow, in 4 1-2 minutes."

* * * * * * * * *

Two Feathers Wins Wrestling Bout

Indian Secures Two Falls Out of Three, and Curran Is Knocked Out.

In the wrestling bout at the Union last night Two Feathers threw D. A. McMillan twice, securing the second and third falls. The handicap wrestling match went to Jack O'Neill, he throwing Jack Curran into the chairs after 34 minutes and 10 seconds of wrestling and putting the latter down and out for the evening. The fall was to all appearances an accidental one, Mr. Curran striking the back of his head against one of the chairs and completely losing consciousness. Drs. Buckley and Glasgow were hurriedly summoned and these men, together with the assistants to the wrestlers, worked over the injured man for fully an hour before consciousness was restored. After the end of the match Mr. Curran had so far recovered that he was able to walk to his apartments.

The conditions of the match were that O'Neill was to throw Curran three times in an hour of wrestling, but the form showed by the two men last night indicated, according to Mr. Curran's admirers, that O'Neill could not throw his opponent three times during a night of wrestling. The sympathy of the crowd was with Curran and he showed far better form and did better work than in any of his matches which he has had heretofore in Missoula. At the time of the unfortunate accident he was still as strong and wiry as he was when he first went on the mat and it looked as if it would go on indefinitely before a fall could be scored. While Mr. Curran worked on the defensive for the greater part of the time, on two or three occasions he had O'Neill in chancery and came near scoring the fall.

The match went to O'Neill under the rules, which say that an opponent must come back after ten minutes and this time was given. In the match last night Mr. Curran had all of the time taken in the scoring of the two last bouts in the main event in which to recover and go on, but he was too badly knocked out to do so and the match was awarded to O'Neill, the gate receipts being divided equally between the two men.

At the conclusion of the match Henry Matt, in behalf of his cousin, Will Matt, challenged O'Neill to wrestle for $100 a side, $25 to be posted as forfeit. Afterward it was announced that the challenge was accepted and that the two men would meet in this city on May 26 for any part of $500.

Two Feathers and McMillan appeared on the mat promptly at 9 o'clock and a minute afterward Referee Sontag called "Time." They went after it hammer and tongs, each struggling for the mastery, there being no unnecessary fiddling for holds. McMillan took the bout, but it required 25 minutes to do the trick, which was done with a half Nelson and a scissors.

Two Feathers' rest appeared to do him good, for he showed up on the mat fresher than ever and, though McMillan had him in danger on a number of occasions, he turned the tables on his white brother and bore his shoulders to the mat after 18 minutes and 7 seconds of wrestling.

The stock of Two Feathers took an upward lunge among the spectators after this occurrence and when the wrestlers appeared on the mat for the third bout the two men were equal favorites. Both men wrestled carefully; they did not appear to care to take any desperate chances, but Two Feathers proved to be the better man and in 19 minutes and 20 seconds he pinned McMillan's shoulders to the mat with a rolling twist and the match was over.

* * * * * * * * *

UNION OPERA HOUSE

A. H. HARTLEY Manager MISSOULA, MONTANA

Friday Evening, May 26

GRAND DOUBLE

Wrestling Match

CHIEF TWO FEATHERS Champion Indian Wrestler
vs. JACK CURRAN, of Missoula

JACK O'NEILL, of Kalispell, vs.
WILLIAM MATT, of Arlee

Prices, 50s, 75c, $1.00. Stage Seats, $1.50
Seats on Sale Thursday, 4 p. m.

Source: "Union Opera House," *The Daily Missoulian*, May 23, 1905, page 6, col. 6-7

* * * * * * * * *

O'Neil Is Defeated by Wm. Matt

Sturdy Son of Reservation Has His Own Way After Two Bouts.

Handicapped by about 15 pounds of brawn, William Matt defeated Jack O'Neill in the wrestling match at the Union theater last night, winning three out of the five falls. O'Neill started in strong and took the first two falls after a hard struggle. After that he was all in, the sturdy son of the reservation taking the remaining three falls with comparative ease, winning the match.

Afterward he challenged either Jack Curran or Two Feathers, offering to throw the former four times in an hour of wrestling and being willing to take his chances with the Flathead chief in either two out of three or three out of five falls. Neither of the challenges were accepted last night.

Matt had the sympathy of the audience throughout. Every time he gained a point he was roundly cheered and every time he got away from O'Neill, who was the bigger man, the audience went wild and the members of the tribe of Young America jumped up in their chairs and cheered with delight and the older members of the same tribe were not slow to follow the example.

O'Neill worked hard to gain the victory, but he was up against a younger and a stronger man, even though he was a lighter one, and victory perched upon the banner of the Indian.

The match between Two Featehers [sic], and Curran was won by the latter. The big Indian had difficulty in throwing the Missoula boy two times during the hour of wrestling. The first fall was secured by the chief in 34 minutes and the second time that Curran's shoulders touched the mat was 12 minutes later. There are those who believe that Curran, should he act other than on the defensive, can throw the big chief from the Flathead, who has been touted so long as a winner. How the falls were secured is told briefly as follows:

Time of Falls.

First fall — O'Neill, leg and nelson. Time, 20:10.

Second fall — O'Neill, half nelson and crotch. Time, 11:00.

Third fall — Matt, half nelson, crotch and arm roll. Time, 10:50.

Fourth fall — Matt, scissors around head with crotch and body hold. Time, 16:35.

Fifth fall — Matt, scissors, crotch and body hold. Time, 12:40.

Timekeepers — Rhoades and Stoddard.

Referee — J. Lang.

Two Feathers–Curran.

First fall — Two Feathers, body hold and scissors. Time, 24:06.

Second fall — Two Feathers, scissors. Time, 12:22.

Third fall — The Indian had 23 minutes, 32 seconds, in which to gain two falls, but he failed to accomplish it and the referee called time. Two Feathers had a half nelson and leg hold at the call of time.

Timekeepers — McMillan and Rhoades.

Referee — William Wyman.

* * * * * * * * *

Curran Is Winner of Match

Secures Third Fall in the Liveliest Sort of a Bout at Union Opera House.

In the third bout of probably the fiercest wrestling match ever witnessed between two middleweights in this section of the state, Jack Curran was awarded the decision over Will Matt, the man who has defeated all comers since wrestling became a favorite sport in Missoula. Curran was given the third bout in 3:27, having two of Matt's points down with a crotch hold.

Friends of Matt protested vigorously, saying that it was a raw steal, contending that the articles of agreement were not adhered to, inasmuch as pin falls were to govern. In the fall that lost Matt the match, his two legs were in the air, the points of his shoulders touching so quickly as to leave doubt in the minds of some who were not observing very closely. Referee McCarthy's decision, however, was final and the men were ordered off the mat.

Both Matt and Curran were in the pink of condition and from the time they shook hands until the end of the bout it was a fierce struggle. Matt assumed the aggressive from the very start, working like a demon, and forcing Curran into many critical positions, but the latter showed more than his ordinary vitality and squirmed out of a number of precarious attitudes. The first fall was gained by Matt in 11 minutes and 27 seconds with a scissors hold.

In the second bout it took Matt just 7 minutes and 50 second to do the work, flooring his man with a double Nelson and a crotch hold. In this bout the leg work of Matt was simply marvelous, and while the audience was with Curran, they could not help but applaud.

At the beginning of the third bout Curran had rested considerably, one of the preliminary matches between "Big Henry" Matt and O'Neill having intervened. Curran came to the center fresh, and Matt had all of the self-assurance of a man that had the biggest kind of a snap. He did not go after Curran as vigorously as in the preceding bouts, but it was apparent from his actions that he was waiting for a deadly opening. During the maneuvers Curran got a half hammerlock which he turned into a crotch and in an instant Matt's two points were declared down by the referee.

Curran was declared the winner. Matt stepped to the front of the stage and protested and challenged the Missoula man again, but the latter would not entertain any proposition for the time being at least.

Matt, it is said, had a number of side bets up on the match and as a result is considerable of a loser.

In the preliminary match, "Big Henry" Matt and Jack O'Neill gave an excellent exhibition, the former winning the third bout, and thereby the contest.

O'Neill gained the first fall in 12:57 with a hammerlock and leg hold.

The second bout was won by O'Neill with a scissors hold. Time, 9:40.

Third by O'Neill, crotch and body hold. Time, 12:25.

Fourth, O'Neill, half Nelson and hammerlock. Time, 15:40.

For the last bout the participants had approximately 10 minutes to go. In the mixup "Big Henry" got a leg and neck hold on O'Neill and slowly forced his points to the mat and was declared the winner of the bout and of the contest. Time, 4:53.

Owing to the inclement weather the attendance was small, but those who were present agree that they were never given a better night's entertainment, and of the Matt–Curran bouts it may be said that they were the snappiest that have been seen in this section for years.

Matt's Challenge.

Will Matt ap[p]eared before the footlights during the progress of the match and announced to the audience that he was ready to accept D. A. McMillan's challenge to wrestle, but would not enter into an agreement whereby there would be more than two in it, but that he would wrestle McMillan alone. McMil[l]an in replying stated that this would be a harder proposition than to wrestle all four of them, thereby intimating that Matt was the swiftest man in the bunch.

Up until a late hour last night no match had been arranged.

Document 62

Indian Hunter Kills Three Bears

November 23, 1904

Source: "Brave Crawled Into Bears' Den," *The Daily Missoulian*, November 23, 1904, page 6, col. 2.

Editors' note: Charles Finley had a great hunting story in killing three bears and bringing the hides to Missoula for the bounty.

Brave Crawled Into Bears' Den
Killed Mother and Two Cub Bears After an Exciting Time.

For daring and recklessness, the story told yesterday by Charles Finley in Tyler Worden's store, has few equals. Finley is a big Blackfoot [sic] brave and he brought three of the finest bear hides to the bounty inspector yesterday for the purpose of securing the bounty upon the same. The animals were killed at Bonner Monday and the way Finley went about it showed that he does not know the meaning of the word fear.

He had discovered the trail of an old bear and her two cubs leading into a cave in the rocks. All of the tracks pointed inward and Finley knew that his meat was inside the cave. Accordingly, pushing his gun ahead of him, he wiggled his way into a borrow which was so small that he could hardly crawl through. When he had gotten the full length of his body into the cave he lit a match and saw three pairs of eyes glaring at him through the darkness. Picking out the one which was nearest and most convenient, he shot and instantly there was a roar of pain and then Finley backed out of the hole as quickly as he possibly could.

Finley was not a bit too quick in getting out of the hole. Two other bears were after him with growls of rage that fairly made his scalp lock stand on end. Before he could regain his feet the animals were upon him, scampering over him in their blind rage. But Finley was not frightened. He kept his presence of mind throughout and when the bears passed him, he opened up with his Winchester and killed both of them before they had gotten fifty feet away from the mouth of the cave.

Then he rested for a bit, got his wind, and, hearing no more sounds from inside the cave, he made another investigation, finding one of the bear dead just within the entrance of the cave. He dragged it to the open air with considerable difficulty and piled all three of the "varmints" in a heap. Then he went to his camp and sent the s....s out and they brought the three animals to the camp on travois. Once at camp there was the biggest kind of a feed, when the hides were stripped from the carcases.

Yesterday he brought the hides to town. They were those of a mother bear and two cubs and were black and glossy. Bounty Inspector Worden says they were the finest hides that have been brought to Missoula in many a year, and as he is an expert, his opinion goes.

The bears were all comparatively small ones, but the audacity of the Indian in crawling into the bears' den and his not only coming out alive, but killing all three of the bear, has seldom been equaled in the hunting annals of the state.

Chapter 3

Documents of Salish, Pend d'Oreille, and Kootenai History Between 1905-1906

Document 63

Chief Charlot Protests Opening of Flathead Reservation January – March 1905

Source: Samuel Bellew to Commissioner of Indian Affairs, January 12, 1905, letter received 4,318/1905, finance division, RG 75, National Archives, Washington, D.C.; "Flathead Council Is Now in Session Considering Future Conditions," *The Daily Missoulian*, February 5, 1905, page 4, col. 5-6; "Council Continues on Reservation," *The Daily Missoulian*, February 6, 1905, page 2, col. 2; "Flatheads' Council Comes to End," *The Daily Missoulian*, February 9, 1905, page 2, col. 2; "Chief Charlot Is Going East," *The Daily Missoulian*, February 10, 1905, page 4, col. 4-5; "Charlot to Have Place of Honor," *The Daily Missoulian*, February 21, 1905, page 1, col. 5; "Chief Charlot Returns from Capital and Will Call Council," *The Daily Missoulian*, March 18, 1905, page 3, col. 1-2.

Editors' note: Charlo and the other chiefs were outraged that the government was proceeding to allot the Flathead Reservation without the consent of tribal members and leaders and wanted to go to Washington to stop the opening. The *Missoulian* reported the tribal council and Charlot's resulting 1905 trip to Washington, D.C., in detail, but the early reports made it sound like Charlot was only seeking to secure a small timber reserve for the tribe. As the last article made clear, Charlot and the chiefs and headmen were totally opposed to the allotment policy and opening the reservation to white homesteaders.

Department of the Interior,
United States Indian Service,
Flathead Agency, Jocko, Mont. Jan. 12, 1905.

Hon. Commissioner of Indian Affairs,
Washington, D.C.
Sir:

Charlo, Chief of the Flatheads, desires to visit Washington, taking with him Judge Antoine Moise and accompanied by Ed. Deschamps and Pascal Antoine, as interpreters.

The object of Chief Charlo's visit is to protest against the opening of the reservation: It has been explained to him several times, both by Special

Agents who have been here, and myself, that Congress had decided to open the reservation for settlement and to allot the Indians land in severalty, but in face of all this he is still unbelieving and clings to his understanding of the Stevens treaty made in 1855, with his father and at the making of which he was present, and says he will not believe nor consent to it until he is told "face to face by the President."

Should he then be convinced that the reservation will be opened in spite of his protest, he desires to urge that action be taken to preserve some of the timber land for the exclusive use of the Indians, instead of having it all sold as provided in the bill; also that the Indians be protected in their water rights by legislative enactment, that there may not be the same trouble here that he claims exists elsewhere where lands have been alloted and the balance opened for settlement; there are a number of other minor points that he wishes to discuss with the "President."

Charlo is the recognized hereditary Chief of the Flatheads and has considerable influence with them, especially the full-bloods, and should his opposition be placated, considerable petty annoyances might be avoided and the assistance, instead of ill-will of himself and following be gained.

Very respectfully,
Samuel Bellew
U.S. Indian Agent.

****

Flathead Council Is Now in Session Considering Future Conditions Head Men Are Present to Hear Chief Charlot's Plan Regarding an Appeal to President for Setting Aside of Timber for Exclusive Use of Indians.

From authentic sources it is learned that the great council among the confederated tribes of the Flathead reservation at present in progress has been called at the behest of Chief Charlot, who has an important matter to place before the head men and chiefs of the different tribes.

The old chief, who for many years was the recognized head of the tribe and whose father, Chief Victor, signed the Hellgate treaty of 1852 [sic], is desirous of making a trip to Washington and laying before President Roosevelt, personally, a grievance which the Indians have against the bill providing for the opening of the Flathead reservation.

As the measure stands today, through a probable oversight on the drafter of the bill, and through whose efforts the measure became a law of the land, no provision has been made to retain any of the timber lands on the reservation for the use of the Indians.

Chief Charlot, who is recognized as one of the leaders among the Indians of the United States, has given the bill opening the reservation his careful consideration and he has discovered that no provision has been made reserving the Indians any timber rights whatever.

His idea is that within the next few years there will be a scarcity of timber for firewood purposes on the reservation; that when that time arrives the Indians who have been allotted their lands in severality, will be compelled to buy their firewood from the white men who become the owners of the timbered area. To obviate this condition he thinks a personal appeal to the president will result in much good and that a law can be passed during the present session of congress which will carry a provision to the effect that a forest reserve will be created providing that certain lands on the reservation will be the exclusive property of the Indians. This will give a timber supply to the Indian residents of the reservation that will last for many years to come.

Chief Charlo
Source: Photograph by John K. Hillers,
Bureau of American Ethnology, Washington, D.C., 1884
Photograph Archives, Montana Historical Society, Helena, Montana,
detail of photo 954-526

Generally speaking, according to the information secured in Missoula yesterday, the project is meeting with approval among the members of the confederated tribes and it is believed that the Indians on the Flathead will raise enough money to send Chief Charlot and his interpreter, as well as a number of other Indians to the national capital to ask for legislation along the lines above suggested.

The old chief was one of the most bitter Indians on the reservation in opposing the opening of the reservation, but when he was shown the clause in the Stevens treaty which provided that the president could allot the land in severality to the members of the tribe when the proper time arrived, he acquiesced, and although the news was most astounding to him, he made no comment further than to say: "That makes sweat," and he then gave up the lands which he had been taught for many years past was the exclusive property of the Flatheads and the other confederated tribes.

It is believed that Chief Charlot will win all of the other Indians over to his views and that he will leave within the next two weeks for Washington, there to make a formal protest to the "great father" and to place in his hands the petition from the members of the different tribes on the Flathead reservation for a timber reservation to be the exclusive property of the Flathead reservation Indians, and on which there will be no poaching by the white men after the reservation is formally opened.

* * * * * * * * *

Council Continues on Reservation

Flathead Indians Have Not Concluded Their Discussion Regarding Timber.

The council of Flathead Indians and chiefs of allied tribes is still in session. Those engaged in the deliberation of the questions which have arisen, maintain absolute silence regarding the proceedings. No white men are permitted in the council tepee and even Agent Bellew is ignorant as to the secret proceeding. That there is friction among the headmen of the tribes, is evidenced by the fact that so much secrecy is being maintained. Chief Charlot is known to wield considerable influence among the older men in the council and he is in earnest in his efforts to secure from President Roosevelt a forest reserve which shall forever remain the exclusive property of the Flathead Indians. Chief Charlot's plan is to go to Washington in person and present the Indians' side of the question prior to the issuance of the proclamation declaring the reservation open for settlement.

Charlot has frequently complained regarding the failure of congress to provide a protection for Indians' firewood and building logs and at the time runners were sent out to summon the chiefs in council, Charlot stated his plan. Since that time the question of the rights of selection of land in severalty has come up in connection with the enrollment which is now in progress.

It is intimated that Charlot stands for allotment of land to full bloods only and that the privilege extending the right to all who have any trace of Flathead blood in their veins, is extremely opposed by the old chief. Charlot is said to be a brainy man and the final result of the council may mark an epoch in the checkered career of the Flathead and allied tribes. The whites look for an announcement tomorrow.

* * * * * * * * *

Flatheads' Council Comes to End
Result of Conference Is Safely Guarded by Those Present.

The great council of the Flatheads, which has been in progress near the mission for the past several days, and at which a number of matters of interest to the confederated tribes have been considreed [sic], has come to an end but whether or not Chief Charlot has carried his point and will be sent to Washington as a delegate from the tribe to lay his proposition for a forest reserve for the use of the Indians in the future before the president can not be learned in Missoula, although it is generally conceded that Charlot has won out in his proposal and will go to Washington if the consent of the d[e]partm[e]nt can be secured. It is stated, however, that the government has flatly refused its permission.

Another important matter which was before [t]he council was the considering of who among the mixed bloods are eligible to enrollment and who will come under the head of members of the tribe eligible to allotment of land when the reservation is opened for settlement. Quite a large number of claimants, who allege they are entitled to enrollment, have not yet been adopted into the tribe according to the custom which has been in vogue for centuries and as a result of the conference a number of adoptions may be made in the near future, but this is opposed by Charlot.

While Charlot is no longer recognized as the hereditary chief of the Flatheads by the government, he is nevertheless considered as the dean of all the chiefs of the confederated tribes and what he stands for is generally considered good enough for the other chiefs and head men to follow. He is vigorous and determined in the pushing of any project he may undertake and his friends in

Missoula — and he has a lot of them, too — are all sanguine in their belief that the old man will do considerable good if the government will allow him to go to Washington and personally talk to the "Great Father" concerning plans he has which will result in benefit to the members of the confederated tribes.

* * * * * * * * *

Chief Charlot Is Going East

Ruler of Flatheads Determined to Tell President of Tribe's Needs.

Chief Charlot, hereditary chief of the Flathead tribe and dean of the chieftains and head men of the confederated tribes on the reservation, accompanied by his interpreter, Antoine Paschell, is in the city on his way to Washington, where he will personally lay certain matters before President Roosevelt in regard to the opening of the Flathead reservation. All of these matters were discussed at the big council which was held near the agency last week, the story of which has already been published in the Missoulian.

Yesterday, through an interpreter, Chief Charlot talked interestingly and stated that he expected to accomplish considerable good by his trip to Washington. He is one of the most able Indians alive today and he thoroughly understands all of the conditions which prevails in the political world. He knows that President Roosevelt, by reason of his resident in the west, is better acquainted with the conditions which prevail in Montana than any other man who has ever been in the presidential chair, and by reason of this fact he expects his petition will not fall upon deaf ears.

For some time past the old chief has been endeavoring to secure permission from the department to go to Washington, but this has been refused him. On account of this refusal the council last week was called. At the council enough money to send him and his interpreter to see the "Great Father" was pledged and Charlot has gotten this far on his journey. He will remain in Missoula for a few days, until another message is sent the department asking that Agent Bellew be also allowed to go to Washington with the chief. If this request is refused then Charlot and his interpreter will make the journey together.

There seems to be little desire on the part of the department to absolutely prohibit Charlot from going to Washington, the messages which declined to authorize the trip advising him that owing to the short session of congress, he will be able to accomplish but very little in the righting of the wrongs he alleges and the plans for the betterment of the condition of the Indians which he proposes. In this matter he is advised to wait for a more propitious time.

However, Charlot is of the opinion that there is no time like the present to do a good deed, and if advices authorizing Agent Bellew are not received in the city within the next few days, the journey to the national capital will be begun by the noted Indian.

In addition to the forest reserve which is desired by the Indians and which has already been exploited in the Missoulian, Chief Charlot has other projects which he desires to bring to the attention of the president. One of these is the preservation of the water rights which the Indians have acquired on the reservation. Quite a large number of Indian ranchers have learned the value of irrigating ditches and at no little trouble and toil they have brought the water upon their lands. As it is these water rights are not of record; the Indian has the right of use and no more, and the recommendation will be made to the president that a special act of congress be passed guaranteeing the right of irrigation and preserving the rights already in use to the Indians who have acquired them. In addition, as there are a number of excellent reservoir sites on the reservation, some action will be asked from the national government to guarantee their use to the confederated tribes.

Another matter which Charlot discussed yesterday was that in the Flathead opening bill no provision is made for the care of the poor, crippled, blind and infirm residents of the reservation — and there are quite a number of them too — and he will ask that some provision, such as the county uses in the care of its poor, be provided for the Indians.

Charlot asserts that the Indians will all have some money coming to them when the reservation opens, but he and the others who were promised money when they gave up their lands in the Bitter Root valley thirty years ago have had experience which they do not relish and are still awaiting the money which was promised for the sale of the lands which they relinquished. He thinks the same methods may prevail with the opening of the Flathead, and if it does, then the old and infirm members of the tribes will starve to death while they are waiting for the money which has been promised.

Charlot is still hale and hearty and is very vehement in his opinion that good will result from his visit to Washington. He is one of the few members of the Flathead tribe who cannot speak the English language, keeping an interpreter with him whenever he is away from the reservation. He is very pronounced in his views in regard to people of mixed blood being allowed allotments on the reservation and asserts that the white men have already gotten enough graft from the Indians; that they should not be allowed to come to the Flathead because they have a little Indian blood in their veins and, through their superior business judgment and knowledge of soil, select the cream of the lands of the reservation. This is another matter he will bitterly oppose when he gets to Washington and talks with the "Great Father" regarding the woes of the Flatheads and the procedure which should be following in their rightment.

For a while Charlot was in consultation with an attorney of Missoula yesterday and, though his trip to Washington may be made in opposition to the wishes of the Indian department, it can be depended upon that he will keep well within his rights and will secure an audience with the president, even should his petition be turned down again, as it was on the occasion of his last visit to Washington, when he, in company with a number of the reservation stockmen, lodged a protest against the collection of the grazing tax which is exacted from all of the stockmen of the reserve who own in excess of 100 head of horses or cattle.

* * * * * * * * *

Charlot to Have Place of Honor

Special to The Missoulian.

Washington, Feb. 20. — Chief Charlot arrived Saturday with Pascale, his interpreter. To-day they called upon Congressman Dixon at the capital.

Mr. Dixon is arranging an interview for them with the president and commissioner. Charlot says he will not believe the reservation is to be opened until the president tells him so. He will remain several days.

Mr. Dixon is arranging with the inauguration committee to give Charlot a place of honor in the parade.

* * * * * * * * *

Chief Charlot Returns from Capital and Will Call Council
Famous Flathead Will Protest Against Opening of Reservation and During Interview with President Stated His Reasons Which May Result in Investigation.

Chief Charlot and Interpreter Michael returned from Washington yesterday afternoon on No. 3. The old chief was so weary when Missoula was reached that he decided to stop off and rest for a day before continuing his journey to the reservation.

Interpreter Michael says the inauguration ceremonies were particularly interesting and that Chief Charlot enjoyed them, though he was not in the parade. The chief had a short talk with the president, explaining his views. He met Senator Carter, Congressman Dixon, Judge Knowles and other Montanans.

The interpreter says it is a mistake to suppose that Chief Charlot went to Washington to insist upon a timber reserve being set aside for the use of the Indians. That was attended to before he and Charlot reached Washington, Mr. Dixon having had the bill amended to include a timber reserve for the Indians.

The fact is, Charlot does not want the reservation opened at all, and will do all in his power to prevent its being opened. He says that under the plan of allotment provided for in the bill too many breeds are getting a finger in the pie. He has no objection to the half-breeds of the three tribes on the reservation getting land, but there is an innumerable host of quarters and eighths, and many with just a trace of Indian blood who have been enrolled and who will be given land. Again, there are a number of Nez Perces on the Flathead reservation who claim to have been transferred there and they also demand enrollment and land. Indians from other lands are there who demand enrollment, but it not known whether any of them have succeeded in their desire or not.

Charlot asked for a congressional committee to investigate, and the interpreter says that while this may not be given, there will be a special agent sent to Montana and that he may be expected some time during the coming summer. Meantime, Charlot will call a council, which will be held on the reservation some time next month. He will endeavor to get the council to petition the government to delay the opening of the reservation until such time as a commission can examine and report upon the feasibility of opening the land to settlement. If it be decided that the reservation must be opened, Charlot will then endeavor to have only a portion of the reservation opened. He is bitterly opposed to the Indians being forced to select lands. He says that it is unfair to make Indians lose their tribal rights and become white men. They are unfitted as a rule to become farmers and need the assistance the government now gives them. Charlot says it makes no difference what the other Indians may decide to do, his band, removed from the Bitter Root valley, now in the southern portion of the reservation, along the Jocko, will never consent to receive lands in severalty. The whites took their land, good land, and forced them to go on the reservation, where they did not want to go, promising them that the land should be theirs and their children's forever, and that land they expect to keep, unless the government goes back on its solemn pledge.

The interpreter was asked how Charlot enjoyed his trip and in reply said that the old chief didn't enjoy all of it. He was thinking, thinking all the time. He is getting old and dislikes traveling. He would not have taken the trip had he not been convinced that he could stop the reservation being thrown open to settlement. He doesn't care for a timber reserve, or for a farm or for anything else in particular, except to retain the reservation as it is.

Asked if in the council held before Charlot went to Washington it was not decided that the Indians would be satisfied with the plan to open the reservation, provided they were given a timber reserve, he said that no such an argument was reached. Charlot did not believe that the reservation was to be opened until he reached Washington. He says he can't understand it. Although the treaty provides that the reservation can be opened, Charlot says he never knew that provision was in it, and can't understand how it got there.

When the old chief reaches the reservation he proposes to make a personal canvass of the situation. He says that while he may not prevent all the reservation from being thrown open he believes he can stop all of it from being opened to settlement. He remains implacable. He will never consent to have his people alloted land in severalty.

Document 64

Indians Spend Bitter Root Land Money in Missoula March 1905

Source: "Indians Spend Coin for Gee-Gaws," *The Daily Missoulian*, March 1, 1905, page 6, col. 2; "Money Well Spent by Indian," *The Daily Missoulian*, March 3, 1905, page 6, col. 4.

Editors' note: Payments for sales of Bitter Root Valley lands resulted in business for Missoula merchants. Some of the money was spent for alcohol, but others spent their money on farm equipment and household supplies.

Indians Spend Coin for Gee-Gaws
Bucks Secure Liquor from Some Source with Money Obtained from Lands.

During the past few days a number of the Indians of the Flathead reservation have been in the city spending money. Recently $5,000 was distributed among a number of the families, the money having been derived from the sale of the Bitter Root valley lands which were relinquished at the time Chief Charlot and about forty other heads of families moved from the Bitter Root valley to the Flathead reservation.

All of the Indians who have been in town during the past few days have been in funds. The bucks, and some of them wore the uniform of the United States, indicating that they were in the service of the government as agency police, evidently invested a considerable amounnt [sic] in booze, as many of them were in a more or less drunken condition. The s....s purchased new silk handkerchiefs for headgear, silk skirts and number of such other gee-gaws which went to their ornamentation — all the same as their white sisters.

Some of the money which has been distributed on this occasion will be sent to Chief Charlot at Washington, who, in spite of the assertions made by knockers and sore-heads, is in Washington in the interests of the tribe and will make a determined effort to have the "great white father" take some recognition of the needs of the Indians — provide them with firewood reservation, look after the priority of their water rights and make some provisions for the care and maintenance of the poor and needy.

The money which the red men received this week has been a long time coming. Many years ago about forty families of the Flatheads, Chief Charlot being the leader, refused to leave the Bitter Root valley and accept the reservation which the tribe at present occupies. After the lapse of a number of years the Indians were induced to leave their ranches in the Bitter Root, the government promising to sell the land at its true worth and pay the same to the Indians who relinquished it. After the lapse of a considerable time this was done and the money distributed this week is one of a series of payments which will be continued as long as there are any lands to be sold in the Bitter Root which are classed as Indian lands. Some of this land has been appraised as high as $20 per acre and the cheapest of it is valued at $6 per acre by the government agents and citizens who twice placed an appraised value upon the lands throughout the valley.

* * * * * * * * *

Money Well Spent by Indian
Prosperous Red Man Uses Coin to Secure Farming Implements.

There is at least one Indian of the reservation who put the money he recently received from the government to good use and he drove out of town last evening as proud a man as ever left the city. And he had reason to be. He had a brand new Schuttler wagon, painted the brightest red, and it was drawn by two white horses that would average up well in any country, provided they were in good flesh. Inside the wagon rode his s.... and she held the horses while the buck looked after his different purchases. In addition, she held a baby in her lap and from time to time her spare attention was taken up by two new dogs which the couple were taking out to the ranch. Occasionally one of the dogs — they were both tied to the seat — would jump out in spite of the efforts of the s.... and he would hang himself until the woman could dispose of the baby and lift the canine back into the wagon, where it would gasp and struggle for breath, only to try the same trick again at the first opportunity. In addition, the wagon contained a new plow and, strange to say, a baby's high chair, carefully wrapped in paper and gunnysacks, to keep it unsullied until the home wickiup was reached.

The Indian is one of the prosperous ones on the reservation, being a rancher and self-supporting.

Document 65

Michel Pablo Not Liable for State Taxes

April 24, 1905

Source: "United States v. Heyfron, County Treasurer. (Circuit Court, D. Montana. April 24, 1905.), No. 690," *The Federal Reporter*, vol. 138, (July-September 1905), pages 964-968.

Editors' note: This decision represented another defeat in Missoula County's efforts to extract taxes from Flathead Reservation mixed bloods. The decision also included biographical information about Pablo.

United States v. Heyfron, County Treasurer.
(Circuit Court, D. Montana. April 24, 1905.)
No. 690.

Indians — Adoption of Half-Breed Into Tribe — Tribal Rights.

> The various acts of Congress relating to Indians, including those relating to the Flathead Indian Nation, as well as the practice of the executive departments of the government, recognize the right of a tribe to adopt as a member thereof an Indian of the half blood who has continued to reside on the reservation as an Indian, and one so adopted has all the rights of a tribal Indian and a ward of the United States, including the exemption from state taxation of his property held on the reservation, so long as his tribal relation continues.

In Equity. Suit for injunction.

Carl Rasch, U.S. Atty. (Marshall & Stiff, of council), for plaintiff.

Woody & Woody, for defendant.

Hunt, District Judge. The United States brought this bill against the county treasurer of the county of Missoula, within the state of Montana, praying for a writ of injunction to restrain the said treasurer from enforcing the collection of certain taxes which he was seeking to collect from Michel Pablo. It is alleged that Pablo is an Indian person and a member of the Flathead Indian Nation, and was such during the year of 1903, when the defendant attempted to collect taxes; that, under the laws of the United States and the treaties heretofore entered into by the United States with the Flathead Indian Nation,

Michel Pablo
Source: Photograph Archives, Montana Historical Society, Helena, Montana, photo 944-242

the said Pablo became, and, as a member of the Flathead Indian Nation, is, a ward of the United States and entitled to own and hold personal property on the said Indian reservation in his own right, free from taxation by the state and the county of Missoula. The answer denies that Pablo is an Indian or a member of the Flathead Nation, and denies that he is entitled to own and hold property on the Flathead Reservation exempt from taxation.

There is but one question presented by the pleadings, which is, was Michel Pablo a ward of the government of the United States, by reason of his being an Indian and maintaining tribal relations with certain Indian tribes? The facts are these: Michel Pablo was born about 58 or 60 years ago, east of the Rocky Mountains, in what is now known as part of the state of Montana, and which was at the time of his birth a section recognized as Indian country, occupied by Blackfeet Indians. His father was a Spaniard, and his mother a full-blood Piegan Indian. His father died when he was young, and after the death of the father the boy accompanied his Indian mother to the Coleville Reservation, in the territory of Washington. His mother died there, and he remained on the Coleville Reservation until he was about 13, associating in his boyhood with Indian boys. Then he went to De Smet, Mont., which is now within Missoula county; and after staying there a short time he went to the Flathead Reservation, and has lived there ever since, or for about 42 or 43 years. About 4 years after he removed to the Flathead Reservation a council of Indian chiefs of the Indian tribes and Indians was called for the purpose of considering the question of the adoption of Pablo. This council was held in 1864. Pablo himself was present at the council. The chiefs announced his adoption after the council, and ever since that time he has been treated as a member of the tribe by the Indians themselves, and has complied with all the laws, rules, and regulations of the tribe. He married a member of the tribe, and has reared a family, and never has severed his tribal relations, but without interruption has maintained the habits and customs of the Indians. The government of the United States has made no difference in its treatment of Pablo from that accorded to Indians of the tribe, and Pablo has participated and acted with the tribes and nations in tribal affairs and councils and otherwise. His name appears upon the official roll and the annuity roll of the government of the United States, and about 20 years ago, when the Northern Pacific Railroad Company obtained a right of way through the reservation, and paid the Indians about $21,000 therefor, Michael Pablo received a share in the distribution of the fund, participated in the council of the Indians held in respect to the matter, and was in all respects recognized as entitled to the privileges and rights of membership in the tribe.

From these facts, and the law to be applied to them, I conclude that Michael Pablo was adopted by the Indians rightfully upon the reservation, and that he became tied to the tribes by a relationship lawfully made, and was and is, in law, an Indian sustaining tribal relations. That the Indians had right of adoption, without doing violence to the Stevens treaty of 1856 [sic], is inferable from the several acts of Congress bearing upon rights of Indians, and particularly from the provisions of section 1 of "An act to provide for the removal of the Flathead and other Indians from the Bitter Root Valley in the territory of Montana," approved June 5, 1872, c. 308, 17 Stat. 226, wherein it was provided that the President should remove as soon as practicable "the Flathead Indians (whether full or mixed bloods), and all other Indians connected with said tribe, and recognized as members thereof, from Bitter Root Valley, in the territory of Montana, to the general reservation in said territory (commonly known as the Jocko Reservation), which by a treaty concluded at Hell Gate, in the Bitter Root Valley, July sixteenth, eighteen hundred and fifty-five, and ratified by the Senate March eighth, eighteen hundred and fifty-nine, between the United States and the confederated tribes of Flathead, Kootenai, and Pend d'Oreille Indians, and was set apart and reserved for the use and occupation of said confederated tribes."

The right accorded to all persons who are in whole or in part of Indian blood or descent, who are entitled to allotments of land under any law or treaty, to sue in the Circuit Court of the United States, is also recognition of Congress that those who are but part Indian in blood or descent may be entitled to rights of allotments of land accorded other Indians under laws or treaties. Act Cong. Feb. 6, 1901, c. 217, 31 Stat. 760, amending Act Aug. 15, 1894, c. 290, 28 Stat. 286; 3 Fed. Stat. Ann. p. 503. The act of Congress approved April 23, 1904 (St. 1903-1904, c. 1495, 33 Stat. 302), providing for the survey and allotment of lands within the limits of the Flathead Indian Reservation, expressly authorizes allotments to be made "to all persons having tribal rights, with said confederated tribes of Flatheads, Kootenais, Upper Pend d'Oreille, and such other Indians and persons holding tribal relations as may rightfully belong on said Flathead Indian Reservation, including the Lower Pend d'Oreille or Kalispel Indians now on the reservation under the provisions of the allotment laws of the United States"; and by section 14 of the same act provision is expressly made for certain expenditures "for the benefit of the said Indians and such persons having tribal rights on the reservation," etc. Taking these several acts of Congress together, I gather from their language that Congress has dealt with the Indians and persons having tribal rights on the reservation with the clear intention to make no distinction between them in the extension of benefits of allotment provisions, and, by expressly including Indians and such persons as have tribal rights on the reservation, it is manifest that Congress intended and did recognize that tribal relations might be created in a way recognized by other acts of Congress or by executive and judicial interpretation.

We find another instance of the recognition of the practice of Indian tribes, in section 1 of the act of Congress approved June 7, 1897, c. 3, "making appropriations for current and contingent expenses of the Indian department, and for other purposes" (30 Stat. 90), wherein it is provided "that all children born of a marriage heretofore solemnized between a white man and an Indian woman by blood and not by adoption, where said Indian woman is at this time, or was at the time of her death, recognized by the tribe, shall have the same rights and privileges to the property of the tribe to which the mother belongs, or belonged at the time of her death, by blood, as any other member of the tribe, and no prior act of Congress shall be construed as to debar such child of such right."

Turning now to the opinions of the courts regarding the status of persons claiming to be members of Indian tribes, we find that in the case of Sloan v. United States (C. C.) 118 Fed. 283, Judge Shiras held that:

> "Recognition of persons as members of an Indian tribe might be had and allotments of land might be made where the tribe clearly deemed such person as a member; and the right of the Interior Department in making an allotment to persons other than actual resident members of the tribe was recognized where the Indians had acted in open council, and had declared persons to be members of the tribe, and entitled to share in the allotments of tribal lands."

The learned judge distinguishes between the rights of persons not recognized by the Indians as members of the tribe and those that had by action of the council been placed in tribal relation on the reservation.

In United States v. Higgins (C. C.) 103 Fed. 348, after a careful review of the class to which half-breed Indians belong, Judge Knowles used this language:

> "Considering the treaties and statutes in regard to half-breeds, I may say that they never have been treated as white people entitled to the right of American citizenship. Special provision has been made for them — special reservations of land, special appropriations of money. No such provision has been made for any other class. It is well known to those who have lived upon the frontier in America that, as a rule, half-breeds or mixed-blood Indians have resided with the tribes to which their mothers belonged; that they have, as a rule never found a welcome home with their white relatives, but with

their Indian kindred. It is but just, then, that they should be classed as Indians, and have all the rights of the Indian."

In 7 Op. Attys. Gen. 746, it is said, "Half-breed Indians are to be treated as Indians, in all respects, so long as they retain their tribal relations."

The Supreme Court, in Roff v. Burney, 168 U.S. 218, 18 Sup. Ct. 60, 42 L. Ed. 442, recognized the Chickasaw Nation of Indians, and reaffirmed previous decisions declaring that the Indian tribes possess attributes of nationality, holding them to be not foreign, but domestic, dependent nations. Effect was there given to a legislative act of the Chickasaw Nation, and the validity of an Indian law, withdrawing citizenship from the wife of the plaintiff, and the consequent withdrawal from the plaintiff of all the rights and privileges of citizenship in the Chickasaw Nation was decided as determined by the authority of that nation, without being subject to correction by any direct appeal from the judgment of the Chickasaw courts.

In Nofire v. United States, 164 U.S. 657, 17 Sup. Ct. 212, 41 L. Ed. 588, it was decided that the Cherokee Nation had a right to recognize one as a citizen by adoption of the nation, and that, where there had been such adoption, jurisdiction over certain offenses was vested in the courts of the Cherokee Nation.

In Raymond v. Raymond, 83 Fed. 721, 28 C. C. A. 38, adoption through intermarriage under the laws of the Cherokee Nation was also recognized.

It is true that the stipulations and treaties entered into between the Cherokee Nation and the United States are especially referred to in these decisions, but I cite them upon the general principle that, no treaty provision to the contrary existing, the courts have recognized a general right of adoption by Indian tribes of certain person who have lived upon the reservation and married members of the tribe, and who have affiliated with the tribes, who are themselves mixed bloods, and whose habits and associations have been and are similar to and with the adopting tribe or tribes.

Counsel for the treasurer of Missoula county relies with some confidence upon the decision of the Supreme Court of Montana in the case of Stiff v. McLaughlin, 19 Mont. 300, 48 Pac. 232. There it was generally said in an opinion rendered by Justice Buck that the provisions of article 2 of the treaty of 1855 with the Flathead Indians provided that there might be placed on their reservation "other friendly bands of Indians of the territory of Washington," who might agree to be consolidated with the Flathead Nation, did not authorize the adoption into the tribe of a quarter-breed Chippewa who was married to a Flathead woman. But in the case as it was presented to the Supreme Court the question of the authority of the various tribes which constituted the Flathead Nation to adopt other Indians as members of the tribes was not discussed as necessary to a decision. Upon the sufficiency of the pleaded defense the court rested its decision. If the answer had set up adoption and the right of adoption, and had pleaded more fully, I do not believe the dictum of the learned justice who wrote the opinion would have found the place that it has.

We find, too, that the executive authority of the general government has recognized the status of person situated as Pablo is as that of tribal Indians. In an opinion rendered by Atty. Gen. Olney, reported in 20 Op. Attys. Gen. 711, he advised the Secretary of the Interior that the laws and usages of the tribe of Indians should determine the question whether any particular person was or was not an Indian, within the meaning of an agreement that had been entered into between the Sioux Nation and the government of the United States. He regarded those questions as rather of fact pertaining to local usages, and, citing the decision of the Supreme Court in Smith v. United States, 151 U.S. 50, 14 Sup. Ct. 234, 38 L. Ed. 67, advised that "presumptively a person apparently of mixed blood, residing upon a reservation and claiming to be an Indian, is in fact an Indian." In the United States v. Higgins, supra, Judge Knowles also followed the doctrine that courts will generally conform to the executive and political departments of the government in their recognition of persons as Indians, where they are at least half bloods, whose fathers were white men, and where the half blood has lived and resided with the tribe to which the mother belonged.

As a result of these several considerations, I conclude that under the facts Pablo is a ward of the government, that his ties with the Indians were long since established, and, being unbroken, still exist; and that he is therefore entitled to immunity from state and county taxes.

The injunction will be made permanent.

Document 66

Allen Sloan Not Liable for State Taxes

April 24, 1905

Source: "United States v. Heyfron, County Treasurer. (Circuit Court, D. Montana. April 24, 1905.), No. 691," *The Federal Reporter*, vol. 138 (July-September 1905), pages 968-969.

Editors' note: This federal court decision paralleled the one for Michel Pablo and supported the right of the Flathead Reservation Indian tribes to adopt members from other tribes. Also see the biographical information about Allen Sloan.

United States v. Heyfron, County Treasurer.
(Circuit Court, D. Montana. April 24, 1905.)
No. 691.

Indians — Adoption Into Tribe — Tribal Rights.

> A quarter-blood Indian, who has during the most of his life resided with the Indians, and who, on his marriage to a member of the Flathead Nation, was adopted by such nation, and has since resided on the reservation, and has been treated as a member of the tribe and by the United States is entitled to the same rights as other members of the tribe, including the exemption of his property from state taxation.

In Equity. Suit for injunction.

Carl Rasch, U.S. Atty. (Marshall & Stiff, of counsel).

Woody & Woody, for defendant.

Hunt, District Judge. This case involves questions similar to those just decided in the case of the United States v. Dan J. Heyfron, as County Treasurer of Missoula County, in the State of Montana, 138 Fed. 964, but the injunction here sought is to restrain the treasurer of Missoula county from collecting taxes alleged to be due by one Allen Sloan. Sloan, whom the government claims is its ward, is 40 years old, and was born at Crow Wing, Minn., where he lived until he was 10 or 11 years old. Crow Wing was at the time a trading post in the Indian country, and inhabited by Mississippi Chippewa Indians. Sloan himself is a quarter-breed Chippewa, his mother being a half-breed Chippewa.

When the boy lived at Crow Wing he associated with Indians. When he was 10 or 12 years of age he moved to St. Cloud, Minn. St. Cloud was a village in the state of Minnesota. He lived there until he was 17 years old. He then worked as lumberman and at various pursuits in Dakota, and came to the Flathead Reservation in 1884, where he has lived ever since; having married in 1884 a half-breed Kootenai Indian woman. In the same year of his marriage he was adopted by the Flathead Nation, two councils having been held for the purpose of such adoption. At one of the councils there were present Chiefs of the Pend d'Oreille Indians, while the second was a general one of the Flathead Nation. Ever since his adoption, Sloan has been treated as other members of the tribe have been. He has drawn rations, annuities, and payments, and has enjoyed the privileges accorded to full-blood Indians on the reservation. The government and the Indians have regarded him as a member of the Flathead Nation. He has participated in the Indian councils as a member of the tribe, and voted on matters transacted by the councils. He was enrolled as a member of the Flathead Nation upon a roll prepared by a special agent of the Indian Department of the United States, and, after special evidence had been called for by the general government, in order that it might be better satisfied of his right to be placed upon the roll before its approval by the Indian Office in Washington, additional testimony was sent, and thereafter instructions were given to have Sloan's name placed upon the roll, provided he should relinquish his rights on the White Earth Reservation.

Upon the facts, Sloan's case is not as strong as Pablo's; yet, upon the authority of the decision in Michel Pablo's case, it is ordered that the injunction prayed for by the United States be made permanent.

Document 67

Land Surveys Begin on Reservation as Prelude to Allotment April 26, 1905

Source: "Many Parties Are Out on Survey of Reserve," *The Anaconda Standard*, April 26, 1905, page 12, col. 1-2.

Editors' note: The first step in applying the allotment policy to the Flathead Reservation was to survey the land according to federal government standards. The article does note that tribal members opposed allotment.

Many Parties Are Out on Survey of Reserve
Indians in Many Cases Object to Work.
They Do Not Understand
And Resent the Appearance of Surveyors on the Lands
They Have Possessed So Long —
One S.... Puts Up a Fist Fight.

Missoula, April 25. — Ernest R. Page, one of the surveyors who contracted for part of the work on the Flathead reservation and who was the first surveyor to run a line of the survey preparatory to the opening of the reservation, has just completed his contract and brought his party in from the field this morning. Mr. Page has been operating from a point near Arlee and running 18 miles north and 12 miles west from that place. The greater part of his work was done last fall, as his first lines were a base upon which the other surveyors worked, and this spring it has only taken him about two weeks to finish. He has had a party of six men and a camp outfit of two wagons and nine horses.

C. E. Redfield of Missoula has a contract for several townships on the reserve and will leave Missoula in about two weeks with a party of seven men and full outfit to begin operations. Mr. Redfield has been on the reservation several times in connection with some of the other contractors, and in an interview with a Standard correspondent gave considerable information on this work.

Mr. Redfield stated that there were 12 contracts let already for surveys and that most of the contractors were already in the field. Each contract consists of from four to six townships, according to the location and kind of country to be worked, no single contract exceeding $5,000. It is the wish of the government to have the work completed as soon as possible, but according to contract the work must be finished by Oct. 31, 1905, and the field notes must be filed in the office of the surveyor general at Helena by Dec. 31, 1905. A great many of the contracts will be finished before the required time, as, of course, each contractor will rush his work as fast as possible. The work of the engineers is to first run the township lines and then subdivide them into sections, corners being set and plainly marked on all of the lines every half mile.

Most of the parties consist of from six to eight men and their camp outfits generally include two wagons with four horses each. The country will allow of the wagons being driven nearly everywhere and pack outfits are necessary only in a very few instances. There is a portion of the reserve, however, on the west side of the Mission range of mountains, where the country is exceedingly rough, but as yet no contracts have been let for this work.

The outfits now on the reservation supply at Missoula, Plains, Ravalli, St. Ignatius and Kalispell, according to the location of the part of the reserve upon which they are working.

Mr. Redfield says that in a good many instances the Indians of the reserve resent the appearance of the surveyors on the lands they have for so long claimed as their own and sometimes threaten the parties with violence if they do not leave. In one instance some members of a party were run off an Indian's land at the point of a gun. Another time several of the bucks came to the camp while the party was all absent but the cook and the camp-tender and attempted to make them pack up and drive away, but after having it explained that it was the men out in the field that were doing the damage they decided it would do no good to drive the two men off the land. At another time the surveyors were running a line which ran directly through the center of an Indian's house and when they came into the yard one of the s.... inmates put up a stiff fist fight with one of the men.

As a general rule, however, the work of the contractor and his men is very pleasant and in several cases the families of those at work accompany them and make the work a summer's outing.

Speaking of the prospective mineral resources of the reservation, Mr. Redfield stated there was but very little definitely known as to the extent of the mineral deposits. No prospectors have ever been allowed upon the reservation for the purpose of investigating and the only samples that go to show the existence of mineral are what have been found by the Indians themselves and exhibited to some of their friends. From this source stories have been in circulation for some time about a fabulously rich copper field situated close to St. Ignatius mission, but these reports have not been verified to any extent.

Document 68

White Businessmen Claim Flathead Lake Dam Site May 13, 1905

Source: Jeremiah Miller to Commissioner of Indian Affairs, May 13, 1905, from file 74,927/1907, Flathead 371, part 2, Chief Clerk to G. L. MacGibbon, December 14, 1909, from file 74,927/1907 Flathead 371, Central Classified Files, RG 75, National Archives, Washington, D.C.

Editors' note: As mentioned before, the ink was barely dry on the President's signature on the Flathead allotment bill before white businessmen were swarming to claim the Flathead Lake dam site as their personal property. The battle over development of the dam site was to continue into the 1930s. The 1909 letter pointed out the legal justification for reserving the dam site for the tribes.

Montana Water Power and Electric Company
Kalispell, Mont., May 13th. 1905.

Hon. Francis E. Leupp, Esq.
Commissioner of Indian Affairs,
Washington, D.C.
Dear Sir:—

There is enclosed herewith, the following: Certified copy of "Notice of appropriation of Water Right" as appropriated June 29th. 1904; filed for Record on July 2nd. 1904, at 9:00 A.M.; certified copy of "Appropriation of Water Right" appropriated June 30th. 1904, and filed for Record July 2nd. at 9:05 A.M., both in the office of the County Clerk and Recorder, in and for the County of Flathead, State of Montana. Also certified copy of a "Joint Quit Claim Deed" transferring the rights of the original appropriators in and to said appropriations, to the **Montana Water Power and Electric Company**, Incorporated, as filed in the office of the County Clerk and Recorder, in and for Flathead County, Montana, on the 11th. day of May 1905.; Certified copy of a certified copy of the Articles of Incorporation of the said Montana Water Power and Electric Company, Incorporated, together with Amendment thereto, as now on Record in the office of the Recorder of Deeds, for the District of Columbia.; Company's certificate as to survey and field notes of the survey of the said Company's right of Way, dam, and grounds for electrical purposes; certificate of organization of the Montana Water Power and Electric Company, Inc., and certificate of list of officers of said company. Also field notes, and Engineer's certificate or affidavit and field notes, of the survey of said grounds for electrical purposes, right of way and dam, as shown on the map accompanying said field notes, enclosed herewith; copies of all of which has been filed in the local Land Office (U.S.) in Kalispell, Montana, on this date. Maps have been filed in triplicate, with accompanying field notes &c. to be transmitted to the Department of the Interior, Washington, D.C.

We pray you to give us due consideration in this matter, and we are willing to give all information within our power, that you may desire.

It is our purpose and desire to carry out the requirements of the Law, in every particular, and we desire to obtain a right of way, grounds, and a permit to construct a dam across the Pend D'Oreille River, within the Flathead Indian Reservation, at the location shown upon the enclosed map and described in the accompanying field notes. This we desire for the purpose of developing electric power to be transmitted to points off of the said Indian Reservation. The survey and maps showing line of transmission will be made after the Government survey of the said Reservation is completed, at which time the survey can be described and shown by reference to the Government survey.

We will be thankful for information as to requirements in matters of this kind, and will be glad to receive a copy of the Act of March 3rd. 1901, (with amendments thereto, if any,) Stat., 31. — 1083.

Papers filed here in U.S. Land Office should reach Washington in a few days. Trusting we may receive due consideration at your hands, we are

Very truly yours,
Montana Water Power and Electric Company, Inc.
By, Jeremiah Miller,
President.

* * * * * * * * *

Dec 14 1909

Power Site.

G. L. MacGibbon, Esq.
c/o American Bank & Trust Co.,
Sixth & Oak Sts., Portland, Oregon.
Sir:

The Office has received, by reference from the Department, your letter of December 4, 1909, in regard to the application of the Montana Water Power & Electric Company for a power site right of way on the Pend d'Oreille River, Flathead Indian Reservation, Montana.

On September 8, 1909, the Department referred to this Office, for consideration and action, a similar letter dated August 31, 1909, from Jeremiah Miller, president of the Company. On September 28, 1909, the Office wrote to Mr. Miller, and called his attention to the Act of March 3, 1909 (35 Stat. L., 781, 796), which provides:

> That the Secretary of the Interior be, and he is hereby authorized, in his discretion, to reserve from location, entry, sale, or other appropriation all lands within said Flathead Indian Reservation, chiefly valuable for power sites or reservoir sites, and he shall report to Congress such reservations.

In view of the fact that the power site sought by the Montana Water Power & Electric Company had been reserved in accordance with the provision of law quoted, Mr. Miller was advised that the Office was without authority to consider the application. The letter was addressed to Mr. Miller was at 80 Sixth St., Portland, Oregon, which appears to be the location of the American Bank & Trust Co., from whose office your letter of December 4, 1909 was written.

The Office has since received a copy of the decision of the General Land Office dated November 17, 1909, addressed to the Register and Receiver, Kalispell, Montana, rejecting the application of the Montana Water Power & Electric Company on account of the withdrawal of the power site.

Very respectfully,
(Signed) C. F. Hauke,
Chief Clerk.

Document 69

Bitterroot Harvest Continues for Tribal Members May 17, 1905

Source: "Flatheads Begin Pilgrimage," *The Daily Missoulian*, May 17, 1905, page 6, col. 1.

Editors' note: Despite all the political events swirling around the reservation in 1905, the traditional bitterroot harvest continued.

Flatheads Begin Pilgrimage

Many in Town on Way to Valley to Gather Bitter Root Herbs.

During the past few days quite a large number of the Indians from the Flathead reservation have been in the city buying supplies in readiness for their annual pilgrimage into the foothills surrounding the Bitter Root valley for the purpose of gathering the roots of the bitter root, Montana's state flower, for medicinal and gastro[no]mical purposes. Yesterday fully 100 members of the allied tribes were in the city and they came in all manner of vehicles from dilapidated wagons to fine top buggies, some of the poorer members of the tribe making the journey on foot.

The bitter ro[o]ts are gathered in large quantities and preserved throughout the year with jealous care by the Flatheads. They are used for medicine as well as food and until the time the flower is in blossom and the seed pods begin forming, they are highly prized. The roots are pulverized and made into a paste and also dried and packed away for future use.

A conservative estimate places the number of Indians who will visit the Bitter Root valley during the flowering season of the bitter root at at least 300. During this time the s....s will do the work, the time of the bucks being consumed in hunting for ground squirrels and snaring bull trout from the Bitter Root river.

Document 70

Thomas Downs Completes Flathead Enrollment

May 25, 1905

Source: Thomas Downs to Commissioner of Indian Affairs, May 25, 1905, from U.S. Bureau of Indian Affairs, "Selected Records of the Bureau of Indian Affairs Relating to Enrollment of Indians on the Flathead Reservation, 1903-08," National Archives Microfilm Publication M1350, reel 1, frames 208-226.

Editors' note: This is Special Indian Agent Thomas Downs' final report on the new roll of Flathead Reservation tribal members. Downs made clear the prominent role played by the traditional tribal chiefs and headmen in assembling the roll and deciding on adoptions of questionable cases. See above for the minutes of two examples of such councils on September 1, and October 19, 1904. The roll which Downs transferred to the Commissioner of Indian Affairs with this letter can be found in the National Archives Microfilm Publications M1350, reel 1, frames 1-63.

Department of the Interior,
United States Indian Service,
Flathead Agency,
Jocko, Montana, May 25, 1905.

Honorable Commissioner
of Indian Affairs,
Washington, D.C.
Sir:

In compliance with the instructions contained in your several office letters of the following dates and numbers, to wit: February 16, 1905, Land 63792-1904; and 1175-1905; March 17, 1905, Land 17887-1905; and in which said letters I was instructed to prepare an entirely new roll of the Indians entitled to rights on the Flathead reservation, Montana, I have the honor to say that said roll has been completed by me and I have the further honor to submit this my final report thereon as well as in relation to the work upon which I have been engaged for the past four months:

I was first directed to proceed to the Flathead reservation by wire from your office and under date of January 11, 1905, Land 1175-1905, a large mass of papers (being applications for enrollment on the rolls of the Flathead reservation, supported by testimony in each case) was sent to me for investigation as to the rights of all the applicants involved in said papers; and on January 26, 1905, I submitted to you my report, which was in detail, covering each applicant as did I make subsequent reports on the various applications which were submitted to me while engaged on this work both by your office and persons here.

As I have heretofore reported to you, in arriving at conclusions upon which were based my recommendations in the above cases, I first very carefully examined the testimony submitted, then examined some of the witnesses shown in each application, saw and talked with the interpreters who acted as such in the various cases and, finally, talked with the chief of the tribe of which applicants claimed to be members, or some of the judges and headmen where such chief was not available, with a view of either sustaining or controverting the claims of applicants. I also saw one or more members of each applicant family. In addition to this I had before me the instructions heretofore issued to Special Agent McNichols at the time he was engaged in making a roll of these Indians, as also was I governed by the instructions given me by your said office letters above referred to.

Therefore, where recommendations are found covering these cases it will be known that the rights of all applicants have been carefully investigated by me on the lines just stated.

At about the time I had completed this investigation, I received your office letter dated February 16, 1905, Land 63792-1904 and 1175-1905, wherein I was instructed "to make a new roll including thereon the names of all Indians who are entitled to rights as members of the Flathead tribe." The blanks necessary to prepare this roll were forwarded to me and I have, as nearly as it was possible to do, followed closely the instructions contained in your said letter, keeping before me at all times the suggestion contained in the concluding paragraph of that letter, to wit:

> "The rights of these Indians should now be permanently established in order that no wrong or injustice may be done them when the lands are opened for settlement and the Indians are allotted. Much of the dissatisfaction and trouble occurring in the Indian Service has arisen from the fact that a proper enrollment of the various tribes has not been made at critical times.
>
> "A change is impending in the relations of these Indians to the Government and it is very important that the preliminary steps taken shall be done so that no trouble or complaint can arise hereafter."

Therefore, in preparing this new roll I have deemed it important to see, if possible, every person whose name I enrolled, or the heads of each family; and where this was impracticable, to talk with the chiefs, judges and headmen of the respective tribes of which the person enrolled was a member or claimed to be a member. It may therefore be accepted as a fact that every person enrolled has had his enrollment approved by the chiefs, judges and headmen of the tribe of which he is shown to be a member.

In order to do this work properly and correctly I have gone to every portion of the reservation, the tribes of the Flathead reservation living in bands on various portions thereof.

I first proceeded to what is known as the Camas Prairie country, a section of the reservation occupied by the Kalispells or Lower Pend d'Oreille Indians. At this place, which is about sixty miles from the Agency, I spent sufficient time to see practically every member of the band, there being present during all the time these Indians were being enrolled, Big Louie, the present Chief of the Kalispells (Chief Michel having died about a year ago) and all of his headmen.

I next proceeded to the territory on the reservation occupied by the Upper Pend d'Oreilles, of which tribe Charley Michel, is the Hereditary chief, going first to Ronan, at which place is located the sub-Agency, and then to Polson, at the Foot of the Lake.

The Spokanes have no Hereditary Chief and Chief Charley Michel is the accepted and recognized chief of the members of that band living on the Flathead reservation.

I next went to the Kootenai country, which is on the west side of the Flathead lake, in the extreme northwestern portion of the reservation and in what is known as the Dayton Creek country. At this place Chief Koos-tah-tah, the Kootenai chief, all of his headmen and a large number of the Kootenai band were present during the enrollment of the Kootenais.

Returning, I proceeded to the portion of the reservation occupied by the Flatheads, going first to St. Ignatius Mission where are located Judges Ka-ka-shee and Joseph Standing Bear, and then to the Agency. Chief Charlo had theretofore been consulted and conferred with concerning certain applicants and particularly those whose applications had been submitted to your office and transmitted to me for investigation; however, he was conferred with relative to the enrollment of the Flathead claimants, as also were Chief Antoine Moiese, the sub-Chief of all the Flatheads, Judge Louison, Louie Vanderburg, Alex Big Knife, Big Sam and Michel Revais, the latter the official interpreter of this reservation for a number of years.

In my report dated January 26, 1905, I recommended that the Agent in charge of the Flathead reservation be instructed to convene a General Council of the Indians of this reservation with a view of having them pass on all claims of those person therein mentioned who possess the blood of some other than the Five Confederated Tribes of this reservation, and that said persons be notified in order that they may have an opportunity to be present at such council and present themselves for such action as the council might deem proper; and by your said letter of date February 16, 1905, Land 63792-1904 and Land 1175-1905, I was instructed "to take charge of this work and at a suitable time to be determined by you (me) call a council and notify all parties of interest and dispose of these cases."

In compliance with said instructions, I issued a call to all of the Chiefs, Judges and Headmen of the Five Confederated Tribes of the Flathead reservation, notifying them that a General Council of all the Indians of the Flathead reservation was to be convened at the Agency, on said reservation, at nine o'clock in the morning of April 18, 1905; that said council was called for the purpose of considering the claims of persons for adoption and enrollment on the rolls of the Flathead reservation and that it was very important that they and as many members of their respective bands as could be present should attend said council; and in response to said call there were present, on April 18, 1905, about two hundred Indians representing all of the tribes on the reservation.

Every Chief, Judge and Headman of all of the Five Tribes was present and acting, being:

Flathead Tribe: *Charlo*, the Hereditary Chief of the Flatheads.

Antoine Moiese, Second Chief of the Flatheads.

Big Sam, Headman.

Judge Ka-ka-shee, Headman.

Judge Joseph Standing Bear, Headman.

Judge Louison, Headman.

Pend d'Oreille Tribe: *Charley Michel*, the Hereditary Chief of the Upper Pend d'Oreilles.

Joseph Soap-seen, Headman.

Btiste Ka-teel-poo, Headman.

Paul Ka-ka-shee, Headman.

Kootenai Tribe: *Koos-ta-tah*, Hereditary Chief of all the Kootenais.

Antise Dominick, Headman.

Kalispell or Lower Pend d'Oreille Tribe: *Big Louie*, the present recognized chief

Joseph Little Stone, Headman.

Spokane Tribe: *Charley Michel*, Chief of the Upper Pend d'Oreilles, being recognized chief of the Spokanes living on the Flathead reservation.

Peter Mag Pie Cap, Headman.
Joseph Hi-hi-tah, Headman.
Eneas Con-kaw, Headman.

I also served written notice on all persons referred to in my several letters who were recommended to stand for adoption and stated to them that they would be afforded an opportunity to present themselves and their claims to adoption and enrollment to the members of said council.

As before stated, in addition to the sitting members of the Council, there were present at least two hundred Indians who remained during the entire deliberations of the Council.

The Council was in session two full days, Tuesday, April 18th and Wednesday, April 19th.

The weather was of such a character that the proceedings were conducted on the campus or lawn in the Agency enclosure.

The Agent and His Financial Clerk were present during the deliberations.

It was said to have been the largest Council ever held by these tribes; and my object in having as large a Council as was possible at this particular time was two-fold, to wit:

First. — To have them pass on all persons then presenting themselves; and,

Second. — To have them pass, as a body, on the roll which I had prepared and upon the enrollment of every name appearing on said roll, the chief and headmen having therefore approved the enrollment thereof.

Therefore, just prior to the noon recess on the second day, the nineteenth, I announced to the members of the Council that I had about completed the work upon which I had been sent by your office to the Flathead reservation, to do; that they were familiar with what that work was; that it was the preparation of a roll of all the Indians and persons who would hereafter have a right on the Flathead reservation; that during the preparation of this roll every Chief and Judge and most of the Headmen now at this Council were present during the various stages of making this roll; that these Chiefs, Judges and Headmen knew every name on that roll, but that this reservation was soon to be opened to settlement and the Indians were to be allotted lands and there might be a distribution of money, and the officers of the Government at Washington had instructed me to make a roll of only those persons who had a right to be thereon; that in order to determine this it was necessary that I have the help of the Indians; that each of the Chiefs, Judges and Headmen did assist me to the end that they have said that every person whose name appears on that roll was a member of his respective tribe; that there were present over two hundred members of their different tribes and that I wanted them, during the recess, to talk the matter over and if there were any names on that roll which they considered should not be there, they should so indicate to me; that the whole roll would be re-read to them if they so desired, and that as one of the proceedings of this Council I would ask that said roll be approved or disapproved by them; that in order that the President, the Secretary of the Interior and the Commissioner of Indian Affairs might know whether or not ever[y] name on the roll which had been prepared by me had been approved and sanctioned by the Chiefs, Judges and Headmen, the Chiefs of the Five Confederated Tribes of the Flathead reservation would be asked by me to sign a certificate on the roll to that effect; that if there was any objection or doubt as to the enrollment of any person on that roll, now was the time to so state, as Washington would consider every name thereon approved by all the Indians after the Chiefs had signed the certificate.

I deemed this very important in view of the change impending in the relations of these Indians to the Government as suggested by you in the concluding paragraph of your said letter of date February 16, 1905; and at the conclusion of the proceedings of the Council, I requested that Chiefs Charlo, Charley Michel, Koos-tah-tah and Big Louie come to the Agency office where said roll would be exhibited to them and said certificate read. They came to the Agency office and in the presence of the Agent, his Financial Clerk and three interpreters, the certificate was read by me and translated by the official interpreter, Michel Revais, to these four chiefs. In order that no misunderstandings might arise in the future with reference to this matter and to avoid "the dissatisfaction and trouble occurring in the Indian Service" which "has arisen from the fact that a proper enrollment of the various tribes has not been made at critical times," I deemed it very important to not alone have this roll certified as containing only the names of persons who were recognized members of the tribes to which they claimed to belong, but to have present at the reading of the certificate two interpreters in addition to the official interpreter.

After the certificate had been read, these chiefs were asked whether they understood fully what its contents and purport were and upon answering in the affirmative, they signed their names, by mark, touching the pen in the hand of John L. Sloane, the Financial Clerk of this reservation, and their signatures were also witnessed by the Agent, myself, my clerk and the three interpreters, all of said chiefs witnessing, also, each others signatures.

I have but one criticism to make concerning the action of this Council and but one recommendation to offer in relation thereto and it is with reference to the unfavorable action had on Isadore Ladderoute, Paul Lucier and Mary Howlett and children.

Isadore Ladderoute was placed on the McNichols roll, his number thereon being 256, and he is shown to be an Oregon Indian. He is also referred to by the Honorable Secretary in his letter addressed to you of date October 3, 1903. He is a half breed Indian but of what blood he is unable to state; he has lived among these Indians for thirty-four years but for some grievance held by some member of the Council, he was refused adoption. At this Council meeting he stated that he had theretofore been adopted at a Council presided over by old Chief Arlee. This, of course, I learned for the first time when he made the statement to the members of the Council. He is an old man, has Indian blood, is stricken with an affliction which renders him incapacitated to do any work and, if it can be done, I recommend that he be enrolled.

Paul Lucier is a half breed, having a trace of Flathead blood. He has married into these tribes, has lived on this reservation for twenty-five years continuously and, I was informed after the adjournment of the Council, he was refused recognition and adoption because of the fact that he served in the Indian Wars during the fifties. He is an old man over seventy years of age and I recommend his enrollment.

Mary Howlett was born among the Flatheads in the Bitter Root Valley; her father and mother were life-long neighbors of Chief Charlo. She was sick in bed at the time the Council was held which, in my opinion, was responsible for her failure of adoption. Her full brother, Joe Dumontier, was adopted by this Council; her full sister, Philomene Hustin, whose number on the roll transmitted herewith is 1740, was adopted at a Council held at the Agency October 19, 1904, and it is respectfully suggested that pages 2, 3, and 4 of said Council Proceedings be read in connection with the application for enrollment of this woman and her children on the rolls of this reservation. While she is of Piegan blood, she has lived among these Indians all of her life, has a number of immediate relatives on the roll and her only home is on this reservation. I deem it a manifest injustice to this woman and her children to not enroll her, and I have the honor to recommend, if it can be done legally, that they be placed on the rolls. The papers in this woman's application were transmitted to you with my letter of February 21st last.

In preparing the roll transmitted with this report I have the honor to say that I have followed, as nearly as practicable, your instructions and suggestions relative to the manner of its preparation. It was impracticable to undertake to retain the numbers as they appeared on the McNichols roll and make them conform to those on this roll for the reason that there have been a number of deaths since the McNichols roll was prepared, there are some double enrollments which I discovered, some eliminations have been made by refusals to adopt and as many as ten numbers, in one instance, were omitted in the McNichols roll. However, I have made a column in which is shown the number the person enrolled had on the McNichols roll, the number the person may have had on the Smead roll, another column which shows the office file number of all cases involving that person's application for enrollment where the application has been considered by your office, as also a remarks column in which is shown dates of Council Proceedings and dates of enrollment recommended by me. Separately, and marked "Enclosure No. 1," I have pre[p]ared a list of all eliminations, double enrollments, &c., from and on the McNichols roll; this paper, in connection with the data shown in the McNichols column on the roll herewith transmitted, will account for every number appearing on the McNichols roll.

Complying with the instructions contained in your said letter of March 17, 1905, Land 17887-1905, I have prepared a separate roll of those person upon whose claims I reported adversely and indicate opposite each name the office file number of those papers, evidence, &c., and also the date of my report thereon where the papers originated at this end and have no office file number, or had none at the time I considered them.

I have also prepared and transmit the same with the other papers, a roll of those persons whom I enrolled while at Bonner's Ferry, Idaho, to which place I went under authority granted by your letter of date May 1, 1905, Land, Authority 93955-1905. I asked authority to proceed to Bonner's Ferry at the urgent request of Chief Koos-tah-tah, of the Kootenai tribe, who stated that there were a number of members of his tribe living there whom he desired enrolled. When I reached Bonner's Ferry, I sent for some of the Indians and drove in the country to see others. There were only three whom Koos-tah-tah recognized as members of his tribe, the others he had in mind at the time he made the request having died during a small pox epidemic at Bonner's Ferry about two years ago.

However, in making the request to proceed to Bonner's Ferry for the purpose indicated, I had in mind the importance of giving to the Indians on the Flathead reservation every reasonable opportunity and facility they might ask looking to the enrollment of persons on the roll at this time who were actually bona fide members of their tribes, thus avoiding dissention and dissatisfaction in the future in view of the impending change of the relations heretofore referred to. . . .

[Downs' detailed description of the other enclosures has been omitted here.]

I have prepared, and made the same a part of the roll transmitted to you of even date herewith, a "Recapitulation" of the Indians and Mixed Bllods [sic] of the Flathead reservation which, in view of the contemplated opening of this reservation, I assumed might be of some importance to your office; and in this connection I have the honor to make the following recommendations with respect to conditions which, in my judgment, should prevail relative to the allotment of land to the full blood Indians of this reservation:

Most of the full blood Indians are old, a number of them are infirm and very few, if any, of them have the slightest conception of land values, or which land would be the best to have selected for themselves; a number of them have not the ability to select and fence their lands before the alloting agent is sent to make allotments in order to have a prior right to the land, nor do they appreciate the importance of doing this; and with a view solely to their protection, I have the honor to recommend that some person be employed in this section who is familiar with land values in this part of the country and who is a surveyor or who has some knowledge of locating corners, whose duties it shall be to select for the full blood Indians the best lands obtainable on said reservation, the selections, of course, to in no wise interfere with those lands selected by bona fide claimants where the same are actually improved or have some improvements thereon. I also recommend that the compensation of such person be $5.00 per day and the per diem $3.00.:

I have the honor to recommend further that if it is determined to adopt this recommendation that the Honorable Joseph M. Dixon, Congressman from Montana, who has been a resident of this county for many years, the father of the bill providing for the opening of the Flathead reservation and who has conferred with me realtive [sic] to the matter herein referred to, be requested to assist in the selection of this person, he being desirous of having extended to the full blood Indians especially every facility looking to the selection of the best lands for them, as is he also able to determine who in this vicinity would be best suited for this character of work.

There may be some persons entitled to be enrolled on the rolls of the Flathead reservation whose names and rights were not presented, some children, for instance, born after I had visited that portion of the reservation upon which the families live; there will be some births, as a matter of course, subsequent to the completion of this roll; and in instances of this character, to preserve accuracy, I have the honor to recommend that the Agent by instructed that where the birth is a full blood, he, the Agent, shall satisfy himself that such birth has occurred and where the birth is a Mixed Blood, the father or mother be required to furnish to the Agent either a certificate of birth from a physician or an affidavit of such birth; that the Agent then place the name of the child on the roll, giving it a number consecutive to the last one appearing on the roll, noting the genealogy on the roll and showing the numbers, as well as the names, of the father and mother as they appear on this roll, making such additional data in the remarks column as may be necessary to properly locate and identify this child and furnish your office on the first of every month a duplicate of this information; that in the cases of death, he be instructed to eliminate the name and number by drawing a red-ink line through the same, and to furnish your office monthly this information.

That in cases other than full bloods, where persons present themselves to the Agent for enrollment, they be required to furnish written testimony as to their right to enrollment the same to be transmitted to you for your consideration.

The surveys of this reservation are fast nearing completion and as this is the time of year when those persons who have a right to be alloted desire to know just what their rights are and make their selections, it is recommended that the roll transmitted to you herewith be acted upon as speedily as practicable.

In conclusion, I have the honor to express the hope that the roll I have prepared of the Indians of the Flathead reservation, Montana, — in view of the importance that it should be as accurate as it is possible to have it at a time when the relations between these Indians and the Government are about to change — has been made to conform to your views; that it contains the names only of those persons who have a right to be enrolled thereon under instructions issued from your office, I am morally certain; that every person whose name appears thereon is a recognized member, either by blood or adoption, of one of the Five Confederated Tribes of the Flathead reservation, is evidenced by the certificate to that effect, made a part of the roll and signed by all of the chiefs of the Flathead reservation.

Very respectfully,
Thomas Downs.
United States Special Indian Agent.

Document 71

Indian Inspector Reports on Flathead Reservation Economy in 1905 June 5, 1905

Source: Excerpt from Arthur M. Tinker to Secretary of the Interior, June 5, 1905, Interior Department, Inspection Reports, RG 48, National Archives, Washington, D.C., 6103/1905.

Editors' note: Tinker's report is especially valuable in evaluating the economic progress on the reservation before allotment was forced on the tribes. Tinker found that "they were prosperous and in good financial condition." He also noted that, while some mixed bloods were very rich, almost everyone had some stock. Of course, with allotment the open range would be ended.

Department of the Interior,
United States Indian Inspection Service,
Flathead Indian Agency,
Jocko, Montana, June 5 1905.

The Honorable,
The Secretary of the Interior.
Sir: —

According to instructions contained in your communication under date of February 16th 1905, I have the honor to report the result of my inspection of the Flathead Indian Agency, Montana.

These Indians have in the past and do at the present time, attend to their own business affairs in their own way, they buy, sell and trade for themselves, the never consult their Agent unless they get into trouble; most of them drink intoxicating liquor to excess which they seem to have no trouble in obtaining when they have the money to pay for it. All the males save a few old full bloods speak English; most of the full bloods, both old and young, wear their hair long and paint their faces.

The Indians of this reservation, with but very few exceptions, live in good log houses and have fair outbuildings. Judging from all visible indications I should say they were prosperous and in good financial condition. Most of them are industrious and for Indians are good farmers. They have a large amount of land enclosed with good fences and cultivate large fields.

During the past few years the amount of land cultivated has steadily increased, last year it was estimated that there were 28,000 acres under cultivation, this year 30% more land has been plowed and seeded than ever before.

The crop produced consists principally of wheat, oats, potatoes and vegetables, they also cut and stack large quantities of hay to feed their stock during the winter, some seasons they bale a considerable amount of hay that they sell to white men residing off the reservation.

It is said that every Indian owns stock of some kind. I am informed that they have about 28,000 head of cattle, but no one knows how many horses and ponies they own, but it is estimated that they have in the vicinity of 21,000.

They usually take good care of their cattle and a few of their best horses. They herd them during the grazing season, cut hay to feed them and care for them during the winter months. With the ponies it is different, they usually run wild and are obliged to rustle for themselves, but few of them are caught and are of no use to them, they are small and of little value, their owners and the reservation would be better off were they all disposed of.

During the past few years they have sold a large number of ponies and some few horses, for which they have received a fair price, last year more than 4000 were sold to horse dealers and shipped to Eastern Markets. It is said that all the Indians understand that in a short time the land of this reservation will be allotted, and when they have received their allotments and the surplus land thrown open to settlement there will be no range for them to keep the number of ponies they now have, and seem anxious to dispose of those they do not need as fast as possible.

At this time there are several horse buyers at various points on the reserve purchasing horses, they have bought and shipped so far this season between 700 and 800, it is expected that several thousand will be sold during the present year.

There are about 2000 cattle grazing on the reservation owned by non residents that have approved grazing permits for which they have paid $1.00 per head.

The Indians have never had grazing permits issued to them but they are required to pay a grazing tax on all the stock they own in excess of 100 head and are now paying the grazing tax of $1.00 per head for 9445 cattle and 50¢ per head for 406 horses the same as the non residents.

When the collection of the resident grazing tax was first proposed at this agency, it was very unpopular. Most of the full bloods and a large number of mixed bloods, especially the old men, were bitterly opposed to the collection of this tax, it was a new idea and they did not like it; the opposition was confined principally to those that would not be affected by it, except to receive their share of the money paid in. Trouble was anticipated in some sections of the reservation if it become necessary to attempt to collect the tax by force, they pretended to believe that the agent would keep the money collected and they would never receive their share of the money paid in as promised. There was never any serious trouble in collecting this tax, and since each person has received their share of the money, they are perfectly satisfied. The agent now has little or no trouble in making collections. The stock owned by the Fathers at St. Ignatius Mission do not pay a grazing tax. . . .

Very respectfully,
Arthur M. Tinker
Indian Inspector.

Document 72

Magpie Objects to Survey of Reservation Land

June 1905

Source: "Flathead Objects to Surveyors," *The Daily Missoulian*, June 10, 1905, page 2, col. 3; "Peter Magpie Case Is Dismissed," *The Daily Missoulian*, June 14, 1905, page 2, col. 1.

Editors' note: This seemed to involve a case of opposition to the allotment policy imposed on the reservation.

Flathead Objects to Surveyors
Peter Magpie Accused of Obliterating Monuments
Made by Civil Engineers.

Peter Magpie, a Flathead brave, has apparently gotten himself in serious difficulty by the strenuous method in which he is protesting against the preliminaries of the opening of the Flathead reservation. Magpie was brought to Missoula by Deputy United States Marshal Young and lodged in jail. This afternoon he will be arraigned before United States Commissioner Wallace P. Smith on a charge of interfering with the United States deputy surveyors who are running lines on the reservation and surveying the ground in accordance with the bill providing for the opening of the reservation.

Magpie is one of the malcontents. He does not want to see the reservation opened and with the evident belief that he could delay matters indefinitely, he is said to have systematically obliterated the marks made by the surveyors as fast as they were made. When a tree was blazed and the bearing marks recorded, Magpie would promptly cut down the tree and the post which had been officially designated as a section corner. When a corner was located in the prairie and the monument set in place in the mound, Magpie is said to have watched his chances and as soon as the surveyors got a safe distance away he would dig up the monument, carry it a long distance away, and then obliterate the mound which was constructed so carefully a few days before by the surveyors.

Finally patience ceased to be a virtue and complaint was made by the surveyors to the agency and Magpie was arrested and lodged in the agency jail, afterwards being brought to Missoula on a warrant issued from Commissioner

Peter Magpie
Source: Photograph Archives, Montana Historical Society, Helena, Montana, detail from photo 954-573

Smith's court. It is understood that he has retained an attorney to defend him and that he will plead not guilty when arraigned this afternoon. His preliminary examination will probably be fixed for Tuesday, June 13.

* * * * * * * * *

Peter Magpie Case Is Dismissed
U.S. Attorney Concludes There Is No Case Against the Indian.

Peter Magpie, the Flathead Indian who was accused of obliterating the marks and monuments of the Baker surveying party on the reservation, has been dismissed on motion of Deputy United States Attorney J. Miller Smith and returned to the reservation last evening, accompanied by his daughter, Susie Magpie, who acted as interpreter for her father during his arraignment before United States Commissioner Wallace P. Smith.

According to Mr. Baker, who was in the city yesterday, there seems to have been considerable of a mistake and some exaggeration in connection with the arrest of Magpie. As far as he is able to learn, only one corner stone was disturbed during the progress of his survey of the reservation. The United States surveyor general and the agent of the Flatheads were notified of this occurrence, and afterwards the arrest of Magpie followed.

Previous to his arrest Magpie and the surveyors had reached an understanding, and for some time the surveyors had been camped on Magpie's ranch. When the monument was destroyed no one was closer to the Indian who destroyed it than half a mile, and no one could recognize whether or not it was Magpie.

Afterwards, when the surveyors returned to their work, they found that the Indians were trying to right the wrong they had done the surveyor, and they put the rock back in its place, but got the mound of earth on the wrong side of the stone in their effort to square themselves.

Speaking of Magpie yesterday, Mr. Baker said that all of the members of his crew looked upon his [sic] as a friend of the surveyors instead of one who desired to oppose their work on the reservation.

Document 73

Nazaine Courville Assaulted on Reservation

June 13, 1905

Source: "Shooting Scrape Near Ronan," *The Daily Missoulian*, June 13, 1905, page 8, col. 2.

Editors' note: The row between Nazaine Courville and Dave Finley was fueled by alcohol.

Shooting Scrape Near Ronan

Nazaine Courville Suffering from a Scalp Wound as Result of Row.

Nazaine Courville was brought to Missoula last night suffering from a severe bullet wound in his scalp, inflicted, it alleged, by Dave Finley near Ronan, last Friday evening. Courville will appear before United States Commissioner Smith today and will swear to a complaint charging Finley with assault with attempt to kill.

According to the story given The Missoulian last night by the injured man, a number of half-breed Indians had been imbibing freely of liquor at the home of August Finley, about a half mile from Ronan, Friday afternoon. Courville, with his partner, Cook McRea, had been in that vicinity during the afternoon and had encountered Dave Finley, a brother of August Finley, who was quarrelsome. He made a number of insinuating remarks to Cook, after which the latter endeavored to administer a thrashing to him.

Dave Finley, according to Courville, then ran to the home of his brother and procured a 30-30 rifle and began firing at him (Courville) and Cook. One of the shots took effect in Courville's head, striking his forehead and glancing, going through the top of his skull. According to his story, he was on his horse at the time, and when struck by the bullet fell to the ground, unconscious, where he remained for upwards of an hour, until friends picked him up.

The agency doctor, who happened to be at Ronan at the time, was summoned, and dressed the wound, and Courville was removed to the home of a friend, where he has been under the care of a doctor until coming to Missoula last night.

Dave Finley made his escape immediately after the shooting, and is still at large. Rumor had it yesterday that he was seen going in the direction of the agency, which gave rise to the theory that he went to give himself up.

After Courville fell to the ground Cook, his partner, spurred his horse, but in making his escape several shots were fired at him, one of which penetrated his saddle. Cook first reported the matter to the agency officials.

Courville's injury is not considered a serious one, but until medical aid had been rendered he suffered greatly from the loss of blood, and it is stated that had it not been for the timely appearance of the agency physician he would undoubtedly have died.

Document 74

Closing Exercises for St. Ignatius School

June 20, 1905

Source: "Closing Exercises at Mission," *The Daily Missoulian*, June 20, 1905, page 2, col. 1.

Editors' note: The program for the closing exercises by the students was included in this newspaper article.

Closing Exercises at Mission

Program Arranged for June 25 to Mark End of School Year.

Several of the sisters of the St. Ignatius mission were in the city yesterday arranging for the closing exercises at the House of Providence, which will take place Sunday, June 25. The sisters state that the past year has been the most successful year that the institution has ever experienced, and the attendance was larger twofold than in any preceding year. An elaborate program has been arranged, and many of the pupils will participate. The program as arranged is as follows:

Greeting song	Chorus
Welcome — Recitation	E. Larose
Gossip Pantomime	Minims
Vocal solo — "Just Like Grandmama"	A. Felsmann
"The Reverse of the Medal."	
Countess Errard	Ida Miller
Isabelle, her daughter	Clara Parent
Mme. Morville, governess to Isabelle	Agnes Asseline
Phillips, maid to Countess	Imelda Morrison
Ellen, housemaid	Mary Pilkoo
Mother Alarum, farmer's wife	Theresa Wilhite
Jane, her little shepherdess	Mary Joseph
Recitation, "Playmate"	L. Larose
Dialogue — "Higher Education."	
Pa	F. Dumontier
Ma	A. Parent
Darling	E. Hull

Dialogue — "The Better Part."

Queen and Seven Fairies.

The Word That Was Not Too Late.

A Girl in Despair	Lucy Lanctot
The Tempter	F. Dumontier
Guardian Angel	A. Barland
The Sweet Little Girl	Eleanor Hull

Cantata — School Festival.

Queen	A. Parent
Punctual Scholar	M. L. Matt
Tardy Scholar	F. Dumontier
Perservering Scholar	A. Asselin
Quarrelsome Scholar	J. Gariepy
First Scholar	Clara Parent
Second Scholar	Esther Larose
Third Scholar	Irene Michaud
Generous Scholar	Jane Bousquet
Selfish Scholar	I. Morrisean
Farewell Address	M. L. Matt
Our School, Song	Chorus
Tableau	Patrons of the School

Document 75

Death and Celebration at the 1905 Powwow

July 1905

Source: "Too Much Dancing Causes Death," *The Daily Missoulian*, July 7, 1905, page 8, col. 2; "'Twas a Lively Fourth and a Long One on the Reserve," *The Anaconda Standard*, July 16, 1905, page 13, col. 3-5.

Editors' note: The story of an Indian who danced himself to death at the Arlee celebration in 1905 was played up in the newspaper. The *Anaconda Standard* account was biased, but did describe the sham battle, as well as the alcohol problems at the celebration.

Too Much Dancing Causes Death
Indian Giving Hilarity Full Swing During Celebration
Succumbs to Cramps.

Out on the Flathead reservation where the five tribes are at present holding high carnival, one of the braves Kootenai Darsoe shuffled off this mortal coil yesterday afternoon and passed to the happy hunting ground. The Indian had been one of the factors in the big demonstration and according to information received from the agency last night he danced himself to death.

Darsoe started in celebrating the first day, participating in all of the dances on the board, until he became almost fatigued. Friends told him to stop, but he was receiving so many compliments from his audience and from the Indian maidens that he insisted on continuing his happy occupation.

Along toward evening he became physically incapaciated [sic] and could could [sic] dance no more, and after partaking of some ice cream he went to the river bank to stretch his weary form so that he might rest and come back again and indulge in the pleasurable pastime. But he never recuperated.

Lying on the river bank in the cool of the evening without any covering on him he took cramps and in agony passed away.

People coming in last night on the belated No. 6, stated that the celebration is one of the largest that has been held on the reservation in years and that the hundreds of whites who have gathered from all sections of the western part of the state are enjoying it immensely. A considerable portion of the time yesterday and the day preceding was devoted to weeping for the dead who have passed away since the last big dance held a year ago. The s....s do all of the weeping while the bucks ride about the sixty or more tepees around which the carnival is being held.

* * * * * * * * *

'Twas a Lively Fourth and a Long One on the Reserve

Missoula, July 15. — There were some exciting times upon the last days of the big Indian celebration on the Flathead reservation, which passed into Montana history Wednesday. In response to numerous entreaties one of the storekeepers on the reservation sent to Plains and secured 80 gallons of good old cider. This cider has passed the mellow stage and was so "hard" that it would make the drunk come almost as quick as peach brandy.

Once it was on hand it sold on the gallon plan to a number of youngsters who had the good fellowship of the Indians, and in less time than it takes to tell it happiness began among the reds. The cider sold readily at 10 cents per small cupful, and in less than six hours there was not a snootful left unsold on the reservation, all of it having been snapped up readily.

It Made Trouble.

It took but a few minutes for it to get in its work, and for a while the Indians were the happiest lot of bucks and s....s who ever danced on a reservation. Afterwards the mood changed and they became devilish and went around looking for mischief. The prompt arrival of the agent, who had been summoned by telephone, prevented the trouble which for a while had been brewing, and a strict investigation of the matter will be made to determine who was responsible for bringing the cider on the reservation. Anyway, the Indians found that hard cider, while it has an excellent taste in the cup as it goes down, is productive of many headaches, and almost rivals the good old booze sold in Missoula when it comes to entrancing effects.

The Sham Battle.

When it comes to spectacularism the reservation Indian can give any stage manager cards and spades and then beat him out several city blocks in the effects produced. During the progress of the dances which took place near the agency during the past week a scene which occurred over 100 years ago in Western Montana was depicted, with all of its realism. This was an Indian battle which took place between the Flatheads and some of their anceint [sic] enemies.

With but scant ceremony rival parties of Indians lined up for the fray. None were armed with firearms, but all had their spears and bows and arrows and war clubs and shields. All were decked out in the gaudiest of war paint and feathers. The fight was bitter and was carried out in true Indian fashion. For a while it was a battle of skirmishers, and each side skulked behind shelter and took advantage of the opportunity offered to pot shoot an enemy. Finally there came a hand-to-hand encounter. Indians fell on every hand and the war crys were almost deafening. The awful pantomime of war club meeting war club and men dying in agony on every side were depicted with frightfulful [sic] accuracy, and for two hours the mimic battle continued. Then it was that the Flatheads gained the advantage and, slowly at first, drove their enemies from the field. Soon the retreat became a rout, and before the defeated party had run very far many prisoners were taken. Afterwards these prisoners were brought to the big Flathead camp by their captors, and the ceremony of burning them at the stake was gone through with.

Old Grudges Settled.

Residents of Missoula who were present throughout the mimic battle say that the onslaught was fierce and it had every appearance at times of being the settlement of more than one old grudge which had been held between the bucks in times past. Some of the blows which were struck with the old, gnarly war clubs were a little too hard to have been done in play, and more than one Indian went down and out in earnest, afterwards recovering to nurse a bunch on the top of his cranium several times larger than a hen's egg.

In the Varnished Cars.

Quite a large number of the Bonner's Ferry Indians belonging to the allied tribes on the reservation were present throughout the big celebration, and these returned to their homes yesterday, some of them riding on the varnished cars and apparently quite indignant because the trains were so crowded that they were obliged to use the smoker or else stand up on the platforms.

Preparing for the Big Hunt.

Some of the reservation Indians came to town yesterday, and nearly all of them while here laid in a good supply of ammunition, in readiness for their annual flit off the reserve to the mountains of the Coeur d'Alene section and the Clearwater, where they will have their big deer hunts, during which hundreds of the timid animals will be slain, their hides converted into buckskin and their flesh into "jerked meat."

Document 76

Young Indian Horseman

August 1, 1905

Source: "Champion Kid Rider of the Reserve," *The Anaconda Standard*, August 1, 1905, page 12, col. 3-4.

Editors' note: This celebration of a young Indian rider gives a glimpse of another aspect of reservation life in 1905.

Champion Kid Rider of the Reserve

Missoula, July 31. — Louie is a young Indian boy who lives on the Flathead reservation at St. Ignatius, and he has attained considerable notoriety among the members of the Flathead tribe for being an expert horseman. Louie is but 12 years old, and his many daring feats performed on horseback undoubtedly class him as one of the best riders for his age to be found anywhere in Western Montana. The horse which he is riding in the picture is his favorite cattle pony "Zip," and although appearing very meek and lazy, he is one of the fleetest and most sure-footed animals on the reserve. During the roundup season, when the cattle on the ranges are gathered in, Louie and "Zip" are always much in evidence, and the horse, guided by the light touch of the reins on his neck, is an expert in cutting our [out] stock from the bunch.

Louie is also an expert with the lariat, and many a young steer has he roped by the front feet and thrown during the branding season. Young coyotes and wolves are also frequent victims of his noose and, in fact, Louie is an adept at all of the cowboy's arts. He rides with a careless grace, seemingly unconscious of his talent and nerve, and is the object of envy by many of his older associates.

Document 77

Peter Matt Shoots Boy in Ankle

August 4, 1905

Source: "Crazy Breed Shot a Boy," *The Kalispell Bee*, August 4, 1905, page 1, col. 3.

Editors' note: Another case of alcohol and violence on the reservation. Court cases were easily accessible to reporters and received more publicity off the reservation than did the peaceful conduct of most affairs on the reservation.

Crazy Breed Shot a Boy
A Lad at Polson Maltreated by a Drunken Indian.
Ordered the Boy to Dance
And Playfully Fired a Couple of Shots Into the Ground Close to His Feet to Set Them Moving — Pete Matts Is Arrested and Will Be Tried for the Offense.

A drunken half-breed with a gun, and a scared little boy, who he was threatening to shoot unless he would dance, almost resulted in a tragedy, at Polson, Sunday. Pete Matts, a breed of dubious reputation, who had imbibed freely of the squirrel whiskey on sale at Polson, ran across the 12-year-old boy, Eugene Anderson, as he was passing the front of Gray & Co.'s store, and playfully pulling a gun, ordered the boy to dance. He enforced his remarks by shooting into the ground in front of the boy and the second shot, the bullet probably glanced, or Pete's aim was poor, and the little fellow received the bullet in his left ankle. The boy was brought to Kalispell by Mrs. W. M. Cramer, who filed a complaint against Matts, and a warrant was issued charging him with assault in the first degree. Judge Sullivan issued the warrant and it was served by Deputy Sheriff Donahue, who went to Polson Wednesday and had no trouble in arresting his man, Matts is lodged in jail and will probably be arraigned tomorrow. He stated that the shot was accidental as he had no intention of more than scaring the boy.

Eugene was taken to the Kalispell hospital where he is being treated and no serious results are anticipated unless blood poisoning should set in.

The Anderson boy and an older sister were brought out from Milwaukee by Ben Cramer a short time ago, and the children are naturally afraid of the Indians and breeds who are numerous about their new home.

Document 78

Reservation Indians Visit Circus in Missoula

August 10, 1905

Source: "Indians in Town to See Circus," *The Daily Missoulian*, August 10, 1905, page 7, col. 1.

Editors' note: When the circus came to town, it was a big event for Indians and whites in western Montana. Note also the information about the importance of Indian business for Missoula merchants.

Indians in Town to See Circus
Many of Them Ride Ponies on the Merry-Go-Round
and Have Good Time.

All trains from the west yesterday brought members of the Flathead tribe from the reservation to witness the circus performance today, and many bucks, s....s, and their papooses rode in on their cayuses. Probably as large a representation of the Flathead tribe is in town today as has been seen here in years. They started to celebrate early and it was really a treat last evening to see the Indians in their gala attire, riding on the merry-go-round on Higgins avenue. All of them had money and appeared to enjoy themselves to their heart's content.

It was a diversion that the Indians are not accustomed to and when they mounted the little hobby horses, swiftly revolving, they gave evidence of being elated, but it is a question whether they or the spectators enjoyed the incident most. The little papooses appeared fairly deligthed [sic] with the exhilirating [sic] sport and it was when their pocket books were empty that they gave up the pastime.

The members of the Flathead tribe have had a very successful season and when all of their crops will have been harvested they will have considerable money to spend among the merchants. Many of those coming to town last night, had sufficient money with them to see the circus and have a good time and it is likely that they will do considerable shopping today and tomorrow. A few of them succeeded in getting hold of a little "red eye' shortly after their arrival and the police were successful in collecting a few bottles from them.

Document 79

Industrious Indians Harvest Crops on Reservation September 5, 1905

Source: "These Red Men Are Industrious," *The Daily Missoulian*, September 5, 1905, page 2, col. 1.

Editors' note: The harvest was good on the reservation and Missoula merchants were anxious for the business the tribal members would bring to the town economy.

These Red Men Are Industrious
Hum of the Threshing Machine Is Heard on the Reservation.

Those who are of the opinion that all Indians are inclined to shirk manual labor should take a trip to the Flathead Indian reservation at the present time. Parties coming in from there yesterday say that it would be an agreeable surprise to people to see a number of members of the tribe industriously engaged at this time in harvesting their bountiful crops.

Between Ronan and Polson three of the latest improved threshing machines are engaged in work and the way that the wheat and oats are being made ready for market would make many believe that there [sic] were in an Iowa or a Dakota wheat field.

The crops on the reservation this year have been bountiful and when harvested the Indians will have a respectable sum of money. They are already looking forward to three weeks hence when all of their products will have been marketed when they will be afforded the opportunity of coming to Missoula and spending it among the merchants for their red blankets and such other commodities as appeal to the hearts of the redskins.

The merchants here, to are awaiting with considerable interest the harvesting of the crops for it is well known that the Flathead Indians are good spenders and as a result of their purchases the bank accounts of the merchants are usually enriched.

It has probably been one of the most successful seasons in years on the reservation and the acreage under cultivation eclipses by far that of any previous season. The Indians now having more improved methods for handling their crops, having during the early spring made provision for the latest improved machinery such as may be found upon the farms of the more skilled white men.

Document 80

Indian Hunters Prepare for Fall Hunts

September 9, 1905

Source: "Indians Going After Big Game," *The Daily Missoulian*, September 9, 1905, page 8, col. 4.

Editors' note: Despite declining big game populations in western Montana, Indian hunters were still usually successful. The business they brought to Missoula when shopping for their hunting supplies was much appreciated.

Indians Going After Big Game
Victor Charlot and Alexander Bigknife Leave for Mountains.

Victor Charlot, son of Chief Charlot of the Flathead tribe, and Alexander Bigknife and Mrs. Bigknife were in Missoula yesterday doing considerable shopping before starting on a six weeks' hunting trip on the west fork of the Bitter Root river. Charlot is conceded to be one of the best shots on the reservation and there have been but very few instances when he has gone hunting that he has not brought back an abundance of game. Last year he and his friends went into the Clearwater country, where they hunted for a number of weeks, bringing back a number of deer and a few elk.

He likes to hunt in the Clearwater country, but, he states, there are too many of the palefaces in there this year, which detracts from an Indian's pleasure in hunting. He and his party have a complete pack outfit with them and they are supplied with provisions to last them for fully two months, should they desire to remain in the hills that long.

A vast majority of the bucks from the reservation and their s....s are at present in the hills hunting for big game, as this is the time of the year they usually start out after their winter's supply of meat. They cart the carcases of the dead animals home with them, where they have a process for drying the meat, and if they are at all lucky they usually get a big enough supply to last them throughout the winter season.

The Indians are going much further into the hills this year than the white men and if there is any game to be had at all, it is pretty near certain that the redskins will get it.

Hunting on the reservation has not been good this year and the Indians have found it necessary to go to other parts, even after smaller game.

Document 81

Large Cattle Shipments From the Reservation

September 22, 1905

Source: "Shipping Centers on the Flathead Reserve," *The Anaconda Standard*, September 22, 1905, page 11, col. 3.

Editors' note: In 1905, reservation ranchers sold a large number of cattle to buyers for markets around the country.

Shipping Centers on the Flathead Reserve
Their Importance Has Been Thoroughly Demonstrated.
A Conservative Estimate
Gives the Number of Beef Cattle Loaded Out This Season
as Five Thousand Head —
All in Good Condition for the Market.

Missoula, Sept. 21. — The importance of Flathead reservation points as stock shipping centers has been thoroughly demonstrated this summer and fall. Few people, even those living in close proximity to the reservation, realize the vast number of cattle being shipped. It is estimated that 5,000 head have been shipped this season. Regarding this important industry, the Plainsman has the following to say in its last issue:

"Few people, even those living right here adjacent to the reservation, realize the vast number of beef cattle which is shipped out of the reservation from this point every fall. A conservative estimate made by one of the principal buyers who makes his headquarters here during the annual fall roundup places the number considerably in excess of 5,000 head, and he also stated that the grade of the cattle from here was very desirable and that they were in fine condition for the market. The shipments for which cars have been ordered to be sent out this week, so far as we could learn, were: George Moore, to Carsten Bros., Tacoma, 10 cars; John Kennedy, to Frye-Bruhn Co., Seattle, 16 cars; John Wenger, for his own firm at Anaconda, to be shipped to Chicago, 18 cars; and several cars which will be sent out to near-by local points, making a total of about 48 cars for this week and the first few days of next. F. B. Ball loaded out 8 cars from Ravalli the first of the week, and will send out about 20 more cars from there in the course of a few days. Mr. Ball also buys for Carsten Bros.

Among the heaviest cattle raisers who furnish this beef on the reservation are William Irvine, Maxine Matt, Angus McDonald, A. Larivee, Ed Lamereaux, Hubbard Cattle company, John Herman, Joseph Morjeau, M. Pablo, Machelle, Beckwith & Sears, A. Jette, Charles Colwell, Z. Corville, Isaac Pauline, Stinger & Sloan and J. Ogden."

Document 82

Flathead Reservation Cattle Roundups

September 1905

Source: William Q. Ranft, "One of the Garden Spots of the Flathead Country," *The Western Homeseeker* (Missoula, Mont.), vol. 1, no. 4 (January 1906), page 11, col. 1-3, and page 15, col. 3.

Editors' note: Ranft was trying to attract white homesteaders to the reservation. He gave a detailed description of the Mission Valley, its farms, and the annual fall cattle roundups on the Flathead.

One of the Garden Spots of the Flathead Country

by William Q. Ranft

A big stretch of fine country lies between Mission creek and Post creek — so big and so fertile and of so much value that it would do this portion of the Mission valley an injustice not to say something about it; and, again to the persons who are interested in becoming familiar with every part of the reservation, it was thought that they should be told of it.

In order to get accurate distances between the several streams, I visited the reservation very recently and took with me an odometer. I assume that every one knows what an odometer is — an instrument which is attached to the wheel of a conveyance and records the distances traveled.

It was found that the distance between Mission and Post Creeks, where the wagon road crosses the latter creek, is 7.62 miles. The road runs in an almost due northerly direction through townships 18 and 19 north of range 20 west. To the west this part of the Mission valley extends to the Pend d'Oreille river and is about 12 miles wide. The lands lying between these points or boundaries — the Mission range forming the east line — where they have been tilled, are most productive, one place in particular which has been cultivated by a Mixed Blood whose name is Tom McDonald, producing this past year nearly three tons of fine timothy hay to the acre and about 40 bushels of hard wheat to the acre.

The lands lying between these two streams are undulating and with very exceptional instances are wholly unoccupied. They lie in a most desirable portion of the Mission valley on the Flathead because of their adjacency both to the largest trading post on the reservation and the Catholic institutions — St. Ignatius — and also to the railroad station of Ravalli, which is but five and one-half miles distant from St. Ignatius.

There are approximately 75,000 acres of first class agricultural lands in this area and, upon an examination of the map of the Flathead, it will be seen that this is but a very small part of the reservation.

The lands are rich and while crops are successfully raised without irrigation, it would be an easy matter to inundate this entire section because of the fact that the waters of St. Mary's Lake, the Mission Falls, Mission and Post creeks could be brought upon it.

St. Mary's lake lies in an almost easterly direction from St. Ignatius about seven miles, the Mission Falls are about five miles due east and Mission and Post creeks flow through this section.

Lake McDonald, which is the main water supply for Post creek, lies just northeast of these lands but a few miles. It is a almost beautiful lake, abounds in mountain trout of peculiar flavor and its waters are as clear as crystals. This lake is very easy of access and can be driven to by a team, it being but a very few miles from the base of the mountains, the ascent is somewhat abrupt but not uncomfortably so. The mountains encircling McDonald lake form a natural reservoir for it and many millions of gallons of water could be stored as the heavy snows which fall in these mountains each year are melted slowly in the spring and summer, insuring more than ample water to irrigate this section of the valley.

It is in this part of the Mission valley, too, that the biggest round-up occurs. There are perhaps 30,000 head of cattle on the reservation and about 25,000 head of horses. In order to "round-up" so much stock naturally requires the practice of some system. There are usually two cattle round-ups on the Flathead — the spring and fall round-ups. It is the custom for the cattle owners — Full Bloods and Mixed Bloods — to assemble at a designated place on the reservation and there discuss the plan and system to be put into vogue in rounding-up on the particular occasion under discussion; the place where the riders are to meet, that is the starting point, the territory to be covered by each rider and to what place the cattle are to be herded.

On the appointed day the riders, owners and their "outfits" meet. The starting point for a cattle round-up is usually in the Little Bitter Root valley. It is the custom to round-up everything on "the other side of the river" as the lands lying west of the Pend d'Oreille river are called. It is also the custom for the riders of all of the owners to work as assiduously in the territory which is grazed over by the cattle of some owner of that stock and in which an owner "on this side of the river" (the east side of the Pend d'Oreille river) has absolutely no interest whatever. It is, in this respect, the most successful practical co-operative plan I have ever seen worked out and to the good and entire satisfaction of every owner of stock no matter how small his herd.

Of course the expense is apportioned as it is necessary to have a large quantity of supplies which are carried in several wagons and several cooks provide the fare.

I have been on some round-ups where there were as many as one hundred riders. And such riding as these natural born horsemen do! About twenty will line up in a group, everybody having breakfasted and the sun is but fairly creeping over some distant hill. Directions to be taken had been agreed upon the night before. Each "cowboy" or rider knew what ground he was to cover and it was his duty to see to it that every head of cattle that he came across was to be "rounded" or driven to the place upon which it was agreed the entire party would meet at about noon.

It is truly remarkable the acumen displayed by these people in knowing to such a definiteness just where the lines of the territory map[p]ed out for them begin and end — it is truly wonderful how a rider will cover all the ground cut out for him on the meagre descriptions given. Yet it is a fact that this is done and the instance is rare, indeed, that a single head of cattle is missed.

At noon, from seemingly all directions, there come thundering to the agreed place hundreds of heads of cattle, many heads of course with recently born calves, and as they are brought to the noon-day resting place, they are taken in charge by the "holders" and kept or corralled in order that those owned by the different members of the party may be "cut out."

After the midday meal, the cutting-out process begins. Those owned by a selected member of the party are first taken. The riders go into the "bunch" and "cut-out" or separate from the herd those having the brand of the owner whose cattle and calves it is desired to inspect and the newly born calves which require branding. This bunch is then taken and the cattle are driven a short way from the balance of the herd and this is continued until each member of the party has his portion of the herd grazing in that section of the reservation cut out and bunched together.

Each "outfit" then takes its own bunch in hand. Many fires are started and "the branding" irons are brought from the outfit wagons. The branding seems cruel, but really is not very painful to the animal, the iron being gotten to a white heat, the calf roped and thrown to the ground and held by two of the party, the hind and fore feet being held tightly together by strong ropes, the head close against the ground and the brand is quickly effected. It isn't often that the head of stock being branded makes known any pain by even so much as a bellow.

The round-up being finished covering the territory of the reservation lying west of the Pend d'Oreille river, the "outfits" are all moved to the east side. Everybody connected with the round-up is glad of this as the real pleasure connected with the work is attached to the round-up in the broad expansive Mission valley.

The first assembling is had at Polson, which is at the foot of the beautiful Flathead lake. Before starting, a day or two in merry-making is indulged in. It is an orderly aggregation of fellows, fearless and all brawn and muscle. Dancing and the Indian Hand Game are the principal sources of amusement. Of course "broncho busting" is indulged in and real and daring feats of horsemanship are witnessed by those happening to be present.

The final, grand round-up of the stock in the Mission valley is almost invariably had in that part of the valley which lies between Post and Mission creeks, and to that portion of the reservation we started across in the beginning of this story of the rich Flathead.

Document 83

Indian Argues Over Ownership of Horse

October 7, 1905

Source: "Indian Loses Horse and Saddle," *The Daily Missoulian*, October 7, 1905, page 8, col. 4.

Editors' note: It is hard to tell whose horse this really was, but the incident does illustrate the challenges of everyday life during visits by tribal members to Missoula.

Indian Loses Horse and Saddle
Gets an Obliging Man to Explain Matters and All Is Well.

"Say, Charlie, are you my frien'?" asked a disconsolate-looking Indian last night, as he stopped a pedestrian who was hurrying along through the wet.

"My name isn't Charlie," replied the pedestrian, "but I haven't any grudge against you. Neither am I conscious of any overpowering feeling of friendliness. It's just about an even bet both ways."

"Das all right," returned the Indian, in pretty fair English. "I wan' you to get my horse, my rope, my saddle. Hees all over dere," pointing toward the Missoula feed corral. "De feller take de whole cheese."

"Maybe it isn't your horse," suggested the stranger.

The Indian almost exploded in expressing his wrath at this. The damp atmosphere sizzled for a few moments.

"Das what dat feller tol' me. He says 'Come off dat horse; eet ees noder feller's.' I say eet ees my cayuse. My name is Johnny Matt. My fadder is old Alec Matt. I leeve on de reservation. We have plent' horse. I pay $45 for saddle myself."

"Well, that's pretty tough, isn't it?" said the stranger. "We'll go over to the corral and ask the man."

It appears that another Indian, whose name is Pete Chippewa, brought the horse to the barn early in the evening and had paid for its being fed. Later Johnny Matt came along, took the horse out and sold the bridle for a dollar. Half an hour later Pet[e] Chippewa came back and demanded the horse. He was informed that another Indian had taken it out. Then there was dire trouble, and Chippewa started out to hunt up Johnny Matt.

Unable to find Matt, Chippewa went home to the reservation. Then Matt appeared again on the street with the horse. The hostler at the barn called him over to the corral and took the animal away from him and put it in the barn.

It took an hour of rapid fire explanation on the part of Matt to convince anybody that he was entitled to the horse and saddle. Finally it was decided to give the animal to him, and he rode home 24 miles at an early hour this morning.

Document 84

More Indians Depart for Fall Hunts

October 1905

Source: "They're Off for the Big Hunt," *The Daily Missoulian*, October 12, 1905, page 2, col. 2; "Indian Band Starts on a Hunt," *The Daily Missoulian*, October 13, 1905, page 3, col. 1-2.

Editors' note: When preparing for their fall hunts, Flathead Reservation Indians were good customers of Missoula merchants.

They're Off for the Big Hunt
Indians Come to Town From the Reservation to Buy Their Supplies.

The Indians of the Flathead tribe are a busy lot these days preparing for their annual hunt in the mountains after deer and other big game to carry them through the winter months. The first fall of snow in the mountains has occasioned a stampede of ammunition and those who have not the best class of rifles have been in the city during the past few days purchasing new ones and are now ready for a three weeks' outing in the hills.

Among the best shots who have been in the city during the past three days outfitting themselves are Three Heads, Lewis Ashley, Swasa, Little Coyote, Look-at-the-Door, Little Rain-in-the-Face, Young-Man-Without-a-Horse, Quis En Kanusua, Sitting Bear, Joseph Standing Bear, Antoine Moise, Nina [Nine] Pipes, Joseph La Moisc [Lamoose] and Little Fronsway. All are said to be excellent shots and whenever they go into the hills they get game if there is any to be had.

Three Heads is conceded to be one of the best shots on the reservation and the occasions have been few when he has not brought back from six to 12 deer from a hunt. He has outfitted himself this year with a pack train and in his party are half a dozen assistants who will help in caring for the game. Last year Three Heads killed four bear, 12 deer, besides an abundance of smaller game. Next to Three Heads, Little Coyote is probably the best shot and Swasa and Look-at-the-Door very seldom go into the hills without making a big killing.

Buying Blankets.

Tyler Worden, who is probably as thoroughly familiar with the Indians on the reservation as any other man in western Montana, states that there will be several hundred of the Indians go into the hills within the next three weeks. About 50 of them are ready to go now, but there is not enough snow to suit most of them. While there has been but little snowfall on the lowlands so far this year, where the deer all appear to be at this time, Three Heads, Lewis Ashley, Swasa and Look-at-the-Door were buying blankets adn [sic] powder yesterday afternoon among the stores and are fully equipped for a six weeks' trip in the mountains.

They expect to go into the West Fork country this year, where, it is stated, there is an abundance of game. The deer are not high up at the present time, so just as soon as the first fall of snow comes they will be on hand to kill them in any numbers. Quite a number will also go into the Clearwater country and those are preparing to remain for a long stretch. Mr. Worden stated yesterday that some of the Indians contemplate remaining in the hills in that section for at least three months.

Jerked Venison.

Jerked venison is to the Indians what chicken and pork chops are to the colored man and those who are frugal lay in a supply during the season to last themselves and their s...s and pappooses for the entire year. The venison is jerked and dried in the mountains close to where the game is killed and in this way they are enabled to pack large quantities back home with them. The heads they usually throw away unless they have orders for them from some of the white folks who desire to have them mounted for ornaments. The hides are packed home and during the winter months the s....s make them into moccasins, which are put on the market for sale.

The Flatheads this year have been purchasing a number of new rifles and Three Heads and Little Coyote now have the most improved 30.30 models. The majority of them are using the 25.35, while only a few are now using the old 45.70 muskets. At least 100 new rifles have been bought during the past year, so that most of the hunters going into the hills will be equipped fully as well as the white men.

Wants a Lot.

Three Heads yesterday stated to a Missoulian man that he expects to kill a great many deer in the South Fork country this season, as there has not been a time in his remembrance when they have been more plentiful. He says there has been a good fall of snow but it is away up in the hills, while most of the deer at present are in the foothills and lowlands where the snow is falling.

Asked how many he expected to kill, he raised his two hands and indicated with his fingers that 10 would be a good number for him. He is probably better equipped for his outing than any white man ever going out from Missoula on a similar trip. He is not depending upon building fires alongside of his tepee but has supplied himself with some of the more modern conveniences. He has, among other things, an oil stove on which he will be able to cook with ease and which will serve also for the purpose of keeping his tepee warm.

Almost all of the Indians are going into the hills this year, he said, and they will all start out in little bands, most of them having signified their intention to leave within the next two weeks.

The members of the Flathead tribe for the most part realize that it is not proper for them to hunt without licenses and yesterday many of them were busy getting their papers. All of them have money with them and are paying their way just like the white man.

* * * * * * * * *

Indian Band Starts on a Hunt

Imposing Array of Braves, S...s and Ponies on Higgins Avenue.

Three Heads with about 40 cayuses, five s....s and 10 assistants, comprising his hunting party, got started on his journey yesterday. At 2:30 o'clock he arrived in front of Tyler Worden's grocery in the Higgins block and within 15 minutes all of his little band had assembled and at once got busy strapping their provisions and paraphernalia onto their horses. About 15 pack horses were used and enough stuff was taken along to last them for two months should they elect to stay in the hills for that length of time.

They brought with them about 400 pounds of flour, 50 pounds of bacon, considerable cornmeal, besides an abundance of food for their cayuses. It was an imposing sight when the little band started out, and fully 200 persons had gathered along Higgins avenue to watch the party as it started for the south over the Higgins avenue bridge. Three Heads led the way with a chestnut cayuse and felt as proud as if he were leading an army to victory. His assistants rode close behind, while the five s....s followed up in the rear, keeping the small ponies and pack horses in line.

They took the route by way of Fort Missoula and over the Buckhouse bridge, thence to the Little Bitter Root, where they will pitch tents for a few days while surveying the country and getting an idea of the location of the deer.

To a Missoulian reporter Three Heads said before starting:

"We not not [sic] looking for best hunting, now but we will be on the ground. There will be heap snow with small moon which comes now before three sleeps. Soon as snow comes we will climb in mountains. We know where best deer are this year. Have been out already."

Asked why he b[r]ought so many cayuses and ponies along with him this time, Three Heads stated that they expected to pack all of the deer heads and antlers of elk, if they kill many, back with them, as he had a great many inquiries from white men for them this year.

Little Coyote and Look-at-the-Door have made all arrangements for outfitting themselves, but they have been detained here for a few days awaiting the arrival of money. They had a check on a bank at Kalispell for $200 which has been forwarded for payment and as soon as the cash arrives they will collect their party and start for the hills. It will not be as large a party as Three Heads, but will consist of about 12 persons and 25 cayuses.

Two other parties will also start out in other directions, but Mr. Worden stated yesterday that he hardly expected to see them move on before next Monday.

Document 85

Indians Fined for Hunting Without Licenses

October 14, 1905

Source: "Guilty of Violating Game Law," *The Daily Missoulian*, October 14, 1905, page 3, col. 3.

Editors' note: In the early twentieth century, Montana insisted that reservation Indians needed state licenses to hunt off the reservation. Tribal treaty hunting rights were denied until court decisions later in the century. Note that in 1905 some Missoula attorneys believed that reservation Indians did not need state hunting licenses in western Montana.

Guilty of Violating Game Law

Two Indians Are Fined $25 Each for Hunting Without Licenses.

Abraham Isaacs and Gabe Sapier, the two Indians from the Flathead reservation who were convicted of having hunted without a license, were fined by Judge Hayes yesterday afternoon $25 each, which with the costs made the penalty for each $27.50, in default of which they were remanded to the custody of the sheriff to serve out the fine in the county jail at the rate of $2 per day.

Abraham Isaacs, the spokesman for the two, when asked if he could give any reason why sentence should not be passed upon him, replied that he had never known before that it was an offense to hunt without a license; that it was not his intention to break any laws and that in the future he would be careful. He also stated that he would make it a point to call on all of his friends after he got out of jail and inform them of the conditions necessary so that they would not get in trouble.

He was the most affable Indian that has appeared in the police court in many a day.

In connection with the cases of Isaacs and Sapier, some of the attorneys here are inclined to the opinion that in accordance with the government treaty once signed with the Indians that they are entitled to hunt regardless of any state legislative enactment, and that if the case were fought the Indians would win. The point, however, was not raised before Judge Hayes and the[y] were treated like white men who might be charged with as similar offense.

Isaacs and Sapier took their sentences philosophically and the only regrets which they had to offer were that they were deprived of the opportunity of going into the hills with the several bands of Indians which have already started and which will leave early next week.

Document 86

School Superintendent Accused of Injuring Pupils October 20, 1905

Source: Samuel Bellew to Commissioner of Indian Affairs, October 20, 1905, letter received 85,701/1905, education division, RG 75, National Archives, Washington, D.C.

Editors' note: Some tribal members believed that the superintendent of the government school at Jocko Agency caused the death of several pupils through his punishments. Bellew rejected the charges, but no investigation was made.

Department of the Interior,
United States Indian Service,
Flathead Agency, Jocko, Mont., Oct. 20, 1905.

Hon. Commissioner of Indian Affairs,
Washington, D.C.
Sir:

. . . . . .

Mr. Holland's statement that the Indians do not like Superintendent Root, and that they send their children to St. Ignatius Mission School in preference to the Agency, is correct. Most of the Indians give as a reason for this that they wish their children to learn the catechism.

As to the punishment of the two boys mentioned, I do not believe that any pupil was punished to his injury. Statement of parents that Mr. Root's punishments caused their death is entirely without foundation.

One of the boys mentioned, Thomas Parker, was sent home on recommendation of Agency Physician on November 10th., 1904, on account of showing symptoms of tuberculosis, and remained home until time of death with pulmonary tuberculosis on June 7th., 1905.

Frank Celuliah, the other boy, was reported sick on April 23d., 1905, and sent home May 1st., and died of cerebro meningitis on May 12th. I am informed by the Agency Physician that there is tuberculosis in this family, and he considers the boy's sickness of tubercular origin.

As to the re-employment of Mr. Root as Superintendent, I do not think it would be to the best interest of the service, as he does not appear to have the faculty of making friends among the Indians or gaining their confidence.

Very respectfully,
Samuel Bellew
U.S. Indian Agent.

Document 87

Two Mixed Bloods Sentenced for Robbery

November 9, 1905

Source: "M'Leod and Stewart Get One Year," *The Daily Missoulian*, November 9, 1905, page 3, col. 1.

Editors' note: Hector McLeod and his partner confessed to robbing the Ravalli railroad station of $45. They each received sentences of one year in the Montana penitentiary.

M'Leod and Stewart Get One Year
For Holding Up Agent and Burglarizing Northern Pacific Depot at Ravalli.

Hector McLeod and L. Virgil Stewart, the two young men who held up the operator and robbed the station at Ravalli of $45 in cash on the night of Nov. 3, confessed to the crime yesterday afternoon to the officers after a thorough "sweating," and subsequently were arraigned before Judge Webster, when they entered their plea of guilty.

Judge Webster then sentenced each to one year in the state's prison at hard labor.

The light sentence given the criminals was the result of extenuating circumstances.

The sheriff's office and Detective L. K. Church, for the Northern Pacific, in inducing them to make a confession, promised them that they would be dealt with leniently by the court. McLeod was told by the officers that if he would plead guilty to the charge that they would recommend to the court and the county attorney that he be given one year, which, with good behavior, would mean 11 months in the penitentiary. He refused, maintaining his innocence. The same argument was then used with Stewart, who agreed to plead guilty, yet he maintained that he was innocent. The officers informed him that they did not want him to do that, but if he put the court to the expense of a trial and then was found guilty that it would be likely to go very hard with him; that he could not expect to get off much lighter than seven years.

He then changed his mind and made a confession of all the circumstances. McLeod later pursued the same course.

Had No Gun.

In their confession it transpired that they did not have a gun at all, but that they only assumed so on entering the depot, which was sufficient to scare the operator and make him run. McLeod was the leader and spokesman. Upon entering the door he shouted to Operator Rosum to throw up his hands, at the same time raising his hand, which was in his coat pocket, pointing it through the pocket at the operator. Operator Rosum immediately ran through the door, effecting his escape. The robbers then emptied the contents of the cash drawer, after which they went west.

Sheriff Davis Graham has been the recipient of many congratulations for his work in making the capture, as he had little if any clue to go on. The operator was unable to give a description of the men as he appeared to have been very excited at the time.

Hector McLeod is a halfbreed Indian and has lived on the reservation for a number of years. Last summer he spent in Oregon, according to his own statements to Judge Webster yesterday. He and Stewart had been together but a short time, the latter coming from Washington, where, he states, he had resided for a number of years. He informed the court that it was the first offense of any kind that he had ever committed and when asked for a reason for his action in this instance he explained to the court that he did not know himself. He is only 24 years of age.

An Old Timer.

McLeod is 27 years of age and, according to his own admissions, he has been through the mill many times. He told the court that he had been arrested for drunkenness and disorderly conduct a number of times on the reservation and also in Oregon while away, but that he had never been confronted with a charge of robbery before.

Before pronouncing sentence, Judge Webster took a great many things into consideration. The officers had practically given the prisoners to understand that they would be let off with a light sentence if they would agree to plead guilty. Under these circumstances Judge Webster informed them he would give them the minimum sentence, although their offense was a very grave one and that under other conditions he would have been inclined to make the penalty much more severe.

McLeod, it is believed, is badly wanted in other places. There is said to be a $200 reward out for him for horse stealing, but when questioned as to this he stated that it was his uncle and not himself who is wanted.

Document 88

Indian Charged with Murder of Another Indian While Drunk November 14, 1905

Source: "Lefthand Is Held to Grand Jury," *The Daily Missoulian*, November 14, 1905, page 6, col. 5.

Editors' note: Louis Lefthand was charged with murdering Lucy Michel during a drunken party in Camas Prairie.

Lefthand Is Held to Grand Jury

Flathead Indian Is Charged with Murder of Chief Michel's Wife.

Louis Lefthand, who is charged with the alleged murder of Lucy Michel, the wife of old Chief Michel, had his preliminary hearing before United States Commissioner W. P. Smith yesterday afternoon and was bound over to the action of the federal grand jury without bail. He was committed to the Lewis & Clark county jail, and will be taken there this morning by Deputy United States Marshal Young.

The alleged murder for which Louie Lefthand will be compelled to stand trial, occurred on or about September 28 last, at the home of old Chief Michel at Camas prairie. At the time of the alleged murder a party of six Indians was carousing and drinking at Michel's place and about 4 days later Lucy Michel, was found dead, presumably from being struck on the head with a heavy instrument and also from bruises which were found on her body.

Assistant United State Attorney J. Miller Smith of Helena, acted in behalf of the state and examined six witnesses yesterday, namely, Louie Wa-ten-me, Paul Isadore, Elizabeth, a daughter of Mrs. Michel, Dr. Lebcher of Plains, Michael Revais and Charlie. Blind Michel acted as interpreter.

Paul Isadore testified that he had seen Louie Lefthand hit the old lady with a club after she had slapped Lefthand, and the Louie had struck her several times. Louie Wa-ten-me testified that Louie Lefthand had told him the he, Lefthand, hal [had] killed the old lady. Charlie's testimony showed that he had seen Mrs. Michel lying in the yard and that afterward he had seen Chief Michel and Louie Lefthand bring her into the house. Dr. Lebcher testified as to the condition of Mrs. Michel when he saw her and examined her a few days afterwards.

Elizabeth testified that her mother had sent her away for the night at the time that all of the men were at their house and that she knew nothing of the alleged murder other than that the men were in a badly intoxicated state when she left.

The defense offered no testimony whatever and Louie Lefthand did not appear to realize the situation at all. Attorney Parsons acted for the defendant yesterday and will appear for his client in the federal court.

Document 89

Indian Hunter Returns After Fall Hunt

November 21, 1905

Source: "Joe Young Moose Has Returned," *The Daily Missoulian*, November 21, 1905, page 8, col. 2.

Editors' note: Some of the reservation hunters had poor returns in 1905, but they attributed the lack of success to the lack of snow to track the game.

Joe Young Moose Has Returned
Indian Hunter Is Back from Clearwater Country After Hard Trip.

Joe Young Moose of the reservation, who headed a party of Indians who went into the Clearwater three weeks ago to hunt for big game, returned yesterday, bringing back the carcasses of three deer, one bear and other smaller game. The remainder of his party will arrive here tomorrow.

Young Moose did not meet with the same success this year that he has in former seasons, and he attributes it to the small snowfall in the mountains. There are plenty of deer, he states, but they are hard to get at, as it is almost impossible track them, as there is no snow on the ground.

While in the Clearwater country he saw three elk and his experiences with one of the big animals is most thrilling. The big buck had put in its appearance on the top of a little hill shortly after daybreak and he was observed by a number of the Indians from their tepees, who started in pursuit. The animal was in just the right position to be made a target of and Young Moose and two of his companions fired three volleys at it. At least two of the shots must have taken effect, for the animal stumbled two or three times in making its escape and upon its trail several clots of blood were found. The Indians traced it to the banks of the creek and later discovered that the animal had died while endeavoring to swim the river. Its carcass floated down the stream until it reached some rocks where it now remains, but the Indians were unable to get to it, as they had no boats and they had no implements with which to cut down timber to make a raft.

Young Moose states that there are at least 50 Indians in that section at the present time who are hunting for game, but that they have met with comparatively poor success. They are patient, however, and are awaiting the arrival of the first snow.

The nights have been exceptionally cool and some of the hunters have been subjected to great hardships. It is the first time in years that they have not been able to kill considerable game by this date, but they attribute it to the scarcity of snow and not to the lack of game.

Document 90

Chief Joseph Objects to Buildings on Right of Way December 1905

Source: Chief Joseph, et. al., to Commissioner of Indian Affairs, December 1905, letter received 8,930/1906, land division, RG 75, National Archives, Washington, D.C.

Editors' note: On February 9, 1906, Agent Samuel Bellew informed the Commissioner of Indian Affairs that John Wightman was planning to build a stable on the railroad right of way for his stage line running from Ravalli to Polson. This petition seems to have been written by a lawyer.

Flat head Res.

Sir:

We, the undersigned Chiefs, headsmen and resident members of the Flathead Confederated tribes of Indians of the Flathead Indian Reservation of the State of Montana, do respectfully petition and request that the Indian department of the United States do forthwith take action to prevent the consummation of a lease and the construction of houses thereunder, as hereinafter mentioned in violation of the treaty rights and other rights of your petitioners.

Your petitioners respectfully represent that under and by virtue of the grant made by your petitioners with the consent of the United States Government, to the Northern Pacific Railway Company for its right of way, through and over said reservation, that said Railway Company, has no right to lease its right of way, or any part thereof, over and across said reservation, to people and persons who shall establish thereon, trading and merchandise stores and posts; and your petitioners further represent that at the station of Ravalli on said reservation, the said railway Company has leased a portion of its right of way to one John Wightman; that said leassee John Wightman is preparing to build and construct thereon, a hotel, a merchandise store and some other buildings to your petitioners unknown, — all done in violation of the treaty rights of your petitioners and without authority of law.

By reason whereof, your petitioners respectfully ask that said John Wightman not be permitted or allowed by you, to erect such buildings and constructions as aforesaid.

x Chief Joseph
x Chief Kekeshee
x Chief Hihita

[Followed by 49 signatures or x's of other tribal members.]

Document 91

Information Agency Assists Potential Reservation Homesteaders January 14, 1906

Source: Frank H. Parr to George D. Linn, January 14, 1906, from file 5,815/1908 Flathead 308.1, Central Classified Files, RG 75, National Archives, Washington, D.C.

Editors' note: The Flathead Reservation Information Agency was one of two businesses set up to sell potential reservation homesteaders information about the lands available. This was one of several ways white businessmen found to make money off the opening of the reservation. William Ranft had been a prominent attorney representing mixed bloods applying for enrollment on the reservation.

Post Office Department
Office of Inspector
Spokane Division
Helena, Mont., January 14, 1906.

Mr. George D. Linn,
Inspector in Charge,
Spokane, Washington
Sir:

I have the honor to return herewith the above numbered case, which relates to alleged violation of Section 1617 Postal Laws and Regulations, 1902, by the Flathead Reservation Information Agency of Missoula, Montana, and after personal investigation on the 12th instant, to submit the following report relative thereto.

This company, or agency is incorporated under the laws of the State of Montana, with a capitalization of $50,000, about $22,00[0] of which, they claim, is paid in. The officers of the Agency are, President, William Ranft; Vice President, Thomas C. Marshall; Secretary and General Manager, H. C. Freeman, all of whom are prominent and reputable men in their vicinity.

I interviewed the President of the Agency, Mr. Ranft, who gave me a detailed verbal explanation of their plans, the principal features of which are incorporated in Exhibit "A" herewith, which is a copy of the statement given to the officers of the United States Land Office at the time of their investigation of this Agency.

The "Flathead Bill" as passed at the last session of Congress, provides, that after the allotment of 80 acres of the reservation to each Indian entitled to same, the balance of the reservation shall be thrown open for entry to such persons as are entitled to that privilege. After the final allotment to the Indians has been made, then a commission, appointed by the President, shall classify and appraise the remaining lands that are subject to "entry."

This Agency has a large map representing the entire reservation, which map shows every forty acre tract of land on same. They do not claim that it is technically correct, but do claim that, should the Government change its present lines of survey, they will conform with such changes and furnish each of their patrons with a correct map. Their plan is to designate on that map, all of the allotments made to the Indians, thereby showing their patrons the sections left for entry; also to show by distinctive colors on each forty acre tract, as shown by the map, the classification given by the Government Commission to that particular piece of land.

In furtherance of this particular feature, they have an index system, consisting of 45,000 cards, representing that number of 40 acre tracts. On each card they expect to show relative to the tract which it represents, the topography of same, kind of soil, adaptability, amount of timber and tillable land, nearest streams, market, post office, church, school and railroad, also the Government classification and price. Mr. Ranft, the President, has spent two years on the Reservation in company with a Government agent, during the enrollment of the Indians, and has, what is purported to be, a complete genealogy of every Indian on the Reservation; he has also acted as counsel for the Indians for some time. These connections with the Indians, and the Reservation, has given him an excellent opportunity to gather such information as he proposes to disseminate to his patrons. The knowledge which they propose to impart, is far from complete, as shown by the above described cards, but Mr. Ranft informed me that his application for permission to thoroughly examine the Reservation is now pending before the Interior Department, and, if it is not granted, he will still be able to gather the necessary and promised data, when it is thrown open for public inspection, although it will then require a larger force of competent men.

They expect to keep such a check on the "filings," that, at a minute's notice, they will be competent to inform each of their patrons as to just what land is open, and to give them such a complete description of it that they will be enabled to make an intelligent selection. This, they claim, will eliminate the necessity of making a personal examination of the Reservation at a large expense; the possibility of selecting a tract already chosen; or the possibility of being victimized by the unscrupulous, so-called locators, as has frequently happened in the past at other "openings."

The numerous endorsements shown in the advertising matter of this Agency, and purporting to be those of prominent citizens of Montana, I believe to [be] authentic, as a result of my personal examination of the original letters. As to that portion of their circular letter, relative to the expression of "Land Office Officials" as to the merits of their system, I desire to say that that statement is based on the expressions of State Land Officials, and not from the United States Officials, as interpreted by the Hon. Acting Commissioner of Indian Affairs. Register Arms, and Receiver Winstanley of the United States Land Office at Missoula, Montana, informed me that they made a personal examination of the office and system of this agency, and the latter informed me privately that he had no hesitancy in saying that it is his opinion, based on his experience in such matters, that this is a perfectly legitimate business, and will be of great benefit to any person desiring to take up this land. This expression, he claimed, did not originate from any friendliness he had for the promoters of this system, but simply as his honest conviction.

I have studied the matter over carefully, and do not believe that they are making any misrepresentations in their advertisements, or any promises that any person, placed in like position, could not fulfil.

In regard to the complaint of William Kelsey against these people, in which he claimed that he understood that this Agency would register its patrons for the "drawing," I desire to invite your attention to a copy of their letter to him, also to his acknowledgment of the return of his $5.00, shown herewith, as Exhibit "B," in explanation of which, they claim that their Kalispell, Montana, agent, D'Arcy, was making misrepresentations, which resulted in his immediate dismissal from their employ.

Inquiry of J. M. Heith [Keith], Cashier of the First National Bank of Missoula, where Mr. Ranft carries his account, shows that that institution has implicit faith in his integrity and business probity, and that they consider that he is financially able to carry out his project. This is practically the sentiment of every citizen I conversed with relative to this subject.

I have carefully examined the literature sent out by this agency, and have substantiated many of their statements contained therein by Government reports.

I am of the opinion that failure to provide reliable and complete information as advertised, is the only contingency that would make this a fraudulent scheme. While they now have a large amount of supposed valuable information relative to this Reservation, they still have a large amount to gather, the latter being inaccessible at this time without permission of the Interior Department, although it will be obtainable at a later date when the land is thrown open for public inspection. It is a recognized fact that it will be cheaper for an organization, backed by sufficient capital and competent officers, to gather such information as the homeseeker desires, and furnish it to individuals, than it would be for any one individual, or small combination of such, to gather it for themselves.

In view of the fact that I have found no evidence of fraud, and as this company has eliminated certain extravagant statements that appeared in their original circular letter, as shown by their letter to the Commissioner of Indian Affairs, herewith, I recommend that the case be closed without further action.

Very respectfully,
Frank H. Parr,
Post Office Inspector.

Report examined, approved and
forwarded to Chief Inspector
Jan. 16, 1906.
G. D. Linn,
Post Office Inspector in Charge. Division.

Document 92

Kootenai Chief Koos-ta-ta's Work Horse Stolen

March 9, 1906

Source: Koos-ta-ta to Samuel Bellew, March 9, 1906, Flathead Agency Papers, letters received, 8NS-075-96-323, National Archives, Denver, Colorado.

Editors' note: One of Koos-ta-ta's work horses was stolen by a tribal member and then sold to a white man who would not return the horse until legally forced to. Koos-ta-ta was not able to put in his crop with only one horse and did not have the money to purchase another horse.

Dayton Mar. 9. 1906

Mr Samuel Bellew U.S. Indian Agent
Flathead Agency Montana
Dear Sir:

I just made a trip to Kalispell to get my work horses that was stolen from me by Gingra, and could not find the man, so I showed my letter that I had from you to the officers in Kalispell and they said it was no good, and said that Doc Hull knew that I could not gain Possesion of my horses. Now I have made three trips after my horse and it has cost me several dollars expences, and I still failed to get the horse, it has been proven that this horse was stolen from me and I shouldn't be out the money that I have to gain possession of a horse that is my own property that I never sold or traded to any one. I will soon be ready to put in my crop and this particular horse is one of my only team I have to work and if I am unable to get him will have to buy one to go with his mate to make me a team and it will cost me $100.00 to buy one as good as this one is, and at this time of year I am unable to get the money to buy one with and if I am not able to get my horse will have to ask you to help me to buy one as I will have to have another horse to put in my crop.

Now as you are my Agt I want you to try and get me my horse as I have failed my self.

Yours Respectfully
Chief Koos-ta-ta

Kootenai Chief Koostatah
Source: Photograph Archives, Montana Historical Society, Helena, Montana, detail from photo 954-573

Document 93

Chief Arlee and His Family Were Tribal History

March 25, 1906

Source: "When the Indians Owned the Land," *The Anaconda Standard*, March 25, 1906, page 13, col. 3-4.

Editors' note: Duncan McDonald related a number of facts about the life and history of Chief Arlee and Arlee's family to the *Anaconda Standard* reporter. He also introduced Arlee's granddaughter to the reporter.

When the Indians Owned the Land

Missoula, March 24. — Among the many interesting chapters of Indian history of the West, perhaps Western Montana has furnished as many happenings for the pen of the historian as any section of the country. Although much has been written concerning the Indian history of this locality, the Bitter Root valley and points on the present Flathead reserve being equally interesting as battle fields or the scenes of peace conferences and treaty making with the government, there still remain many interesting things unwritten; stories which do not deal with the red man on the warpath, but rather of his characteristics and mode of living in this part of the country. Of these unwritten stories, perhaps none are told more interestingly or are more authentic than those by Duncan McDonald of Ravalli, who has lived in Western Montana for many years and has been identified with affairs of both Indians and whites, and whose father, Angus McDonald, was a great peacemaker between the two.

During the recent cold spell Duncan made a visit to Missoula, stating that in such weather steam-heated blocks were good enough for him, and while in the city called at the Standard office to discuss reservation topics with a reporter. While talking an Indian woman passing the window was hailed by Duncan and shyly acquiesced to his beckoning to come into the office, the reporter being informed that this was Mary Sooa-sah, the granddaughter of Chief Arlee, once a prominent chief of the Flathead tribes. After some persuasion the woman consented to "stand" for her picture, which resulted in the above, a good likeness of both Duncan and Mary. After the picture was taken a number of interesting facts in the lives of the Arlee family were related. Mary following the story attentively, occasionally breaking into the speaker's account in her native tongue to correct some error or some detail, the expression of her face at times denoting that the story brought to her mind many sad memories of the past.

Old Chief Arlee.

"Old Chief Arlee was one of the great chiefs of the Flatheads," began the speaker, "and Mary here is one of his few relatives yet living. She is a good, kind woman and is beloved by all her tribe. Chief Arlee, after whom Arlee station is named, came into prominence during the time the first treaty was made by the Flatheads with President Garfield, the treaty in which the Indians promised to move from the Bitter Root valley to the present reserve. Chief Charlot, yet living on the reservation, the chief who made a trip to Washington last year in the interests of his tribe, to ask for certain additions and modifications in the bill to throw open the reservation, was then first chief of the tribes and Arlee was second chief. Charlot refused to sign this treaty, but Arlee believed the move to be a wise one for his people and so signed the agreement, and was from that time until his death recognized by the government as the first chief of the Flatheads. Arlee also figured prominently in several other treaties with the government and was known by his people as the treaty chief.

"Arlee was also a very brave warrior and was in many big battles which took place between the various western tribes in this vicinity during those early days. One of the battles in which he took a prominent part was with the Blackfeet tribes on Ravalli creek. Once in another engagement with the Blackfeet Arlee was the only one from his party of 30 warriors who escaped, all the rest being killed and scalped.

His Sister Living.

"Strange to say, a sister of Chief Arlee is now living on the reservation. Her name is Susan and she is next to the oldest woman living on the reserve, her exact age in years, however, not being known. She is peculiarly marked with what is generally taken for a scar from a deep cut on her upper lip. This, however, is a birthmark and is thought to have resulted in a strange manner. Arlee's father was also a noted warrior of the tribe, but was killed during an unequal fight with the Blackfeet when Arlee was but a boy. The fight began at Evaro. The Flatheads, being equipped with bows and arrows only, while their opponents had guns, were being routed and had been forced back as far as Schly station. At the foot of the hill on Finley creek is where Arlee's father fell, the Blackfeet scalping him and cutting a deep gash in his upper lip with a tomahawk. After the battle was over and the enemy had gone on through the country, Arlee's mother, in spite of the protest of her tribe, went to view the dead body of her husband. Kneeling beside his cold form she raised the blanket with which he had been covered and was deeply affected by the manner in which his face had been cut. A few weeks later, when Susan was born, she bore the birthmark upon her lip resembling exactly the scar upon the lip of her brave warrior father."

Document 94

Alcohol and Murder on Dayton Creek

May 30, 1906

Source: "Pleads Not Guilty and Waives Hearing," *The Anaconda Standard*, May 30, 1906, page 10, col. 2.

Editors' note: Antoino Louis might have killed Modeste in self-defense, but whiskey sellers at Dayton Creek lubricated the affair.

Pleads Not Guilty and Waives Hearing
Antoino Louis Charged with Killing of Modeste.
Plenty of Bad Firewater
Sold to the Indians by Traders on Dayton Creek and Cases Will Be Investigated by the Grand July at Helena Next Week.

Missoula, May 29. — Antoino Louis, the Indian from the Flathead agency who is charged with the murder of Modeste, another Kootenai Indian, was taken before United States Commissioner Smith to-day for a preliminary hearing, but owing to the failure of the witnesses in the case to arrive, Attorney Parsons, who represented the defendant, decided to waive the hearing and enter a plea of not guilty. This action was taken in view of the fact that Antoino is a witness in a whiskey-selling case and will appear before the grand jury in Helena next Monday. Deputy United States Marshal Young took the prisoner over to Helena this evening.

Beating of Modeste.

The crime is alleged to have been committed on May 5 on Dayton creek, on the Flathead reservation. It is alleged that Louis beat Modeste over the head with a club and Modeste died from the effects of the injuries received. It is said that there is not a very strong case against Antoino, the dead man having been the aggressor in the quarrel. The accused man is a "blanket" Indian, and a fine specimen of his tribe. He stated to-day that, while whiskey had caused a number of murders on the reservation, the fiery liquid was not responsible for this one, as he was in the possession of his sober senses. Antoino would not make any statement as to the sobriety of the man he killed.

Reap Rich Harvest.

There are several Indian traders doing business on Dayton creek, who are said to be reaping a rich harvest from the sale of liquor to the Indians. Major Bellew has made several ineffectual efforts to stop the traffic, and the federal grand jury at Helena will make a searching investigation next week and endeavor to bring some of the parties to justice. Antoino admitted to-day that he had purchased whiskey three weeks before the tragedy from at least two of the traders on Dayton creek, and he was admonished by Major Bellew not to suffer from a lapse of memory when he should be questioned by the grand jury at Helena next Monday on this matter.

Document 95

Status of Flathead Lake Dam Site

August 8, 1906

Source: Interior Department to Commissioner of Indian Affairs, August 8, 1906, letter received 68,267/1906, land division, RG 75, National Archives, Washington, D.C.

Editors' note: The years between 1904 and the opening of the reservation in 1910 were filled with efforts of individuals to gain control of the Flathead Lake dam site. White businessmen applied for the development rights and some tribal members worked to obtain adjacent land. The site was finally reserved for the tribes and/or the irrigation project. The battle over control of the dam continued until the twenty-first century when the Confederated Salish and Kootenai Tribes finally obtained ownership.

United States
Department of the Interior
Aug. 8, 1906

Hon. Commissioner of Indian Affairs
Washington, D.C.
Sir:

I am in receipt of your letter of the 3rd instant, in which you refer to letters from F. E. Hilton, formerly of Missoula, Montana, charging that frauds have been perpetrated in enrolling Indians on the Flathead Reservation and alleging that a scheme is on foot whereby the lands adjacent to the Pend d'Oreille River are to be obtained unlawfully by interested parties for a water site, etc.; that these papers were referred to Special Allotting Agent Rankin, and you submit his report. You state that the Allotting Agent says concerning the enrollment generally, if the statements of some of the people are of any value, there is ample ground for the belief that there was a great deal of fraud and there is a scheme on foot to obtain some unjust advantage by reason of fraudulent enrollments, etc.; that in relation to the falls of the Pend d'Oreille river, he has not had time to visit them, but if they are any thing like as valuable as they have been represented, he thinks they should be reserved for the tribe and either leased or sold to the highest bidders, etc.; and in view of these statements you recommend that Chief Engineer Code or Inspector Hill be directed to proceed to the Flathead Reservation and make an examination of the Pend d'Oreille Falls in connection with Allotting Agent Rankin, and that there be set aside such land as may be necessary to conserve the power available from these falls, with a view of asking Congress for appropriate action for their disposal.

In reply to that part of your letter, you are informed that Inspector Code has this day been instructed to proceed to the Flathead Reservation, Montana, for the purpose mentioned by you, and to confer with Allotting Agent Rankin and the Indian Agent in regard to the matter, and you will please give him any necessary instructions to that effect.

In relation to the statement of Mr. Rankin concerning the fraudulent enrollments, you say that they are justified; that in 1901, the population was 1638, in 1903 it was 1670, and there are now on the approved roll in excess of 2100 Indians; that the field work is such that no inspecting employee under your control can be spared, for an examination of the rolls, and you submit this matter for the consideration of the Department, with the hope that an inspector can be detailed to investigate the same, etc.

Replying thereto, you are informed that there is at present no inspector available for detail to examine into and purge the rolls of the Flathead Indians, but as Mr. Yvon Pike of the Interior Department is now on detail to your Office, and, it is understood, is a present on the Blackfeet Reservation, you are instructed to direct him to proceed to the Flathead Reservation, and after consultation with the Allotting Agent Rankin, and the Indian Agent in charge, to take all necessary steps to clear the rolls of the names of those that should not appear there, and you will furnish Mr. Pike with all necessary papers and instructions.

The enclosures of your letter are herewith returned, and a copy of the letter to Inspector Code is also transmitted.

Very respectfully,
Thos. Ryan
Acting Secretary.

Document 96

Charles Allard Wins Relay Race in Spokane

October 8, 1906

Source: "Great Relay Rider Comes to Town," *The Daily Missoulian*, October 8, 1906, page 9, col. 1.

Editors' note: Charles Allard, Jr., just won a relay race in Spokane and had entered another relay race at the Western Montana Fair in Missoula.

Great Relay Rider Comes to Town
Charles Allard, Winner of Interstate Race at Spokane, Arrives.
Cowboy Rider Went Twenty Miles at Average Speed of 2:33.

Charles Allard of Polson arrived in this city yest[e]rday from Spokane and will enter the 20-mile relay race at the Western Montana fair which opens today.

Allard won the $1,500 interstate relay race at Spokane which was finished Friday. His time for the 20-mile run, two miles a day, was 47:06. H. G. Smith of Endicott, Wash., was second, just four seconds behind Allard. Third money went to A. E. Stowell, also of Endicott, Wash. last year's relay winner, and fourth went to Anasta Jim of the Flathead Indian reservation. None of the others finished in the race.

Anasta Jim finished first on yesterday's race, which was perhaps the closest of the entire day's run. All of the four riders finished practically together, only a second's time intervening between them.

The race for first money was practically over several days ago as Allard and H. C. Smith steadily drew away from the rest of the contestants. A. E. Stowell also clinched third place on account of some hard luck of Anasta Jim's. Between Allard and Smith there was very little difference, Smith being if anything, quicker in the saddle. Allard's horses were the fastest however, and probably therein lies the secret of his victory. While not so fast in handling the saddle as Smith, Allard however, took time enough to make sure of his saddle for every fresh mount and did not lose time by any misfortune.

Allard Averages 2:33 a Mile.

Allard's time for the 20 miles, 47:06, means an average of 2:33 for each mile, in which he was by the rules of the race required to dismount, unsaddle, put saddle on a fresh horse and mount again twice in each mile, running four laps of two miles each every day.

By his victory Allard gets 50 per cent of the $1,500 less 5 per cent which is deducted by the fair management as entrance fee. Allard was paid $712.50 H. C. Smith got $356.25; A. E. Stowell, $213.75, and Anasta Jim, $142.50.

The time for yesterday's ride and the total time for the 20 miles:

	Time.	Total.
Charles Allard	4:43	47:06
H. G. Smith	4:44	47:10
A. E. Stowell	4:45	48:32
Anasta Jim	4:42	49:52

Seven Riders Enter.

Seven riders entered the race on the first day. Joe Bickel of North Yakima was 21 seconds ahead of his field on the first three day's ride, but was disqualified by the judges for entering a professional racehorse. Louis Pierre, another Flathead Indian, withdrew after the second day. Frank Fromm rode through the first eight days, but then turned over his time to Louis Pierre, who finished all but the last half of his 20 mile ride. A. E. Stowell broke his ankle in dismounting Wednesday and his place was taken by C. L. Smith also of Endicott, a cousin of H. G. Smith, who finished third for him.

Index